LANDSCAPES OF WAR

The Archaeology of Aggression and Defence

Where is the horse now, where the hero gone?
Where is the bounteous lord, and where the benches
For feasting? Where are all the joys of hall?
Alas for the bright cup, the armoured warrior,
The glory of the prince. That time is over.
Passed into night as it had never been.
Stands now memorial to that dear band
The splendid lofty wall, adorned with shapes
Of serpents; but the strong blood-greedy spear
And mighty destiny removed the heroes,
And storms now strike against these stony slopes.

From the Anglo-Saxon poem *The Wanderer*

LANDSCAPES OF WAR

THE ARCHAEOLOGY OF AGGRESSION AND DEFENCE

PAUL HILL & JULIE WILEMAN

TEMPUS

First published 2002

PUBLISHED IN THE UNITED KINGDOM BY:

Tempus Publishing Ltd
The Mill, Brimscombe Port
Stroud, Gloucestershire GL5 2QG
www.tempus-publishing.com

PUBLISHED IN THE UNITED STATES OF AMERICA BY:

Tempus Publishing Inc.
2 Cumberland Street
Charleston, SC 29401
1-888-313-2665
www.tempuspublishing.com

British Library Cataloguing in Publication Data.
A catalogue record for this book is available from the British Library.

ISBN 0 7524 1963 3

Typesetting and origination by Tempus Publishing.
PRINTED AND BOUND IN GREAT BRITAIN

Contents

Acknowledgements

We first knew that there was a good book in this subject matter when we were teaching similar material on a Continuing Education course at the University of Surrey. Since we announced our intention to write it, our students turned into providers. We discovered to our surprise that they had been to more places than we had and taken more pictures of castles, walls, gun emplacements and pillboxes than we could have thought possible. Without them, it would have been a modestly illustrated volume indeed.

We have received a great amount of help and support from our friends and families during the preparation for this book. We are particularly grateful to the following people for the provision of photographs: Sandra Luff, for her professional work on photographic reproduction as well as some choice picture selections; John Eagle, for his excellent photographs of Greeks at Thermopylae; Jeanette Hicks for her numerous photographic contributions; Sue Walker; Jez Smith; Richard and Liz Hill for braving the wild countryside around Offa's Dyke to bring us revealing photographs of the monument and of Clun Castle; Abigail Robertson for her stunning pictures of the Great Wall of China; and finally, Martin Pegler for his armour photograph.

We are also thankful for the patience of our families during the months of preparation for the book and for offering us advice along the way. One of our number actually fought in one of the battles outlined in the book and revealed to us some invaluable personal recollections of what it was like to fight in a modern war. To Lucy Hill, Douglas and Joan Wileman, we owe the benefits of their close support.

To Simon Davies we owe a special thank you. Since the kernel of an idea of tracing warfare in the landscape through different periods and places came to us, he has been a source of extraordinary knowledge and clarity of thought and has kept us abreast of aspects of military theory that we might otherwise have missed.

Further thanks are due to Steve Dyer for his help and support; Tim Everson; Fairbrass Knowles; Margaret Broomfield; Dave Potts; Chris Hayward; Jenny Newell; Caroline Jones; Bryan Harmer; Judie English; the offices of the Light Dragoons; the Denver Public Library; and the staff of the Cambridge University Aerial Photographic unit.

List of illustrations

Text figures

Colour plates

Introduction

The idea that land warfare is dominated by the constraints and opportunities of the physical landscape is hardly a new one. We have sought here to use archaeology to demonstrate how throughout the ages and at various levels, people have responded to threats of aggression by defending themselves at a personal, kin-group, regional or national level. The physical evidence has been left in the landscape for us to examine: castles, bastles, defended homesteads, hillforts, fortresses, town walls, pillboxes and linear frontiers are all examples of a response to aggression which has left its trace. Archaeology, however, has its limitations. Traditionally, archaeologists have used evidence from ethnographical and anthropological studies, texts and iconography to complement the evidence from the physical remains. Some campaigns and battles in history have left no trace in the archaeological record, despite being huge affairs. Here we have to rely on historical accounts to piece together the story. Where we have no choice but to borrow interpretative tools from other disciplines, we have done so to demonstrate a point. For example, the battle of Mont Pinçon which we cover in chapter 4, fought in August 1944 in the difficult countryside of Normandy, has left only a stone memorial and a few pillboxes to help tell the tale of a fight for the most important hill in the region. Here, we have complemented our material by turning to oral testimony from someone who fought the battle to provide aspects of the story. Our point is always the same, however: each of our chosen areas of focus shows how the landscape is used in warfare and the effects that it has.

But it not just a story of armies on campaign through the woods, across rivers and over mountains. The whole notion of the response to aggression needs to be qualified by an examination of the earliest evidence and the nature of the cycles of dominance in which warfare seems to go. From the earliest times when Sumerian city states were pitting themselves against each other in confrontations over scarce resources, a familiar pattern emerges. By the time people had developed a settled agricultural lifestyle, with houses, villages and fields, they were also developing the need to begin to fortify their homes and communities. Defensive ditches, palisades and walls have been identified at many Middle Neolithic sites across Europe for example, while in the Near East urbanisation brought a demand for raw materials, luxury goods and resources. In turn, neighbours sought to challenge other neighbours in a battle over these resources and for political supremacy. So they built up armies. And then they built walls to keep other armies out. Then the armies learned the first lessons of siege warfare and got to work, providing they were not defeated in the open field before they got there. This example is just one of many cycles of aggression and defence which we look at in chapter 5 that leads to stalemate until circumstances change. Later in prehistory, the arrival of the

1 *Victorian ideas on the origins of human aggression were not without their charm. This print by Cosmo Rowe accompanied an article in* The Idler *by H.G. Wells entitled* 'Stories of the Stone Age'. *The caption read 'Waving the axe of stone, while he chanted of the killing of Uya'*

chariot brought warfare to a new level, making long range campaigns possible and bringing a limited tactical flexibility to armies in the field. The development of trench warfare in the late nineteenth century can be traced from the American Civil War through the siege of Plevna in the Russo-Turkish war, culminating in the appalling attrition in Europe between 1914-18. Defensive measures had got the better of the offensive. The arrival of the tank, which brought mobility back to the battlefield, slowly changed the picture. Between the wars, the experiments of employing tanks in whole divisions and using them as a strike force in their own right would, by the Second World War, shift the balance of aggression and defence back onto the attack.

But have people always been inclined to turn to violence? What of our most primitive ancestors, or the earliest settled prehistoric communities? Did they live

2 *The Tower of London as portrayed in* Old and New London, *1897. What was once the ultimate statement of Norman dominance in England became portrayed in a picturesque and nostalgic manner*

peaceful, co-operative lives or did they, too, resort to fighting and killing to gain resources or express fears and frustrations (**1**)? These questions have, in recent years, increasingly gained attention among archaeologists and anthropologists. Evidence is coming forward to suggest that even the most primitive people, few in numbers and isolated by great uninhabited tracts of land, engaged in violent aggression against each other. A triple Mesolithic burial at Vedbaek in Denmark included the body of a man with a bone point in his neck, suggesting a violent death. At Talheim in southern Germany, a mass grave of 34 men, women and children was excavated in 1983-4. These people had died violently. Over half had been killed by lethal blows to the head, crushing and even piercing the skull. Two skulls also revealed traces of injury by arrows.

It is important to outline what we mean by the term 'warfare' in this book. There are numerous definitions of warfare in the literature ranging from the low-level yet organised aggression, to the state-level warfare recognisable in the texts of Clausewitz. We accommodate a wide spread of these interpretations in the belief that the effects upon and actions by communities in conflict are significant, whether they occur on a local or national scale. We are not concerned with small-scale violence such as family quarrels or bar room brawls, nor are we considering criminal violence. We do, however, recognise that small-scale fights of these types may occur as spurs towards larger-scale conflict and may affect defensive or aggressive behaviour.

Once warfare becomes recognisable in the history of human society, its relationship to landscape and climate becomes equally clear. Decisions about what to protect or attack, and how to go about it, are invariably confined by the dictates of topography and weather. The forms of weapons and armour, types of troops, transport and supply, defences and fortifications, battlegrounds and strategy are all intrinsically linked with practical considerations of geology, vegetation, land use, seasonal change, rainfall and temperature. Equally inseparable are cognitive elements of landscape recognition – the perceptions of sacredness, ownership and land potential, ancestral roots and meaning, wealth and status exemplified by control or access to specific territories and regions.

It should be kept in mind, however, that not every structure has a purely practical military purpose. The picturesque Bodiam Castle in East Sussex (**colour plate 1**) and the red brick castle at Herstmonceux in the same county are both examples of castles built more for show than for defence, despite appearances to the contrary. Another pitfall is to see monuments in the same way that previous generations have (**2**). Sentimentalism will not help us get to the truth about a site.

And what of the evidence which is left on the remains of the victims of war? Here archaeology can shed light on the effects of ancient weapons and the nature of trauma. The evidence is piling up from an examination of skeletal remains over the years from both battlefield cemeteries and isolated discoveries, showing some unexpected and revealing results, and it is with an account of the pathology of warfare that we end the present volume.

There is now a very stimulating environment for the discussion of warfare as a major archaeological topic. The material presented here will provide a framework for some of those discussions in what can no longer be claimed is a neglected subject.

1 Origins of warfare

> In peace prepare for war, in war prepare for peace. The Art of War is of vital importance to the state. It is a matter of life and death. A road either to safety or ruin. Hence, it is a subject of inquiry which can on no account be neglected . . .
>
> *The Art of War*, by Sun Tzu, *c*.490 BC[1]

How did mankind come to be aggressive? What causes us to resort to violence against our own species? This question is a very large one, and many different ways have been attempted to find answers. At the root of the problem lie two major approaches. One holds that aggression in man is not fundamentally different from aggression in other animals, and that sociobiological explanations can be sought for the reasons behind violence in humans. These causes might include competition between males for females, or between individuals or groups for status, or for territory. The other position, broadly, suggests that there is a materialist explanation for aggression, 'starting from the standpoint that warfare is utterly irrational and therefore one would only risk one's life in combat when there was a desperate need for land or more immediately food'.[2]

The nature of aggression has been studied in several ways by researchers with different methodological or subject starting points; observations of primates have attempted to identify warlike behaviour in our closest relatives, while anthropologists have looked in detail at various forms of aggression in primitive and developed modern societies. Archaeologists have tried to draw conclusions based on the interpretation of physical evidence, and historians have studied the documentary material associated with conflicts over time.

None of these approaches is without its problems, either of methodology or of interpretation. We are all products of our time and place and hold views coloured by the experience of the society in which we live. Consequently, our attitudes to warfare and violence change remarkably from generation to generation and from place to place. The discovery in the caves at Makapansgat in South Africa of the remains of *Australopithecus Africanus* bones intermingled with the bones of a number of baboons led Raymond Dart to analyse the cause of death in 58 of the baboon skulls in a series of publications between 1949-1965. His conclusions were that the baboons had been victims of an aggressive and increasingly carnivorous tendency amongst the australopithicenes and that the depressed fractures on their skulls represented a bludgeoning from a right-handed opponent. Also, the weapons with which these hominids carried out their atrocity were fashioned from some of the bones which lay about. The hominids themselves were not without pathological signs of violent injury, indicating that there was probably indigenous aggression in their own community. Mankind's ancestor, it seemed, was the killer-ape, with a predilection for weaponry. The prose with which these theses were presented is somewhat graphic and says more perhaps about the time of its writing than the subject matter itself.[3] Many of the 'injuries' on the bones which Dart analysed were subsequently shown to have been caused by post-depositional phenomena.[4]

The behaviour of apes and monkeys, though undeniably important to the study of human action, must necessarily be different: human society, cognition and above all our use of language present a far more complex set of variables for interpretation than is the case with other primates. Anthropological observations, particularly those of primitive modern societies, may be beset with problems occasioned by the gulf between the understanding of the researcher and the meanings comprehended by the tribespeople, by the preconceived mind set of the researcher founded in Western notions of logic and social expectations, by the limited time span of many such observations, and by the effect that being observed may itself have on the behaviour of the observed, among other things. Archaeologists constantly debate the extent to which a study of physical remains can aid in an understanding of the way people in past societies thought about their world or believed in the appropriateness of their actions; the percentage of real evidence for any one period of the past that survives for our study is incredibly small, and generally each set of evidence tends to be fairly isolated in time and space. Besides these drawbacks, there are also many interpretative problems for archaeologists – how do we known if a skeleton found with a knife stuck between its ribs represents an episode of war, a domestic murder or a tragic accident? Historians have many of the same problems – their evidence is often patchy and incomplete; there is a tendency for most historical material to stem from the conquerors rather than the conquered, and of course there is the problem of assessing the veracity of documents, which may have been at the time the result of propaganda, wishful-thinking, or downright lying. This list is very incomplete – there are hundreds more potential problems to be dealt with in any effort to study the origins of human aggression.

Nevertheless, we can take a common-sense approach and look at some of the most commonly cited causes of aggression, and bring together what evidence we do have for early conflict in man's history to see if we can make correlations, at least at a superficial level.

Some suggested types of aggression in humans include maternal aggression – the way females will resort to violence to protect their young. Predatory aggression is that displayed in the quest for food. The desire to protect or to expand the hunting or feeding range of a group can lead to territorial aggression. Many animals display dominance aggression, especially but not exclusively among males attempting to achieve status or breeding rights, and to create a stable 'pecking order' within the group which helps to maintain internal peace.[5] Aggression can also arise from emotional states: anger, frustration, fear, desire, and even the over-excited state that can arise from activities sometimes characterised as 'sport'. It has also been suggested that the ritual preparation and the conduct and celebration of warfare can have a necessary cathartic value for a society.[6] This thesis proposes that such warfare and its associated rituals serve to bind a society together, release surplus energies, group fear and tensions, and provide an escape from boredom.

How early in the history of mankind does evidence for conflict occur? This question is beset by the difficulties posed by a limited and incomplete set of evidence capable of a number of explanations. Notwithstanding the Makapansgat evidence, skeletal trauma has been identified on *Homo erectus* skulls found at Zhoukoudian in China which may have occurred before the death of the individuals concerned, and it has been suggested that three parietal depressions on the skull of the Middle Pleistocene youth found at Swanscombe in Kent may represent old injuries received through combat.[7] A number of Neanderthal cases of trauma have also been cited as possible evidence for violence – four individuals of the group found at Shanidar in Iraq show evidence of wounds, and No. 4 had sustained a serious head injury, which seems to have been a relatively common occurrence. Keeley[8] notes a study suggesting that 40 per cent of Neanderthal skulls have similar head trauma:

> It would be difficult to explain the various Neanderthal injuries (including those in the original Neander Valley male) as simple accidents, and it seems more likely that conflict was the cause. Such injuries are very unlikely to be the result of family squabbles, but rather of serious, hard-hitting conflict, perhaps linked to territory or hunting rights over game or other resources.[9]

By the later Palaeolithic, there is evidence suggesting the taking of scalps in southern France, the use of projectile weapons against other humans (a projectile point was found embedded in the spine of a child at Grimaldi in Italy) and mass homicide in Czechoslovakia where group burials of men, women and children – the males showing signs of cranial injuries – have been dated to between 34,000 and 24,000 years ago.[10]

This evidence does not add up to war in its generally accepted sense – the deliberate organisation of violence by state-group against state-group – but if all these cases do represent deliberate injury, it becomes clear that the earliest periods of human development were certainly no 'golden age' of peace and co-operation.

By the Mesolithic, the evidence becomes even stronger. Arrowheads found in the ribs and backs of skeletons in the Vassilevka 3 cemetery on the Dnieper demonstrate a period of aggression around 10,000 years ago, and other mass burials that may represent similar incidents have been found across Europe in France, Greece, Denmark, Spain, Germany and Britain.

> The series of injuries attested at Mesolithic cemeteries seems to mirror the extreme forms of conflict waged in the defence of boundaries of individual territories. The wide geographical distribution of Mesolithic injuries shows that what is involved is not a local phenomenon, but a widespread trend in social development.[11]

Studies of Mesolithic artefacts have suggested that there was quite an arsenal available during the period that could be employed to inflict injury on other people – bone-

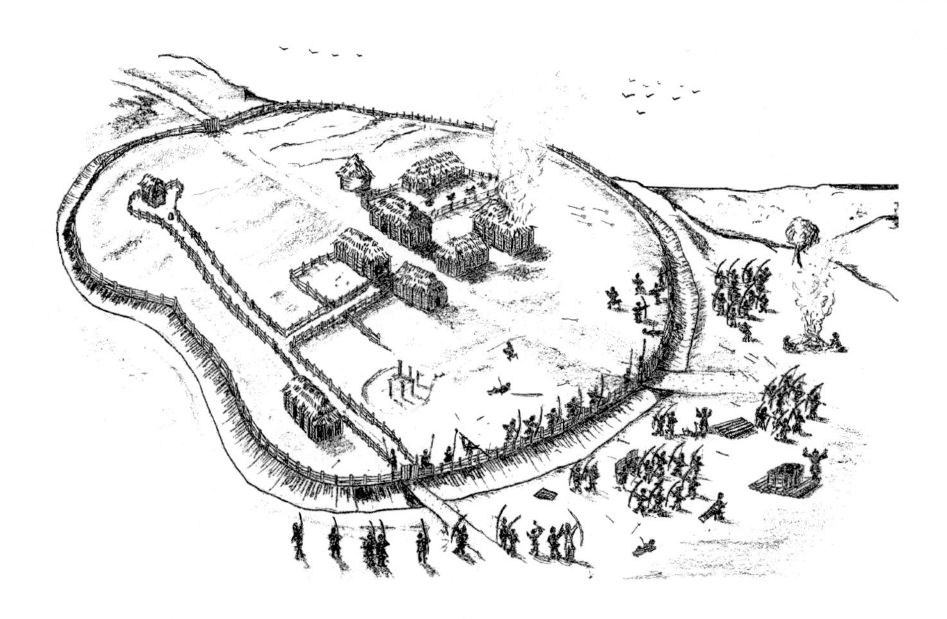

3a The Neolithic settlement of c.2500 BC which followed the original causewayed enclosure at Crickley Hill, Gloucestershire, was destroyed by fire and archery attack despite having a more complete defensive circuit than its predecessor. This reconstruction shows the settlement under attack. Note the sacred shrine at the western end of the fort

and flint-tipped arrows, spears, bone and antler clubs, and, absent from the inventory but no doubt utilised, clubs and spears made of wood. The blunt trauma noted particularly on skulls could as well have been inflicted by timber weapons as crafted maces or axes formed of composite materials. There are a few sites where the building of fortifications in the Mesolithic is claimed, but these are very uncertain.

A site of particular interest is a very early Egyptian cemetery, known as Cemetery 117, assigned to the period of 12,000-4500 BC and belonging to the Qadan culture. Situated in the north of modern Sudan, the cemetery was uncovered during excavations prior to the construction work on the Aswan Dam. Of the 59 skeletons, up to half exhibited wounds inflicted by microliths, assumed to be arrowheads. Some of the injuries were multiple and in two skulls there was evidence for the projectile having entered under the lower jaw. It is assumed that this site, like many other Neolithic sites, was positioned on a good fishing river within reach of rich agricultural lands, and that consequently what Arther Ferrill refers to as CSR, or Competition for Scarce Resources, had a key role to play in the emergence of organised violence in the Neolithic period.[12]

Evidence for defensive structures in the Neolithic, however, is much less equivocal. Crickley Hill, in Gloucestershire, seems to have begun as an undefended causewayed enclosure which came under attack from people armed with bows – their leaf-shaped arrowheads remained scattered over the site (**3a & b**). Subsequent to this attack, a number of phases of re-cutting of ditches was succeeded by Phase 1d during which the site was provided with a single massive ditch whose upcast was used

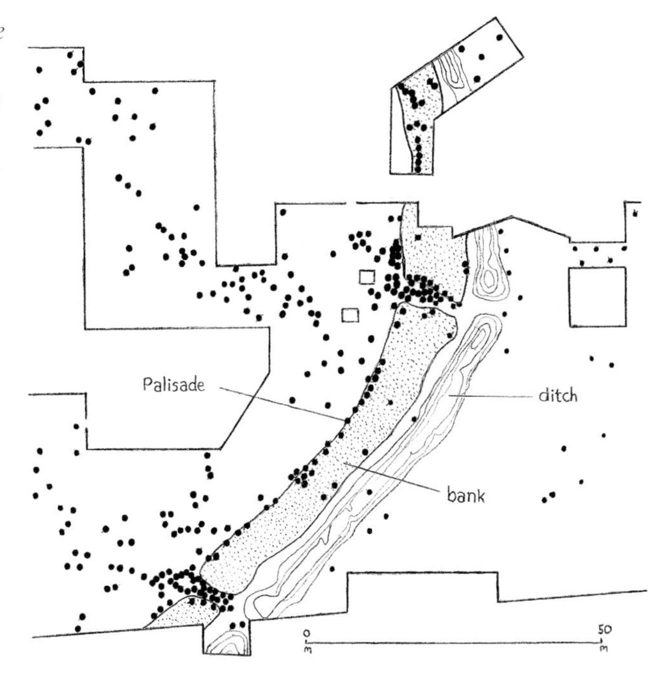

3 The archaeological evidence for archery attack at Crickley Hill is difficult to refute. This map is based on excavation plans and the round dots show find spots of flint arrowheads

to build a rampart 10m wide although only 0.5m high, which was crowned by a timber palisade. Two timber-lined gateways gave access to the centre via fenced and cobbled roadways. Rectangular house foundations suggested a densely packed interior. The site was apparently abandoned after another fierce attack – hundreds of arrowheads were found along the palisade and clustered at the two entrances.

> The enclosure had quite obviously been defended against archery attack and it is highly likely that it was built with this intention, for the low palisade formed no more than a breastwork. The ditches were presumably designed to break up and slow down an assault, and the low bank, or rather platform, would then serve as a killing-ground, at point blank range, against aggressors clambering out of the ditch.[13]

Another site often discussed in Britain in this respect is Carn Brea in Cornwall (**4**). Here, a wall of massive granite blocks (standing perhaps 2m high) enclosed an area of about 7200m^2 in which were cleared terraces with traces of domestic occupation. Carbon dating suggests that the wall was built some time before 3177-2921 bc. This village had been destroyed by fire, possibly during an armed attack, the evidence for which rests on the finds of some 751 leaf-shaped flint arrowheads. The wall had collapsed by about 2867-2627 bc, and the excavator suggests that the settlement probably had a life of about 250-300 years within these limits. Calculations of the effort needed to construct the defensive wall reach an absolute minimum of 31,000 man-hours – this was clearly an important and considerable undertaking for the community, which may have numbered some 150-200 people.

4 *Carn Brae in Cornwall. A Neolithic site with evidence of attack by archery and significant defensive stone structures. On the east side the causewayed enclosure had been blocked-up to make way for a more robust Neolithic fortress*

> As an obstacle intended to impede ingress by man the wall must be considered 'defensive', in that term's broadest sense, and, as defence customarily includes a psychological as well as physical posture, it may well be that the structure was deliberately constructed to present an imposing appearance, and was, in effect, a statement of the status of the community that built it. This suggestion of a positively defensive role is supported by the contemporary addition of a ditch outside the wall on the eastern side of the Eastern Summit. This ditch has no apparent structural relationship with the wall . . . and therefore is presumably set out purely to reinforce the wall.[14]

In his consideration of the reasons for the construction of defences, the excavator cites the wide-ranging contacts suggested by the material assemblage recovered. He considers the evidence from other excavations in Cornwall and concludes

> That other sites were similarly organised and took part in similar exchange schemes seems most likely and the evidence at the Carn Brea Neolithic settlement enclosure might appear to indicate that these parallel communities were close enough and of a similarity of interest to result in competition, direct conflict and warfare.[15]

Further traces of Neolithic fortification have been found at a number of sites in southern Britain, many of which also seem to have a high proportion of relatively exotic artefacts. We may therefore draw a tentative conclusion that warfare in Neolithic Britain, at least on a small and occasional scale, was originally motivated by economic considerations.

The Later Neolithic of continental Europe also saw increased efforts at fortification. Ditches and palisades were placed around a number of settlements such as Iclod and a stone wall was built at Karanovo in Phase V. It has been pointed out that the presence of banks, ditches, walls and palisades does not in itself confirm the incidence of warfare, and there are differences perceptible in an overview of eastern European sites between lowland and upland settlements. However, 'the main causes of warfare would have been resource competition between neighbouring groups, often with a long tradition of exchange and kin alliances, but where the breakdown of peaceful relations leads directly to warfare.'[16]

By the Late Neolithic and Early Bronze Age, warfare had become more formalised and organised in various societies. It is during this period that we start to find evidence in several forms of the development of military thought – strategy, tactics and philosophy. The increased organisation and complexity of ancient warfare in this period seems to be inextricably linked to the emergence and development of the earliest civilisations in the world. The rise of the first city states of ancient Sumeria brings with it evidence for organised warfare.

The evolution of warfare in the ancient period

Archaeological evidence for warfare, by its very nature, can often pre-date historical accounts of battles and campaigns. As well as the evidence of the ruinous city sites themselves in the ancient world, we are served by the clues inherent in memorial fragments, wall paintings, carvings, statuettes, models, weapons and armour. Together with historical material, we may try to piece together a picture of the evolution of organised aggression in the period we define here as 'ancient' – a period stretching from the emergence of the Sumerian City States in the middle of the third millennium BC to the decline and fall of the Western Roman Empire in the fifth century AD.

The written word as a source of evidence for the interpretation of military activity is certainly useful. If we are looking for descriptive or illustrative material, particularly when we are trying to examine how campaigns were fought or how men were equipped, we must turn to relatively unreliable written accounts and to pictorial representations within the surviving material culture. This latter type of evidence requires careful interpretation, since we have to be sure that we know why an artist or sculptor chose to represent a warrior or a battle scene in the way he did. As for contemporary accounts and authorities, these are not without their difficulties. Some chronicles give only scant reference to great feats of military organisation such as the Hittites' march to Babylon, whilst there are those who claim that authorities such as Herodotus, and even Caesar himself, are prone to differing types of exaggeration.[17] If written by the right sort of person, however, some historical documents from the period can shed a great deal of light on matters. The art of war in sixth-century BC China, for example, was already a highly elaborate affair with a creed and philosophy attached, as the writings of Sun Tzu demonstrate.

It is little wonder then, that whenever we come across an ancient text commemorating an aggressive encounter between two warring factions, or a wall painting or

5 *The Stone Bastion at Jericho. This defensive feature is one of the earliest in the archaeological record for any type of proto-urban settlement. Its scale and solidity indicates its builders' serious intent.* Photograph: Robin Luff

relief sculpture, we see a high degree of military preparedness and specialisation already developed in the descriptions and representations of the forces that were present. By the time of the Bronze Age from about the fourteenth century BC onwards, we can see states totally organised for war, with land forces split between infantry, small amounts of cavalry and chariotry, organised into regular units and even equipped with something approaching an Engineer Corps for the task of undermining city walls and undertaking countermining operations. The evidence left by Neolithic warfare, like its Bronze Age successor, also points to a degree of organisation.

The ninth and eighth millennia BC in the Near East saw an increase in land use and improvement in irrigation techniques leading to a form of proto-urbanism which gave rise to the earliest known defences. The impressive walls of Jericho, which is situated in an oasis in the Jordanian desert to the north of the Dead Sea, were built some time in the seventh millennium BC and bear testimony to the protectionist state of mind of some of these early urban settlements. Excavation has revealed a huge stone bastion 8.5m in diameter attached to the wall, built with an internal spiral staircase (**5**). Beyond the stone circuit wall was a V-shaped ditch measuring approximately 8m wide by 2.5m deep.[18] Another roughly contemporary candidate for defensive arrangements in a proto-urban environment was the settlement at Çatal Hüyük in southern Anatolia, which is thought to have been occupied between 6500 and 5500 BC. There are no defensive bastions like there are at Jericho, nor even an independently functioning wall, but the construction of the dwellings, which were entered through the roof and have no doors, has lead to the interpretation that the walls of the buildings themselves would have served as a defensive barrier in their own right.[19] Although these farming settlements ultimately failed to develop into true towns, there seems at least to have been an organisational capability within a structured community enough to procure the building of defences against aggressors. Both settlements produced agricultural surpluses, exploited local resources (obsidian in the case of Çatal Hüyük) and had a certain degree of long-distance trading interests to protect. Whoever built the walls and bastion at Jericho was expecting trouble.

The Sumerians

> He went to the forge and said 'I will give orders to the armourers; they shall cast us our weapons while we watch them.'
> From the *Epic of Gilgamesh*

Unfortunately, it is not until the emergence of the city states of Sumeria in the middle of the third millennium BC that again we come across convincing evidence for organised warfare in the archaeological record. The Sumerians, originally from Persia, had themselves invaded lower Mesopotamia in the fourth millennium BC, setting up urban settlements mainly in the area between the rivers Tigris and Euphrates. By now, true cities had begun to be established in the fertile plains of southern Mesopotamia during the third millennium BC. The city states had a long and varied history, but each is characterised by the ferocity of its competition with the others over scarce resources as well as the political ambitions of its leaders (**6**). The river valleys of Mesopotamia may have been fertile, but they lacked many of the raw materials needed to sustain urban life. There were few mineral resources in the area and no reliable building stone, siliceous rocks, ores or even good timber. The need to import such goods from the mountain settlements and further afield had an important bearing on urban development and on the emergence of powerful kings who could demonstrate their prowess by securing by military means the greatest amount of resources for their city and by protecting their cities from hostile intent. The city states waxed and waned in their dominance. First Kish, then Ur, followed by Lagash and then Umma.

Urbanisation brought with it a sophistication in social and religious organisation, which has left us with the legend of the warrior hero Gilgamesh as well as writings and pictorial representations displaying some revealing military detail. This material shows us how far military organisation had come since the time of the building of the earliest ramparts at Jericho. It is generally considered that the Sumerians were the first to develop the infantry spear phalanx which appears to be depicted on the Stele of the Vultures. It seems certain that the forces of the city states of Sumeria were both regular and organised. The Stele of Vultures, for example, displays serried ranks of close-order infantry (**7**). We can only surmise about the nature of Sumerian warfare before the period of this representation, but it is true to say that by the time of the writing of the great epic of Gilgamesh, weapons and armour had reached a sufficient level of sophistication, with the axe, bow (a weapon apparently fit for heroes yet employed in great numbers if surviving accounts of arrowhead orders are anything to go by), short sword,

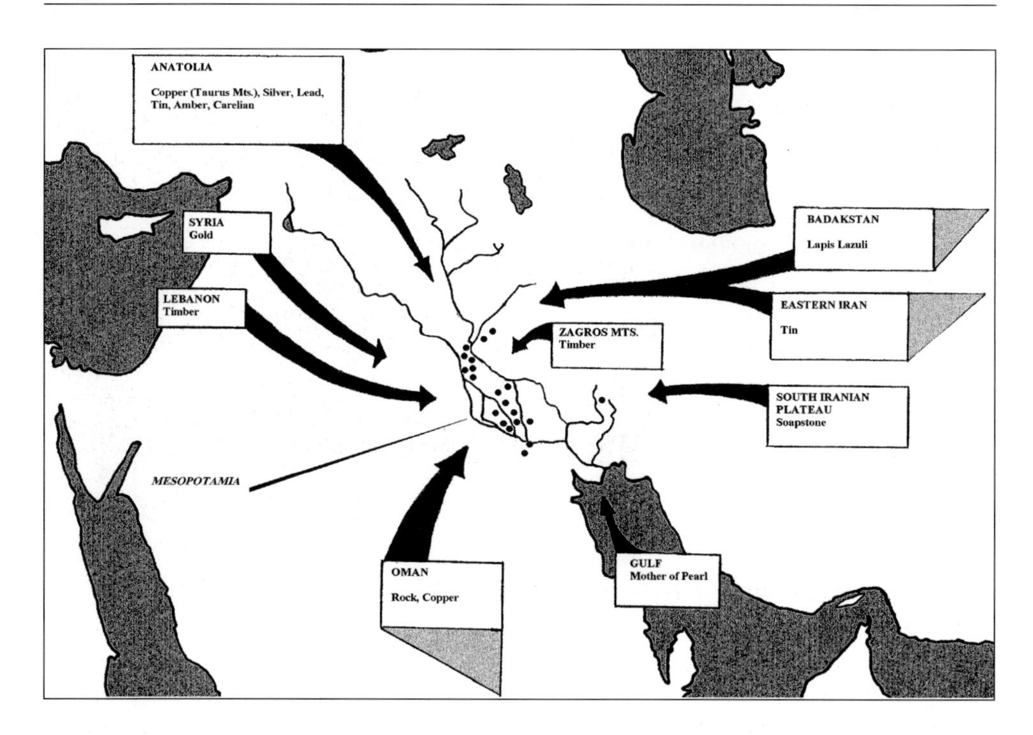

6 Map showing how through trading needs, the city states of Mesopotamia found themselves in a crucible of warfare. Few important resources and materials were available locally and competition was intense

spear and shield in use. For armour, the breastplate is mentioned, which is supposed to have covered Gilgamesh entirely. There is also reference to cavalry of a sort, with mention of mounted warriors upon magnificent stallions. Because the Sumerian cities had walls and were actively defended, it is likely that many military encounters took the form of siege warfare. We know that Sumerian armies on campaign were equipped with siege trains, although we are poorly served for pictorial evidence in Mesopotamia until the period of the Assyrian Empire, which literally teems with illustrative material showing siege engines and sappers at work (**14**).

One of the most perplexing of troop types represented in Sumerian art is the chariot. It is not at all like the chariots of later periods. The vehicles depicted on the exquisitely executed decoration of the so-called 'Royal Standard of Ur' (**colour plate 2**), have four and not two wheels and are pulled by four draft animals often interpreted as onagers, an ancestor of the donkey. Four animals, of course, present a larger target to enemy missile fire than two. There are many questions not sufficiently answered by the available evidence with regard to the Sumerian chariots. We know nothing about the temperament of the onager, although it has been said that it may have been difficult to domesticate.[20] Quite how fast an onager can travel is another question, but it is difficult to see speed as being part of this particular troop type's benefits. The vehicle seems to have four solid wheels, each of three pieces, but there is no indication that the front two wheels

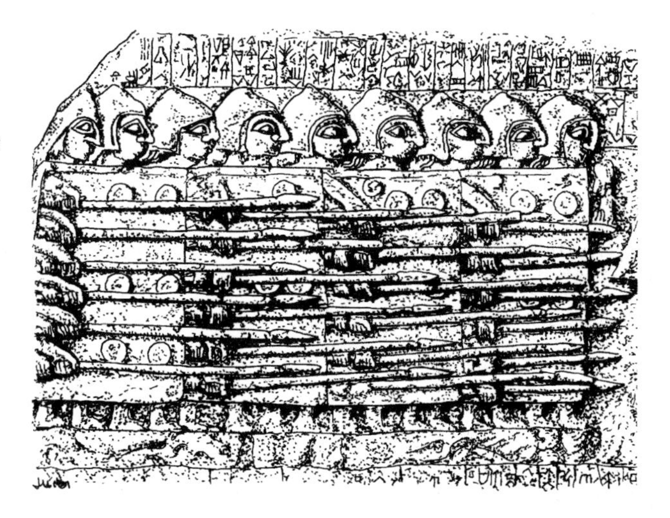

7 Drawing of The Stele of The Vultures, Lagash, c.2500 BC which celebrates the military victories of the king Eannatum. This is one of the earliest examples of the use of shock infantry in close formation, each carrying their spears levelled. The posture is essentially a defensive one

were capable of pivoting. They certainly seem unable to pass under the body of the vehicle, which must have resulted (if the depictions are accurate) in the chariot having an extraordinarily wide turning circle. The only possibility for the vehicle having a tight turning circle would be if the breastwork at the front of the platform pivoted in much the same way as a modern truck driver's cab does, but here we lack sufficient evidence to draw a conclusion. Versatile mobility could not have been this vehicle's strong point.

Given that the Sumerian war chariot is most frequently depicted carrying its two-man crew armed with a giant quiver of spears, whilst riding down fallen enemy warriors, it would be safe to imagine a limited battlefield role for the vehicle, one which saw their employment firstly as an elite warrior taxi service and secondly as a method of chasing down fleeing infantry in areas where battlefield successes required reinforcements.

One oddity in Sumerian chariotry remains. This is the so-called straddle-car, a small two-wheeled vehicle which simply has a saddle for one rider. It is not known how this was deployed in a military context, if at all. Its image survives in the small clay models which were often made to represent it. It does at least represent a more mobile possibility than the four-wheeled chariots depicted in the Royal Standard.

The era of the chariot

If the Sumerian period had seen the rise of armies equipped to take on opposing city states, then the new era was to see a shift in the posture of warfare to a more expansionist mode. It is no coincidence that the rise of the chariot accompanied the rise of the great kingdoms. The war chariot probably had its origins in the area south of the Caucasus, and from there its influence spread to the Hittites, then quickly around the Levant in the seventeenth century BC. The arrival of the new weapon in Egypt seems roughly to coincide with the advent of the Hyksos ('foreign chiefs') around 1650 BC, who are thought to have brought the art to the Egyptians.

Early in the second millennium BC came a series of technological and social developments which saw the usage of the chariot transformed from a transportation to a battlefield tactical role. The arrival of the true chariot is intricately bound up with the histories of the elites in ancient civilisations. The horse was becoming domesticated in many areas and this meant that a chariot drawn by a team of horses would easily be faster than the vehicles of the Sumerian period. Lightweight and bent wood working techniques accounted for the new spoked wheels and curved felloes, replacing the solid wheels of the previous millennium. Built with a new lighter body and incorporating archers armed with the new powerful composite bow, the chariot was utterly transformed. Speed and manoeuvrability characterised the new weapon as it entered its golden era in the early centuries of the second millennium. In general, the weapon was probably used as a mobile firing platform, but in some cases, when the warrior on board was equipped with a long spear, the assumption must be that the chariot delivered him quickly to the battlefield where he dismounted to fight. The side-effect of the newly discovered mobility was an acceptance of the vulnerability of the crew to enemy fire and the development of body armour to protect them. One particular discovery, the Mycenaean charioteers' armour known as the Dendra Panoply (**8a**), which covered its wearer from thigh to chin, accompanied by a boars' tusk helmet, demonstrates the extent to which body armour was used and implies a significant cost in providing this weapon type.

The requirements for the provision of a chariot corps were profound. For all their usefulness, the chariots of the great kingdoms were costly. Horses had to be bred and trained, crew had to be trained, armed and protected, specialist materials needed importing and craftsmen trained in the new technologies. Then there would be the logistical demands of a chariot army on the march, which would need to take with it a workshop and craftsmen for field repairs and maintenance.

War chariots were not just restricted to the ancient Near East kingdoms of the Hittites and Egyptians or to the Minoans or Mycenaeans (**8b**). By the late thirteenth century they had reached China, and by the time of the Western Zhou dynasty around 1050-1025 BC the new weapon was being used to secure a mastery over the Shang dynasty. It is from Chinese writings, particularly those of the rather later T'ai Kung, that we get a good indication of the strengths and weaknesses of the chariot in warfare. The chariot is hamstrung by terrain. T'ai Kung's texts on the 'Six Secret teachings' list ten types of terrain unfavourable to chariots and only eight that are good. Of the eight, none of them are really terrain features as such, but instead represent situations in which one should best employ a body of chariots. Any terrain or circumstance which impedes the chariots' ability to quickly withdraw from a situation is deemed fatal. This includes deploying with treacherous ground to the rear. Narrow defiles are said to lead to fatigue and should be avoided. Marsh, bog, irrigated fields and heavy rain are all supposed to spell disaster since they all deny the chariot its element of mobility. Even when chariots are in their preferred open terrain they need to be numerous, for as isolated individuals they may be cut-off. With these constraints in mind, it might be hard to see how chariots could be successfully employed anywhere except on a level road in great numbers. There are however times when chariots can use their speed to the best effect. Enemy that is unprepared should be struck with chariots as quickly as possible. Enemy that has been defeated and is turning to run should be cut down with chariots.

Chariots should also be used to attack the enemy in their camp, a measure apparently particularly effective at twilight.

Chariots it seems were at their most effective when attacking with the element of surprise, and used their speed to get out of tricky situations. When their retreat was blocked then disaster would follow. We still have to reconcile this convincing picture of chariot capabilities with the images we see of great warrior pharaohs charging down stricken enemy with their chariots in what seems like a frontal assault. In most cases, however, these scenes may be depicting an enemy rout, a situation which chariots are usually well-equipped to exploit.

Two examples from the ancient world of chariot army encounters serve to illustrate the elements of surprise and the inherent weaknesses of the weapon as outlined above. These are the battles of Meggido and Qadesh (**colour plate 4**).

By the time of the 18th Dynasty, the Egyptian pharaohs had established themselves as one of the great powers of the ancient Near East, along with the Hittites of Anatolia. The borders of Lower Egypt were secured with a massive fortification building programme, and by 1600 BC the Libyans west of the Nile Delta were subdued. Attention turned to campaigns beyond the Sinai into the Levant. In 1485 BC Tuthmosis III, Pharaoh of Egypt was on campaign in the Levant and found his northern route blocked by the town at Meggido. Within the walls were many leaders of other city-state forces, offering Tuthmosis a golden chance to bring many of his enemies to battle at once. Tuthmosis chose the narrower of the two approach roads to the town and led his army up it. It was so narrow in fact that the arrival and subsequent deployment of the Egyptian army took its enemy by complete surprise, and in the ensuing battle the Egyptian chariots won the day with swift and decisive actions. The next day there began a seven-month siege of the remaining forces of the town.

With their northern expansionist interests, the Egyptians were bound at one stage or another to come into contact with the Hittites of Anatolia, whose capital was at Hattusas. The Hittites too had chariots and infantry combined. In the early thirteenth century BC, Ramses II (**8c**) undertook a campaign, travelling north via Gaza, turning inland to Damascus and then on to the town of Qadesh on the Orontes. Ramses had received reports that the Hittites were some considerable distance away in Aleppo in Northern Syria, but this proved to be deliberate disinformation peddled by spies. The Hittites had in fact hidden their forces beyond the natural topographical feature of the town itself, behind the downslope of the far bank of the river. The Egyptian first division made camp with the Pharaoh. The second division was caught by surprise in the flank by Hittite chariot units and the ensuing struggle carried some of the first division's camp with it. By good fortune (although Ramses II would have it different), a second Egyptian chariot force, the Na'arn troops, had arrived at the battlefield and took the Hittites by surprise, defeating them and pushing them back across the river.

In the decades around 1200 BC a new change in Bronze Age warfare took place. Infantry were more numerous and well armed. The chariot's weakness in the face of an organised infantry capable of cutting it off and surrounding it, equipped with new longer swords, was to be its downfall. The horse was no longer to be used as a high-speed draft animal, but was to be developed into cavalry. Chariots which

8a (left) The Dendra panoply with associated boar's tusk helmet. Mycenaean charioteer's body armour. Very much the equipment of the elite warrior. This type of body armour was in use between c.1450–1350 BC. He probably dismounted to fight

8b (above) Chariot from crater fragment, Mycenae

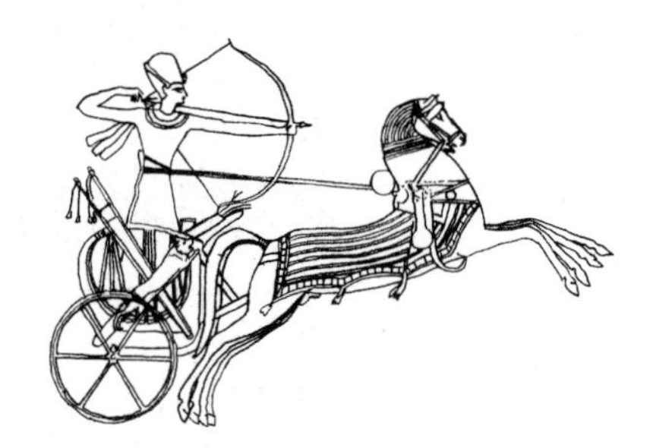

8c (above) Ramses II in his battle chariot at the battle of Qadesh. A glorification of the role of the noble charioteer in warfare. Note the reins around the pharaoh's waist

8d (left) Depictions of chariots in the era after their main pre-eminence. Top to bottom: i) Greek Geometric vase, eighth/seventh century BC. Chariots used in the Greek Dark Ages are sometimes depicted in funeral processions, echoing an elitist Mycenaean past. ii) From a silver bowl, possibly originating in Syria, found in a late eighth/early seventh century BC burial at Palestrina, northern Latium. iii) Bronze Benvenuti Situla Este. Later seventh century BC. Italy

8e Later Assyrian Heavy Chariots riding down enemy archers. Sixth century BC. The weapon was obsolete by the Assyrian period

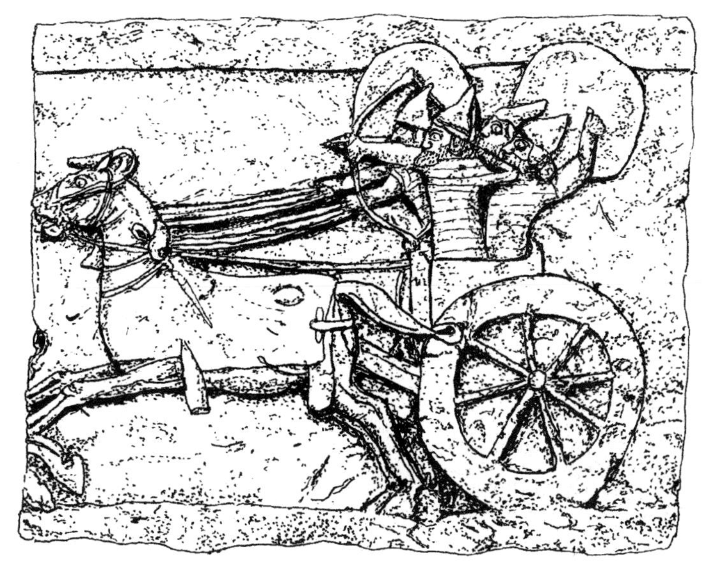

8f Assyrian Heavy Chariot with archer, driver and two shield bearers. Slower than earlier chariots, this Assyrian chariot required one extra shield bearer because of its vulnerability. Cavalry by now had become the main tactical weapon

8g The Vix Crater, French, c.525 BC shows the continued importance of the chariot in the Iron Age as a symbol of wealth. The 1.64m high vessel, for mixing wine, probably originated in Greece and was imported into France where it was included in the funerary furniture of an important woman

appear in later illustrations may still have had a military role, such as those of the Assyrians (**8e–f**), whose heavy chariots are depicted in battle action, but they were not the main arm of the new armies of the succeeding centuries. Other illustrations show the continued importance of the chariot as a status symbol, frequently depicting it in relation to the funerary rites of important people (**8d & g**).

Warfare in the Bronze Age of Europe, north of the Alps

The Bronze Age seems to have been a pivotal era, during which many of the features of the social, political, artistic, geographic and military landscapes that we recognise today were formed. Tantalisingly, although we have a great deal of evidence for the period, there are huge gaps in our knowledge and, of course, we have nothing in the way of historical information. Literacy had not penetrated into the transalpine zones. The study of the Bronze Age in Europe is, at the moment, a very lively area; many new theories are being proposed, much new material is becoming known, and many of our ideas about dating and sequences are in flux. This is, therefore, a period which is throwing up far more questions than answers, and this state of affairs must be borne in mind in any discussion of the warfare of the period. We can perhaps discern some themes, some general patterns of development and change; however, they can all be subject to different interpretations and analyses. The old archaeological adage of 'absence of evidence is not evidence of absence' is never more important than when considering this era.

That the Chalcolithic (Copper) Age and the succeeding Bronze Age were periods which saw great and significant changes is undoubted. These changes manifest themselves in many structures, monuments and artefacts, and imply similar change in social, political and cultural life. For these 'cognitive' areas of the past we lack direct physical evidence, so we must rely on interpretation, analogy and sometimes inspired guesswork. The important thing is to be open to new ideas, different theories and contradictory evidence; the next site to be discovered may always be the one to collapse our hypothetical house of cards.

With this caution in mind, what can we say about the Bronze Age? It seems to have been the period when mankind's ability to manipulate his world made great strides in technology, especially in metalworking, the building of structures, and transportation. From the early flat-cast copper axes of the Chalcolithic in the late third millennium BC to the highly developed and skilful jewellery and weapons of the Late Bronze Age, the ability and technical knowledge of the craftsmen of the period clearly increased at a fast rate, compared with the thousands of years of the preceding lithic technologies. The domestication of the horse, perhaps in the late Neolithic, led to the development of a whole range of forms of wheeled transport and to vastly increased trade, cultural and social mobility. At the same time, it seems clear that riverine and marine transport was also improving rapidly. Among the important finds in Britain in recent decades have been the Middle Bronze Age boats at North Ferriby, East Yorkshire and Dover in Kent. The latter, dated by radiocarbon provisionally to the fourteenth century BC, was originally 13m long and considered to have been capable of Channel crossings.

That crossings were made is certain – the Bronze Age has a great deal of evidence for pan-Continental trade and exchange of ideas. Amber and furs came down from the far north; oil, wine and ornamental vessels came up from the Mediterranean. Distribution maps for particular artefact forms, such as pins and brooches or swords, show close correlations in style and actual imports of material across vast distances. Many of these show that the trade routes made use of coastal contacts (from Scandinavia via the Low Countries, France and the British Isles to Iberia) or river routes (such as the Rhine, the Weser and the Danube). In central upland Europe, the distribution maps show the use of mountain passes, possibly indicating the use of pack trains. Two common artistic motifs of the Bronze Age may relate to the importance of this trading explosion: the ubiquitous 'wheel' symbol and the almost as common 'waterbird', symbols which recur in a variety of forms from Portugal to the Steppes and from Ireland and Scandinavia to North Italy and Greece. It has even been suggested that the Bronze Age saw the development of the 'Celtic' language systems, spread by the traders and sailors, creating a sort of prehistoric Esperanto to facilitate exchange of religious, political and technological ideas, although it is hard to see how this could ever be proven if it were true.

It is during the Bronze Age that we first see clear efforts to delineate territorial boundaries. These are not defensive frontiers, but agricultural divisions – the reave systems of Dartmoor, 'ranch' boundaries of Wessex, and 'Celtic' field systems of much of southern England, for example. The desire to demarcate territory may be related to demographic stress, or to farming difficulties such as soil starvation. Equally, we may be seeing the beginnings of tribalism, formalised group identities, and perhaps the emergence of systems of control and government under warrior elites or chieftains.

An important feature of the Middle and Later Bronze Ages is the appearance of fortified settlements, relatively small at first, but developing into the hillforts usually associated with the Iron Age. That a great many of these monuments originated in the Bronze Age now seems to be certain. Why they were thought necessary is less clear. Many are situated where they are able to dominate trade routes, crossings and passes, although they are generally placed at a little distance on the most naturally defensible sites. Again, are we looking at the emergence of tribal chiefdoms? Were these centres the beginnings of proto-states that would develop in the succeeding centuries into the variety of societies ultimately encountered by the Romans and by history?

When the first traces of the use of metals becomes evident in the archaeological record of Europe, the dominant form of weaponry seems to have been the bow. This is, of course, a hunting weapon, but the evidence shows that its lethal power could have been and was turned against people. Evidence has already been cited from Crickley Hill and Carn Brae in England for the usage of the bow and arrow in human aggression. Recently, however, scans of Oetzi, the Copper Age man found in an Italian glacier, have revealed the presence of a projectile point lodged under the scapula (**9**). A pathologist on the project, Dr Eduard Egarter, has said 'The new data leave little room for doubt that the man died as a result of being struck in the back by an arrow. It was a bull's eye.'[21] Oetzi himself was found with a quiver and arrow fletchings.

Other examples of arrow wounds from the Early Bronze Age have been found in Britain (at Barrow Hills, Oxfordshire, for example), in the Netherlands and Spain. Numerous flint arrowheads appear in graves, along with archer's wrist bracers, espe-

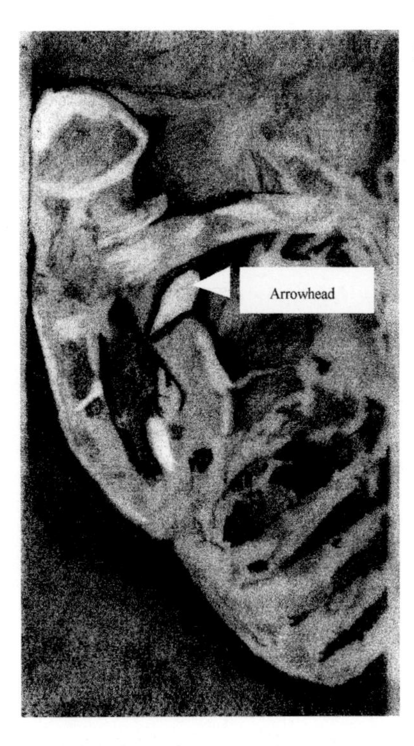

9 Oetzi the Ice Man. Dating from the early Bronze Age, he was discovered in the Alps in 1991. It did not become apparent for some time that lodged in the man's back, under the scapula, was an arrowhead that almost certainly killed him. This drawing is taken from an X-ray

cially in those associated with the Beaker culture. Another frequently-found weapon of the Early Bronze Age is the dagger, either riveted to its handle, or provided with an integrally cast tang. These daggers are often particularly fine; the example (one of three in the grave) from the Bush Barrow near Stonehenge in Wiltshire had a pommel decorated with thousands of minute gold nails arranged in patterns. Its twin was found in Finisterre in Brittany, proving the cross-Channel connection early in the period. The dagger evolved into the rapier, a long thin blade, with a riveted handle. This was a thrusting weapon, one which would have necessitated some skill and training to use effectively, although evidence from tears along the line of the rivets in some examples suggest that attempts had been made to use them as slashing weapons. That close-range combat was becoming more common is demonstrated by the appearance of shields in the later Early and subsequent Middle Bronze Ages. Most early shields were made of organic materials, and so evidence is scanty, but a wooden shield-former, for the shaping of leather shields, was found at Kilmahamogue in Ireland, carbon-dated to 1950-1540 BC, and later examples of both wood and leather shields have also been preserved in Irish peat. Osgood[22] describes the rapier as 'the weapon of champions', and suggests that its use is symptomatic of a change in the way warfare was carried on – from long-range, perhaps almost non-personal, archery, to close-range, formal duels between trained masters of the art, possibly on behalf of the rest of their respective communities.

As the Bronze Age progressed, forms of weapons began to proliferate. New types of spear and sword, halberds and axes appear, and defensive equipment also became more elaborate and widespread. Examples of helmets, organic and bronze shields, greaves to protect the legs, and bronze corselets are found. There are also hints of padded or quilted body armour, perhaps as depicted on the anthropomorphic stelae found at Le Petit Chasseur in Switzerland.

Spear forms range from almost impossibly large to light throwing weapons. They have traditionally been divided into 'javelins' (for throwing) and 'lances' (for thrusting), but skeletal evidence suggests that the manner of use may have depended upon circumstance. The possibility of larger spearheads being hafted to short shafts and used like a Zulu assegai has also been postulated. Evidence for Middle and Later Bronze Age spear wounds comes from many places, such as a find from Over Vindinge, Denmark of a skeleton of a man aged about 50-60 with a bronze spearhead 47mm long and 24mm embedded in the pubis, having entered the body from behind, and the point of a spearhead which remains in the vertebrae of an individual from La Grotte du Pas de Joulie Trèves, now in the museum at Aveyron, France.

The weapon of status for the latter half of the Bronze Age was clearly the sword, however. Typically short (between 50-80cm long), these are very close combat weapons. The heavier slashing-type blades that succeeded the rapier would have taken less skill to use effectively, and therefore may have been weapons used by a wider section of the population, not just champions. By the end of the Bronze Age, a dual-purpose sword was in use over much of Europe, the so-called 'Carp's Tongue' form, which combined the rapier's thrusting capabilities with the weight and edge of the slashing sword. These later swords were generally provided with a solid integral cast hilt. This was a formidable infantry arm, as the depth and severity of skeleton evidence attests. The development of winged chapes has been claimed as evidence that these swords could have been used from horseback, the rider using his foot against the chape to enable him to draw the sword from its scabbard; against this notion are cited the lack of stirrups, and the shortness of the blades. A warrior would lack the stability or reach to be effective from horseback with these weapons, it is claimed. On the other hand, we know little or nothing about the possibilities of saddles at this time, perhaps due to their organic nature, and the Romans, armed with relatively short swords and using moulded leather saddles, coped very effectively with this style of fighting.

> As the Bronze Age progressed weapons became more technologically advanced, and these advances not only necessitated changes in defensive technologies, but also facilitated them. By the onset of the succeeding Iron Age, the Bronze Age warrior was able to call upon a wide range of defensive protection while making use of a varied arsenal of beautiful yet deadly bronze weapons.[23]

A number of helmet forms have been found – cap helmets from France, Spain and Germany, conical and rounded bell helmets from Germany and Slovakia, crested helmets also from France, Spain, Austria, Italy and Germany, and the amazing horned helmets from Viksø in Denmark. Iconographic evidence suggests the use of horned helmets in Sweden and Sardinia too. These are, of course, bronze examples, perhaps reserved for ceremonial use or parades – the likelihood of organic materials used to construct most workaday armour is strengthened by the hemispherical helmet from Cuevas de Vinromá in Spain made of silver and antler.

Shields have been found in many locations too – circular bronze examples from Germany, France, Italy, Britain and Eastern Europe and Scandinavia, particularly the 14 fine shields buried together at Fröslunda in Central Sweden, and organic shields including those attested by patterns of bronze studs in graves in Germany (at Wollmesheim, for example, where a surviving fragment of wood proved the shield to have been about 20mm thick) and from peat finds in Ireland, Sweden and Germany.[24] Also from Ireland is the Clonbrin leather shield which was 50cm in diameter and 5-6mm thick.

The use of greaves to protect the legs is attested from Central and Southern Europe, and as has been already mentioned, it is possible that quilted or padded body armour was worn. Apart from the Swiss stelae, it has been suggested that portrayals of curiously square-bodied warriors in Swedish rock carvings may be representations of this type of protection.[25] The use of chariots is also suggested by iconographic material, though probably as transportation to the battle rather than as a fighting platform.

The move towards fortification of settlements, while discernible in many parts of Europe, was by no means universal at any single period during the Bronze Age. Some sites had received fortification in the late Neolithic. In Chalcolithic Iberia, a number of remarkable settlements enclosed by defensive walls and bastions, and provided with possible arrow slits, suffered devastating attacks leading to abandonment. Late Únětice sites in eastern Germany, Otomani sites in Romania and settlements in parts of Hungary began to acquire defences in the Early Bronze Age. Middle Bronze Age sites in Bohemia acquired ramparts, palisades, ditches and stone-built walls; bastions and towers were built on Sicily and Sardinia. By the Late Bronze Age, ramparted and ditched settlements and defensibly sited hilltop villages appear in many parts of the Continent, notably in the Rhine-Main Basin and the Lausitz area of east Germany and Poland.[26] A site in Moravia, Cezavy Hill, contains many burials thought to be those of slaughtered defenders. In Britain and France, too, defensible locations were being chosen. Well-known examples in Britain include Mam Tor in Derbyshire, Hog Cliff Hill in Dorset, and Ram's Hill in Berkshire, which had a heavily defended gateway and an enclosing rampart and ditch, the latter up to 3.75m wide and 1.24m deep. Increasing evidence suggests that high-quality craft production and trading activities were beginning to be concentrated on these defended locations:

> The considerable variety of pottery styles found at Ram's Hill matched its unusual location at the geographical boundary between different style zones. Some of the finer wares have styles which are geographically distinct. Typically, they cover regions of southern Britain up to 100km (62 miles) wide. Along such corridors where two or more styles overlap or coincide the defended settlements like Ram's Hill are found.[27]

This pattern is also visible in continental Europe, so trade and craft production must have assumed great importance by the Later Bronze Age, and must have been perceived as coming under threat. The big question is – why?

10 The comparison between Scandinavian Bronze Age maritime warriors and those of the later Viking Age is difficult to escape. It is probable that raiding by boat was a frequent occurrence in Scandinavia and Britain in the Bronze and Iron Age, which may explain the building of such defensive features as brochs. This depiction comes from a Swedish rock carving

The changes in the Late Bronze Age right across Europe and the Near East have been much discussed. The proliferation of weaponry and armour (the first 'arms race' as it has been called), the move towards defensive locations, the signs of territoriality and of elite graves occur in almost every society of the period to some extent.

Various theories have been suggested. Upland zones in Britain and elsewhere, settled and farmed for centuries, are found to be abandoned around 1200 BC. Was this the result of a climatic shift leading to poor summers and wet winters, creating the conditions for bog formation that ruined the farmland, and leading to poor harvests and starvation? Was it a result of the eruption of Mount Hekla, the Icelandic volcano, in 1159 BC? Some suggest this could have caused a form of nuclear winter as dust clouds obscured the sun, or that sulphur from the explosion fell as acid rain, causing crops to fail and animals to sicken and die. Other suggestions include the overfarming of poor or light soils (the heavy plough still had to be invented, so most arable farming was restricted to these less fertile zones), population explosions, demographic pressure as a domino effect across Europe originating in the westward movements of people from the Steppes and central Russia, or the result of socio-political changes creating competing aristocracies vying for control of territory and trading profits.

We are also unsure of just how much warfare there really was in the Bronze Age. Burial evidence is scanty overall; although it includes examples of weapons trauma the statistical significance cannot be assessed. The appearance of weapons in graves may suggest that they are status or ritual objects, rather like the Great Sword of State – after all, no one actually expects the Queen to wield the sword in battle. Moreover, many of the fine shields and helmets are thought to be too thin to be of any practical use, and must therefore have been used to underline the wealth and status of the owner rather than (or as well as) his military prowess.

On the other hand, the vast amount of time and effort involved in the building of fortifications, the clearly practical and military developments in weapons technology, and various iconographic depictions of combat, together with the nearly complete dominance of military symbolism across Europe at this time, suggest that warfare was a prevalent aspect of society. If not a matter of battles between cultural or political groups, armed raiding seems to be a particularly likely scenario, especially as facilitated by the use of the horse and boats. Many of the Swedish rock carvings show armed figures mounted on horseback or standing in boats (**10**), some apparently complete with horned helmets, and the carved wooden figures from Roos Carr, Humberside, dated to the very end of the Bronze Age, carrying (probable) wooden clubs and shields, depict warriors standing on a boat. The analogy with the later Vikings is inescapable, and begs questions about the range and extent of the depredations such war bands could have achieved.

The catastrophe of the Late Bronze Age

The notion that the passing of some of the great civilisations of history can be put down to changes in the style of warfare is one which goes in and out of fashion. Of course, the story is a complicated one and with each civilisation that came to a seemingly abrupt end in the decades around the year 1200 BC, there is archaeological evidence to promote theories of both survival and destruction at different times and places. It is, however, generally true to say that the core of the ancient world, with the notable exception of Mesopotamia and the stoutly resisting Egyptians, was utterly transformed by a series of events, not all military, which culminated in a new order in the Near East. Within just a few generations, the old great Empires were broken up, their cities destroyed. Anatolia, the ancient heartland of the Hittite Kingdom, was to see a new Phrygian order. Elsewhere smaller kingdoms sprang up within the areas of ancient empires, many of which are mentioned at length in the Old Testament, such as the Kingdoms of Solomon and David.

Whether or not the violent passing of cultures such as the Myceneans can be put down specifically to the actions of what the Egyptians described as 'the people from the Islands in the midst of the sea', is a moot point. The 'Sea Peoples' are still poorly understood. These islands may have been those which inhabit the Aegean Sea, but what seems to characterise the Sea Peoples are their martial qualities and their advanced and effective weapons and armour. They are variously depicted wielding long slashing swords, carrying small shields and wearing some defensive body armour. It is a matter of some significance that the Naue Type II sword (**11**), a weapon with a possible North European root, with its relatively straight sides and long blade, clearly designed for slashing strokes as well as the thrusting strokes of contemporary swords, should appear

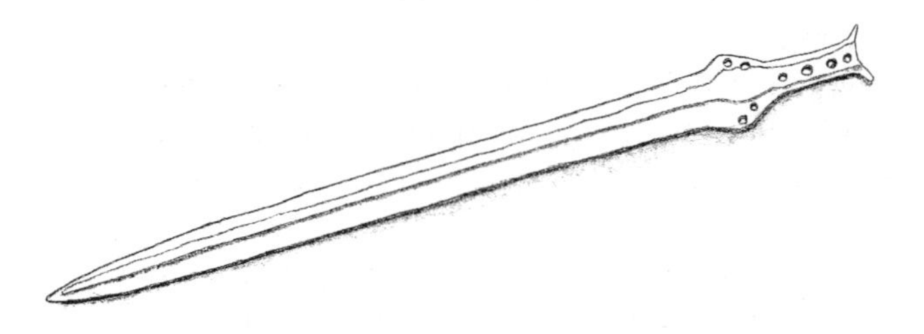

11 *The straight sided Naue Type II sword was at an advantage over the rapiers and tapering swords which preceded it. At around 80cm in length, it was designed as a cut-and-thrust weapon.*

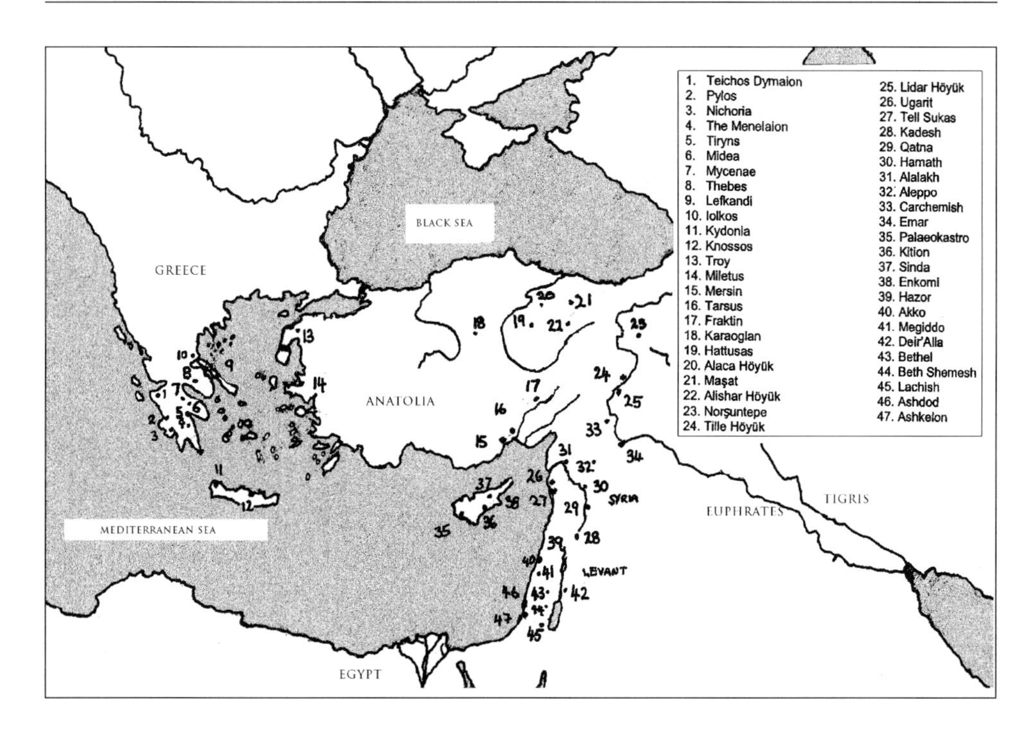

12 Map of the eastern Mediterranean showing the main sites destroyed in the Catastrophe of the Late Bronze Age in the Ancient world

at the time of the collapse of the great civilisations. Indeed, it is often found in the heart of the areas which were destroyed (**12**). Moreover, the obvious aggressive nature of this weapon development, and its morphology, compares interestingly with the development of similar *iron* weapons amongst the Germanic tribes of the Late Roman Iron Age and Dark Ages in Northern Europe. In both cases, we have Empires militarily threatened by irregular tribal warriors with a strikingly similar offensive weapons set, and a penchant for using it. Principal amongst these weapons was the long sword: whether it be a Germanic broad sword of the sixth century AD or a Naue Type II sword from 1200 BC, the fact remains that with such arms, the enemies of an empire need not necessarily be considerable in number, but would be effective in their small warbands. John Hines has sought to prove, on the basis of the Danish Late Roman Iron Age bog deposits, that the average size of a Germanic warband in the fifth century AD would only have been around 200 men, which it is argued here demonstrates how few men are needed to be militarily effective.[28]

The factors surrounding the collapse of the Bronze Age civilisations, in particular the fall of the Palatial civilisation at Mycenae, have been variously accounted for. The military aspect of the 'Catastrophe', as it has now become known, has gained ground recently. In summary, the main proponents for the differing views adopt the following stances.[29] Vermeule,[30] Iakovides[31] and Betancourt[32] favour the 'Economic Factors' argument, while the effects of climate are preferred by Carpenter.[33] Internal social upheaval is put forward by both Andronikos[34] and Mylonas[35] while invasion from outside the Aegean world is favoured by Desborough,[36a-b] Rutter,[37] Winter[38] and Deger-Jalkotzy.[39] Drews,[40] however, prefers to see changes in the nature of weapons and warfare as the main cause with an increase in the availability of powerful weapons amongst the non-elite warriors, citing the Naue Type II sword as one of the principal weapons of the aggressor. While there may be aspects of every argument in the truth, there is undoubtedly a change in the nature of warfare in both the Aegean and Northern Europe in the Bronze Age, and its levelling effects must have been profound.

The Assyrian War Machine

> . . . The tribute of the sea coast – from the inhabitants of Tyre, Sidon, Byblos, Mahallata, Kaiza, Amurru and Arvad [Cyprus] which is an island in the sea, consisting of gold, silver, tin, copper, copper containers, linen garments with multi-coloured trimmings, large and small monkeys, ebony, boxwood, ivory from walrus tusk, a product of the sea – this their tribute I received and they embraced my feet.
> Ashurnasirpal II after a campaign in the Levant, 877 BC

With these words the true founder of the Neo-Assyrian or Late Empire, Ashurnasirpal II (883-859 BC), encapsulated the driving force of Assyrian imperialism. The Assyrians were to become the model for many of the empires of the ancient world including Babylon and Persia. Few cultures mourned the passing of the cruel empire when Nineveh was sacked in 612 BC, but those who had been touched for three centuries by the hand of Ashur knew that the Assyrians had got something right in the way that they approached organised warfare.

The story of the rise of the Assyrian Empire is one that is inextricably linked to the nature of the landscape in which the core cities of Nineveh, Ashur and Arbil found themselves. The Assyrians had to develop an active aggressive military to keep their borders free of punitive and sometimes very penetrating raids. The heartland of Assyria had no real easily defendable features. This policy was further enhanced by the deliberate deportation of populations, a practice which had gone on for some time, but which under Tiglath Pileser III (745-727 BC) and his successors took on a whole new dimension. In 744 BC, 65,000 people were deported from Iran and in 742 BC, 30,000 people were deported from Hamath in Syria and resettled in the Zagros Mountains. Of particular significance was the carrying-off of 27,290 inhabitants of the Israelite city of Samaria. The date is disputed and could either be the three-year-long siege initiated by Shalmaneser V in 724 BC or the action of his successor Sargon II early in his reign in 721 BC. Whatever the argument as to the identity of the aggressor, the subsequent effects upon the dispersed populations who became known as the 'Lost Tribes of Israel' were to be profound indeed.

The geographical disposition of Assyria, despite its obvious weakness, had some great strengths too. If the Assyrians could expand their domination by either securing vassal status on city states outside the area of Greater Assyria, or if they could, as time

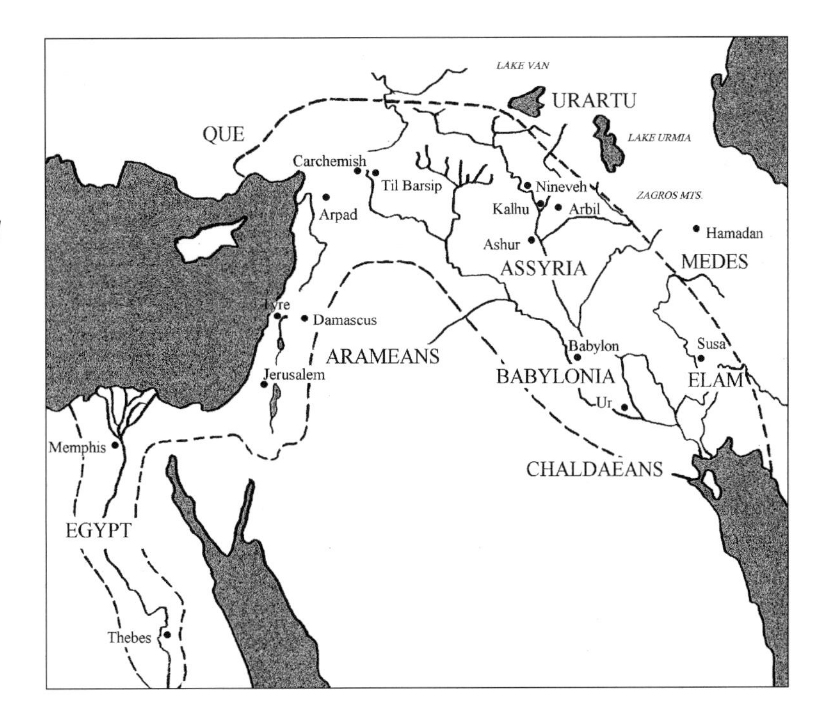

13 Map of Assyrian Empire at its height under the reign of Ashurbanipal (668-627 BC). The dotted line indicates the maximum extent of empire

was to prove, introduce direct rule all the way to the Mediterranean seaboard, then the control they would have over the flow of trade from Anatolia in iron, silver, lead, tin, gold and copper would be immense. It would be possible to redirect the material into the heartland of Empire. This is precisely the motivation behind Shalmaneser III's campaigns in Syria between 858 and 855 BC when he had secured Til Barsip as a forward base for operations. As if proof were needed of the importance of economics to the survival of the Assyrian Empire, it is worth pointing out that when the Empire was going through a period of steep decline and royal weakness, between 811 and 741 BC, it was only when the kingdom of Uratu annexed Assyrian lands on the lapis lazuli trade route and threatened the supply of horses from Mannea that the 'final straw' had come. Hereafter, following the successful coup of the governor of Khalu, the Empire was to embark upon its most militaristic phase. The economic boot could be on the other foot, too; Tiglath-Pileser III placed an Assyrian embargo on timber supplies from the Lebanon to Egypt, redirecting the material to the heart of his own empire.

The notable aspect of Assyrian militarism was not so much in the level of organisation that one would expect for a society geared for almost total war, but in the way in which Assyrian kings prosecuted their political aims, using the military as a primary tool. At its height in the seventh century BC under Ashurbanipal the Assyrian Empire stretched right across the old Fertile Crescent and down into Egypt (**13**). By this time the Assyrian army had changed from the seasonally recruited militia with a professional elite corps to a standing army with royal bodyguard and vassal mercenaries capable of undertaking any kind of operation at any time of the year. The standing army of the later, or Neo-Assyrian, Empire was known as the Kisir Sharruti. Siege warfare was, of course, a significant aspect of warfare in a

14 *The Assyrians were the leaders in the ancient art of siege warfare. This detail from a panel from Nimrud, NW Palace 865-860 BC, shows sappers at work undermining enemy walls with other troops using scaling ladders*

landscape dominated by urban settlements and the Assyrians were without a doubt the ancient masters of the art (**14**). Sieges could be protracted affairs, although it was policy to try to end them quickly with terror if possible. Despite some remarkable siege equipment, they could be costly in terms of manpower and attrition. In the campaign that saw the fall of 46 cities in the Levant under Sennacherib (704-681 BC), the siege of Lachish is known from the evidence of a mass grave to have cost 1500 Assyrian lives. It was not beyond their army to launch amphibious assaults, either: as early as the ninth century there is evidence of infantry having been issued with inflatable skins with which to paddle across rivers, their horses swimming in tow, and their chariots dismantled and floated across on boats of skin, known today as 'keleks' (**15**). In 694 BC Sennacherib attacked the Kingdom of Elam after a long period of trouble using ships built by his Phoenician vassals. The marshes of modern southern Iraq were no obstacle to this professional army. In campaigns against the Chaldeans (who were to be instrumental in the ultimate downfall of the Empire), the Assyrians used a vast flotilla of reed boats to prosecute their wars successfully.

Keeping an empire together was always difficult. The key to success in this regard was unquestionably the ability of the administration to communicate quickly with forces and political leaders at different ends of the vast lands they controlled. To this effect, a network of well-trained messenger riders was formed. Also, under Tiglath-Pileser III (745-727 BC), the old system of allowing vassal status among conquered enemies at the border of the Empire was abandoned in favour of direct rule and the instigation of a patchwork of smaller and less threatening political entities. Eunuchs were often appointed at the heads of these states: their first loyalty would be to the king and, most importantly, they, would have no dynasty which could cause trouble in the future.

15 *Drawing of detail from bas relief, ninth century BC. Obstacles such as rivers were no real hindrance for the Assyrians who are shown here crossing a river on inflated animal skins. Infantry were not the only troops to be carried across. Chariots too, were dismantled and reconstructed on the opposite bank*

Under Ashurbanipal (668-627 BC) Assyria saw its greatest successes and maximum extent of power, but as is often the problem with large empires, it somewhat over-stretched itself. Fratricidal warfare with the King of Babylon and grand designs on Egyptian territory, combined with a punitive expedition into the Kingdom of Elam (which resulted in the sewing of salt over the ruins of the conquered enemy settlements), put intolerable pressures on the resources of even this most resourceful empire. The arrival onto the scene of a new and powerful force in the Near East, the Scythians, brought many problems not just to Assyria. But in the end it was the closest and oldest enemies of Chaldean-influenced Babylon and the Medes who conspired to reduce Nineveh and bring the final capital of Assyria to its knees in a siege, for which some evidence exists. The gates of the town (notably the south-western Halzi gate and the northern Adad gate) had deliberately been narrowed from a 7m width to a 2m width, and there is reference to the river Khosr having been diverted to wash away some of the defences.[41]

Greek warfare

By the time of the Spartan poet Tyrtaeus, writing in *c.*650 BC, Greek warfare seemed to have completed its evolution from the personal feuds of elite warriors engaging in single combat, to the beginnings of what was to become the trademark of Greek armies for hundreds of years, the hoplite phalanx (**colour plates 6 & 7**). He describes warriors as standing shoulder to shoulder, a posture seldom encountered in the writings of the earlier periods of Greek history. Although early hoplite armour seems to predate the arrival of the new tactical philosophy, it seems to most scholars that there was definitely a change in the nature of Greek warfare at the beginning of the seventh century BC.

As with the rise in sophistication of warfare in the Near East, some 1000 years before this era, the changes in Aegean warfare directly resulted from the rise of the city state. The choice of military posture had become the responsibility of the civic community at the heart of the politics of the Polis.[42] Hoplite warfare was characterised

16 Detail from the Chigi Vase in Museo Nazionale di Villa Giulia, Rome, showing one of the earliest depictions of Hoplites in action. c.650 BC

by the appearance of the phalanx, often formed eight deep, but doubled or tripled in depth to suit whichever wing of the army was on the tactical offensive or defensive. The main weapon in this era was the spear and it was wielded overarm as the phalanxes crashed into one another. The last few yards of tactical approach were often executed at the trot, heightening the impact of the forces upon one another (**16**). The Spartans, by far the most organised of all Hoplite city states, are known to have stepped their approach in a more regimented manner.

The probable founders of the new style of fighting, on the Greek mainland at least, were the Argives, who are thought to have adopted it from the Carians of south-west Asia Minor, well-known mercenaries. From the Carians, via Miletus, came the new warfare to Argos. Traditionally it was the Spartans who first fell prey to the new style of fighting in 669 BC when Pheidon, tyrant of Argos (680-650 BC) deployed it to defeat the Spartans for the first (and last) time. When we look at what the wars were fought for, we see that the landscape played a key role in both the way in which the battles were fought and the reasons why they were fought at all. Disputed areas of good agrarian land were often a reason for two states going to war, notwithstanding the political ambitions of individual kings.[43] More to the point, the deployment of close-order infantry could only be executed in relatively flat, open terrain. When hoplites were unable to fully deploy, or were caught by opposing armies in passes or en route in column, disaster usually followed. The Spartans, as Plutarch stressed, through superior training, were often able to turn disadvantageous situations to their own advantage through tactical manoeuvring, although this must have been of limited use given the enormous size of some of the phalanxes. Where the Spartans excelled was in their exploitation of a natural tendency in close-order spear and shield work. As enemies closed upon one another it was noted that men would shuffle their shields over to the right in order to secure the locked-shield appearance of the shield wall. This meant that the phalanx itself would drift to the right as the armies closed. This kind of thing must have happened throughout the long era of heavy infantrymen armed with spear and shield and cannot have been unique to hoplite warfare. Sparta, however, turned it into a tactical manoeuvre, known correctly as an Incline, where the purpose was to get an overlap on

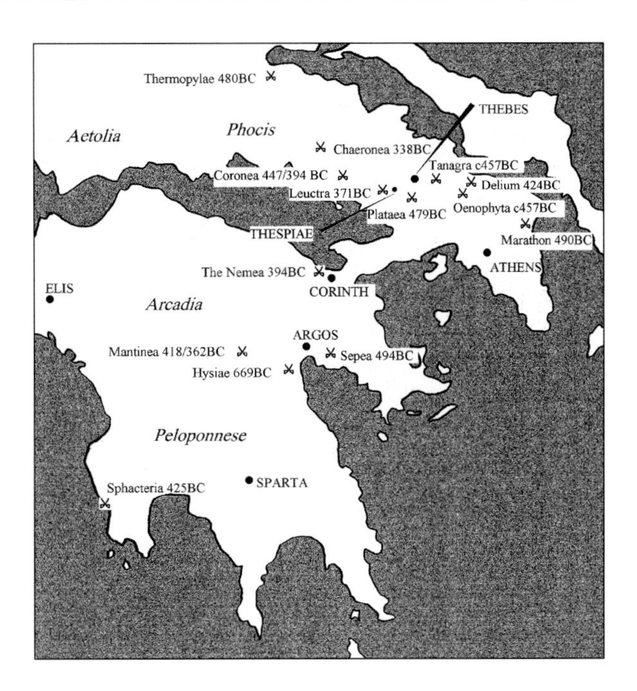

17 *Map of central and southern Greece showing the main battle sites and dates of the Hoplite warfare period*

the right side of the phalanx against the enemy's weaker left. In fact, the right side of most coalition armies was nearly always the strongest side. Those on the left often suffered greatly. The Boiotians, who had lost many men on the battlefield over the years, simply refused to fight at the battle of Nemea in 394 BC until they were put on the right wing, away from the expected Spartan hammer blow.

Despite the fact that hoplite warfare was a highly ritualised affair, often with a series of divinations and sacrifices made before battle, casualties could still be heavy. The numbers killed in single battles were probably quite small compared to the army total, but the effects on groups of hoplites, who were called up from small towns, could be devastating. Recently it has been pointed out that the Boiotian town of Thespiae's walls rose and fell with the fortunes and misfortunes of its hoplites on the battlefield.[44] Given that a city state's infantry muster could represent two thirds of its adult male citizenry, it is easy to see why the Thespians, who were badly mauled at Thermopylae (480 BC), and again at Delium (424 BC), and once more at Nemea river (394 BC), were all but obliterated by hoplite warfare, rarely having enough time to fully recover from compounded losses over several generations (see **17** for map of Greek battles).

Hoplite versus hoplite was a common occurrence in Greek warfare. However, the hoplite system was to be fully tested during the Persian wars. The Persians had fared well in Hellenistic areas away from the Greek mainland, but they were to be defeated on Greek soil. In 490, at the battle of Marathon (**18**), Athenians and Plataeans allied against the Persian forces which had its main body of infantry flanked by two cavalry units. Athenian deployment involved thinning their line to match the length of the Persian block, the consequences being that the Athenian centre was pushed back some distance. However, double successes on both of the Persian flanks saw fleeing Persian infantry take their mounted comrades with them, resulting in the Greek allies

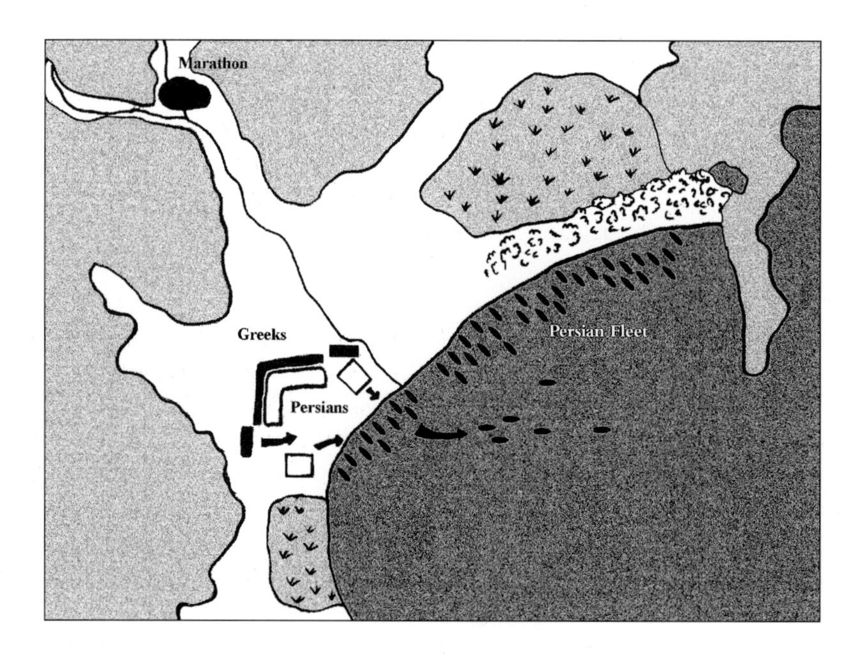

18 The Battle of Marathon 490 BC. The Greek centre thinned itself to match the width of the Persian line. As the Persians succeeded in the centre, their wings collapsed allowing the Greeks to press home their advantage on both flanks

being able to swing into the centre taking the remaining Persian forces in both flanks.

As if to confirm the usefulness of hoplites on the battlefield, the battle of Cunaxa in 401 BC, south-west of modern Baghdad, showed how they could be used in foreign lands against a different enemy. Greek mercenaries, of whom the informative Xenophon was one, fought for the rebel Persian prince Cyrus against the king of Persia, and they evidently swept all before them.

One thing that was not fully developed in Greek warfare of the hoplite era was the use of cavalry. At Tanagra in *c*.457 BC their actions did have an important bearing on the outcome, but only because the Thessalian cavalry deserted to Sparta. Cavalry was rarely present in any great numbers in the hoplite armies, particularly in the case of Sparta. Occasionally it could have an impact if it turned up at the right moment, like it did at Delium in 424 BC where the Boiotian cavalry appeared behind a hill causing alarm in the Athenian flank. There were light troops in the armies too. Slingers and archers numbered but a few in comparison to the overall total of the force, but Xenophon tells us that the Greek slingers in their retreat from the Persians were able to out-distance enemy archers, keeping them at bay. The Thracian peltast, a light infantryman, was a useful addition to the Athenian army too, and very well equipped for operations in difficult terrain.

By the time of the coming of Philip of Macedon and Alexander the Great, Greek warfare was changing once again. No longer would there be a reliance upon the considerable strengths of the hoplite phalanx. The new era would be defined by more balanced forces of combined arms, with missile forces, cavalry and infantry working in unison. The new infantry, whose job it was to pin the enemy down, soon evolved into the famous phalangites, armed with pikes. Now the Greek phalanx, still formidable as a shock force, would have good supporting troops and a greater offensive capability which, as history would show under Alexander, could be carried to the ends of the earth, defeating all before it.

Roman warfare

How Rome rose to dominate the world is one of the greatest and most thoroughly documented stories in history. The secrets to the centuries of Roman endeavour are not difficult to find. Adaptability is perhaps the best word to describe the Roman approach.

When we first come across references to the Roman army in the sixth century BC there is little to distinguish it from the Greek. The hoplite style of fighting, which the Etrusco-Roman armies appear to have adopted, was a familiar site in the classical world. Under Etruscan domination, the phalanx was the principal arm of the force, with lighter Latin contingents on the wings. According to Livy, it is to Servius Tullius, who acceded in 578 BC, that we owe the first of many great shake-ups of the army. It was to be organised on a class-based structure, with infantry of the first class (the wealthiest) through to fifth classes (the poorest), supported by Equites, the Regular cavalry. Still fighting in a hoplite manner, the Tullian army was stronger for its reorganisation and it is worth pointing out that its response to the landscape (despite the fact that there were no great walled cities in Italy at the time) is characterised by the inclusion amongst the 80 centuries of the first class of two centuries of Engineers.

Rome's main concerns for many centuries were local ones. The Etruscan yoke was thrown off by a mixture of Greek forces and Latin League towns (of which Rome was the founder) at the end of the sixth century. The Etruscan city of Veii was captured in 396 BC and it is around this time, with the arrival of new enemies on the Italian peninsular, that the Roman army underwent another of its responsive reorganisations. Just 17km to the north of Rome, the Celtic tribe, the *Senones*, had penetrated deep into Roman territory and defeated a Latin army on the banks of the Allia. Rome was sacked and lessons had to be learned from this new threat. The nature of the threat was that Rome's enemies fought in a style for which the unwieldy hoplite phalanx was poorly suited. The Celts, for example, were equipped with long slashing swords for which the new curved scutum shield with its spindle boss was a much better counter than the round shields of the hoplite soldier. The other enemies of Rome also demanded a new response: the Sabellian hill tribes would simply not allow themselves to be defeated out in the open by a steamroller phalanx. The same applied to the Samnites and Umbrians, who, like other tribes, became Rome's allies after their conquest. Their settlements were to become colonial towns occupied by the Capite Censi, the lowest class eligible for military service. Weapons and tactical organisation had to change.

Under Camillus, the Roman army often fought in three lines: the first of Hastati, armed with pila (heavy throwing spear), sword and scutum, flanked by skirmishers; the second of Principes, with long spear, sword and scutum; and the third, the veteran Triarii, equipped with the same weapons as the Principes. The days of the reliance upon serried ranks of spears had gone. Rome was adapting to the terrain in which she found her soldiers fighting. Rome soon came to dominate the Italian peninsula, but the learning would continue to be hard as the Romans faced their first foreign wars in the third century BC.

After all the reforms designed to combat the new threat of hill tribes and loose formation Celtic tribes, it is perhaps ironic that Rome's first foreign war was not only fought on Italian soil, but was fought against a Macedonian-style phalanx. Arriving in Italy in 280 BC, Pyrrhus, king of Epirus brought with him a pike phalanx and 20 elephants against which the Romans' incendiary pigs (an anti-elephant measure of some desperation) were ineffective. So too, unfortunately, were the Roman cavalry. At Heraclea in 280 BC, the elephants swept the Roman cavalry away, allowing the Epirote cavalry to take the Roman infantry in flank and put it to flight. Pyrrhus took many casualties on this occasion and sustained even more at the battle of Asculum in 279 BC, despite achieving a victory. It was clear that a war against Rome, which was strong at this time in manpower reserves, was going to be one of attrition. Pyrrhus, who gave his name to the concept of the costly victory, despite winning most of his battles, was eventually checkmated by numerically superior forces of combined consular armies.

The first Punic War (261-241 BC) against Carthage was fought for control of Sicily and tested Rome's manpower reserves to the limit, particularly in the naval commitments she made. The second Punic War was also fought at great cost to the human resources of Rome and nearly broke her. This war involved a conflict with the great Carthaginian general Hannibal (218-202 BC). It was to be an educational experience for Rome, whose mistakes sometimes repeated themselves. In 218 BC Hannibal crossed Europe's most formidable natural frontier and marched into legend with around 20,000 infantry, 6000 cavalry and 37 elephants. The Celts of the Po valley came to him and joined his force. On the banks of the Trebbia, near Piacenza, a combined consular force was defeated because it had relied too heavily on a brute-force frontal assault on the centre of Hannibal's Celtic and Spanish line, whilst its flanks collapsed and were routed by the cleverly reinforced Carthaginian wings. After this experience the Romans came up with the curious idea that the iron fist would surely work if it were reinforced by numbers. Consequently, during the shadowing operations of the next year, a very large eight legion force was amassed. By 212 BC this had grown to 25 legions.

In 216 BC the Romans and Carthaginians fought at Cannae (**colour plate 5**), where ingenuity outshone brute force in spades. Hannibal had formed up in the same way as at Trebbia (without his elephants, most of whom had not survived their first winter), and the Romans reinforced their centre. The Romans were going to smash through the enemy line, but Hannibal had already guessed this and had formed up his Celtic and Spanish centre into a crescent with its apex towards the Romans. As the Carthaginian infantry took the expected punishment it gradually gave ground, sucking the Romans into a giant trap. The Carthaginian cavalry had time to drive off the Roman cavalry and turn to assist the units of infantry who had been placed on the wings for the enveloping manoeuvre which cost Rome so dearly.

Hannibal, despite his successes, found his Italian campaign to be an attritional affair, as Pyrrhus had before him. By 207 BC, after a failed attempt at besieging Rome itself and the defeat in northern Italy of his brother Hasdrubal, the great general retreated to the toe of Italy and was soon recalled to Carthage when the Roman general Scipio had invaded North Africa. At Zama, in 202 BC, Hannibal was outwitted by Scipio, who had adapted his own forces to Carthaginian tactics. Rome was master of the Mediterranean.

After the defeat of Carthage, Rome entered a new era of military successes, culminating in the Macedonian wars of the second century BC. This time, the more flexible Roman forces were able to get amongst the cumbersome phalanxes of their enemy on two important occasions and win decisive victories in difficult terrain. At Cynoscephalae in 197 BC new Roman manoeuvring and command and control techniques saw them exploit an accidental encounter on a rough hillside shrouded in rain and mist. At Pydna in 168 BC the phalanx was once again defeated and the resulting hostage-taking exercise gave to history the Achean Polybius (*c*.203-120 BC), who was housed in the residence of the Scipios and who wrote prolifically on the organisation and tactics of the Roman army of his era.

In 107 BC Caius Marius was elected consul and the campaigns which were to follow in the hilly semi-desert of Numidia were to be highly mobile affairs against the king Jugurtha. Marius also had problems with the Cimbri and Teutones, which required his attention lest Rome should be invaded once again by Celtic tribes from the north.

Marius was chiefly responsible for a professionalisation and standardisation of the Roman army. 'Marius's mules', as they became known, were logistically very capable legionaries. Legions would now be 6200 men strong and not the 4000 of previous eras. He extended the length of service of a legionary and is attributed with embuing him with the requisite Roman attitude to a career in the army. This has been seen by some as the beginning of a long history of antagonism between army and state. Yet it remains a testimony to the archetypal Roman general that no further far-reaching reforms were made until the time of Augustus.

Internal troubles occupied Rome for some years at the beginning of the first century BC, with a social war in the 90s which was a campaign for civil rights amongst those Italians who supplied alae sociorum to supplement the legions. The distinction between them and the Regular units soon would no longer exist. Between 80-72 BC the rebel Quintus trained the Spaniards as legionaries and during the years 73-71 BC a slave army trained by Spartacus passed into legend, but was holed-up in the toe of Italy by Crassus who built an enormous 60km wall from coast to coast to trap his enemy.

The first Triumvirate of Caesar, Crassus and Pompey brought many famous military campaigns with it. Crassus, jealous of Caesar's successes in Gaul, undertook a campaign against the Persian successors, the Parthians, in the east and succeeded only in demonstrating the vulnerability of the Roman army when on campaign in difficult areas. In 53 BC he ignored advice as to the route he should take (a route through the Armenian mountains would eliminate the threat of Parthian cavalry, but as Mark Anthony would later find, was decidedly difficult terrain). Instead, he chose a direct route across the Euphrates at Zeugma. Further to the east he encountered the Parthians and formed up into a defensive square. The Parthian horse archers were able to pick off the Romans at will. The result was a tangled Roman withdrawal to Carrhae where Crassus was lured away and killed. Roman standards were captured and the army continued its western exodus in fragments. It was an awful campaign.

Caesar in Gaul, on the other hand, was showing the sort of military skills for which he was to become famous. His siege of Vercingetorix's forces at Alesia is covered elsewhere in this book and demonstrates well the Roman approach to siege warfare. Caesar was able to enlarge his legions from four to eleven and recruited one legion, 'the Larks', entirely from Gauls. Along the banks of the Rhône in 58 BC, Caesar built a linear fortification to check the natural migrating tendencies of the Helvetii. It was 18 miles long and its wall was 16ft high, garrisoned from small forts at intervals. All of this was achieved in just two weeks and the structure could still be seen in the nineteenth century. In many ways, Caesar's great linear fortifications foreshadowed the switch to an entirely preclusive frontier policy in the later Empire by proving that vast stretches of land could be engineered to provide either an encapsulating siege line, or a linear barrier to outsiders. The siege works of Alesia, the fortifications of the Rhône and Caesar and Pompey's opposing lines of continuous fortifications and counter fortifications at Dyrrhachium in 48 BC were micro examples of what was to become imperial policy during the days of Empire.

By the time of the reforms of Augustus (31 BC-AD 14), there were 28 legions in service. Once created, a legion remained a permanent feature. To Augustus can be attributed the creation of Auxilia cohorts and the policy of Preclusive Security. The Empire was not without its revolts, however. The Varian Tragedy of AD 9, where Rome lost three Legions to treachery in the German woods, is covered elsewhere in this book. It was just one among many rebellions which included the Illyrian revolt of AD 6-9, the Boudiccan revolt in Britain of AD 60, the Jewish revolt of AD 66-70, and the Dacian wars of the early second century. Rome took a dim view of rebellion, as was shown by the fate of most of those rebels outlined above.

The complex politics of Imperial Rome are well documented, as are most of the military campaigns of the period. Here, we must concern ourselves with the creeping trend towards the policy of defence-in-depth (an area covered in detail in chapter 3), a concept which runs in opposition to the building of linear fortifications on frontiers designed to keep people out. The establishment in Rome of double-strength cohorts of legionaries under Septimius Severus (AD 193-21) probably marks the beginning of the Roman mobile strategic reserve, which was to grow in importance throughout the third and fourth centuries. Septimius knew that the army was the most important factor for the survival of the Empire, which is why he told his sons from his deathbed to look after the troops. Franks, Alamanns, Goths and Vandals were all pushing up against Rome's frontiers at this time. The next step on the road to a proper mobile reserve came under the troubled reign of Gallienus (AD 253-268), who at times only controlled Italy and Africa. He created an enlarged field army and officer corps, resulting in a greatly increased cavalry contingent and consequently increased mobility.

19 Two Roman infantrymen representing the armies which occupied and then later left Britain. Foreground: with lorica segmentata, pilum and shield c.AD 120. Backgound: Late Empire, round shield, sword. Photograph: John Eagle

External trouble was never far away in the late Empire. Aurelian (270-275) even went as far as building walls around Rome itself, so great was the Germanic threat from the north. Then, however, came Diocletian, who brought some considerable order out of the chaos and reactionary policies of the previous decades. Under him, there would be three field armies with Maximian, Constantius and Galerius at their heads, shortening the reaction time in meeting external threats. Although Diocletian's own Comitatus, or Imperial Entourage, was supplemented by frontier garrisons, it did however provide a mobile reserve under his direct command. After Constantine prevailed over Maxentius in the early fourth century, he changed the military machine again. Recruiting from Germanic areas, he established new units and greatly increased his mobile capabilities. The mobile forces, or Comitatenses, would work in conjunction with the Limitanei of the frontier forts and towns of the Limes, or frontier regions.

Despite the presence of a huge number of Germanic troops in the Later Roman army, it was not until after the disaster at Adrianople in AD 378 where Gothic cavalry soundly defeated the Romans, producing a crisis in available manpower, that Imperial policy looked towards the employment of Foederati. These troops were characterised by fighting as tribal units, probably in their own style, under their own chieftains. The Goths themselves were settled inside the Empire under their own leaders in the Danubian provinces, and the pattern was to spread. The collapse of the Rhine frontier in 406 undid all the containing work of the gifted General Stilicho and saw Germanic tribes flood into Gaul and Spain, strategically cutting off Britain. Rome was sacked by Visigoths in 410 and Britain lost soon after. The end of the Roman Empire in the west was not, however, a quick affair and was not without some successes: Aetius, with Visigothic help, defeated the Huns in Gaul in 451. In the end, the Roman frontiers were breached and the policies of keeping a number of mobile reserves meant that the Emperor could not be strong everywhere. However, the very fact that there was a decline before the fall of the Roman Empire in the west compares interestingly with what had been an immediate collapse of the Assyrian Empire in 612 BC,

20 Roman infantrymen prepare defensive works. From a scene depicted on Trajan's column

and shows that in many ways the military policies of Constantine and his successors must have had something to recommend them.

Human aggression has always gone in cycles of offensive and defensive postures, with one measure providing the answer to the threat of another. We have highlighted some changes in ancient warfare in this chapter which typify this phenomenon and concentrated on some eras where examples can be found. The early city states of Mesopotamia threw walls around themselves in an essentially defensive response to the prosecution of offensive warfare by their neighbours. These measures were taken to protect economic interests in an area where essential natural resources were scarce. Many centuries would pass before the stalemate was broken. Kingdoms began to replace city states in Mesopotamia and elsewhere, and they commanded enough manpower resources to tip the balance in their favour.

Not until the first chariot armies of the great kingdoms in the seventeenth century BC do long-range expansionist tendencies appear, where armies had an offensive (if vulnerable) capability. For all its weaknesses in the field, the chariot remained an elite weapon down to the so-called catastrophe of the Bronze Age in the decades around 1200 BC. The proliferation of warrior elites and the spread of infantry weapons across Europe and the Mediterranean had a profound effect on the direction of warfare in the Late Bronze Age. After this, the rise of infantry became all-important as new Empires were carved-out across the ancient world. The Assyrian story is one which reflects the importance of combined arms and outwardly aggressive policies as a response to circumstance. Capable of long-range campaigns, it used cavalry and infantry and developed the art of siege warfare and amphibious operations to prosecute its political goals. The Greek city states saw the employment of massed ranks of infantrymen in a defensive posture, first against each other and then against the flexible Persian army. The scale of warfare had by now increased and state-level warfare had reached a new level, pitting empire against empire in a seemingly endless cycle with one empire succeeding another. The Romans also built their empire around the infantryman until very late. The Romans learned hard lessons throughout their long history, but their adaptability was the key to their successes.

In chapter two, we look at the many ways in which the idea of defence has been undertaken, from the personal level to a wider role in the landscape.

2 The defensive response

> . . . At the same time Philip, the King of France, sent a letter to him [King William I of England] and ordered him to come to him, and he would give him the castle at Montreuil so that afterwards he could daily do ill-turns to those not his friends.
> *Anglo-Saxon Chronicle.* Worcester Manuscript D. Entry for AD 1075

There are probably just three instinctive responses to being attacked: quickly run away from the danger, try to become invisible, or counter-attack as fast and as hard as possible. To try to ensure survival, mankind has developed a whole series of defensive techniques related to one or more of these natural responses. Animals share the same instincts as man, and have evolved similar strategies – the ability to escape rapidly, various forms of camouflage to render them invisible, and teeth, claws and horns with which to fight back. Some creatures have also evolved armour in the form of thick skin, scales or tough carapaces, and a few have even learned to use weapons, like our close relatives, the chimpanzees.[1]

There are many ways of classifying defences and their development. One way is in terms of scale related to what it is that people want or need to protect. At the most basic level, each person desires first of all to protect their own skin, and so we may regard personal weapons and armour as indicators of the primary level of defence and attack.

Above the level of self comes that of immediate kin – the protection of one's family (**21**). The continued existence of the family depends on more than just personal survival. It entails defence of those incapable of protecting themselves: the very young, the elderly, and any sick or otherwise incapacitated members of the group who may be unable to run away fast enough, or hide themselves effectively, let alone fight back. Additionally, there is the concern to protect the family's potential for future survival beyond the immediate event. This means defending the roof over their heads, their food supplies, tools and utensils, their animals and their crops.

This sort of protection usually necessitates the forming of barriers, psychological or actual, and can also include the use of strategies such as camouflage and the setting of traps. At this level too, systems of early warning of danger may be developed. As societies become more and more complex, the recognition and demands of kinship are extended to wider affinities typified by villages, clans and eventually tribes and nations. Defence of a larger group demands new developments. There may be a need for the building of strong points and refuges, the formalisation of boundaries or borders, and more complex and interconnected strategic action.

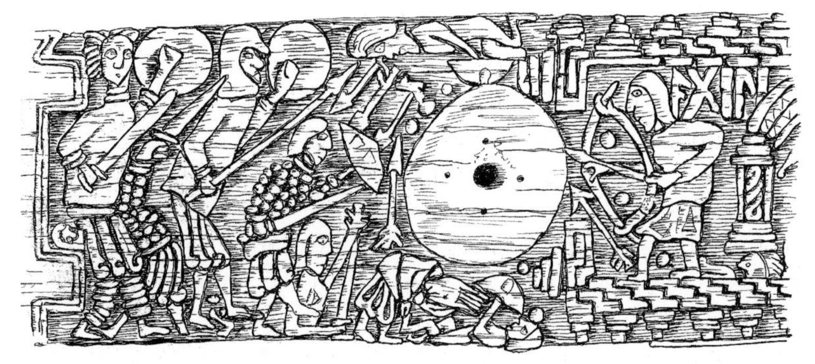

21 Egil the archer defending his home. From the whalebone Frank's Casket. Anglo-Saxon, eighth century

Frequently, larger communities tend to develop specialisations among their members in such spheres as production, social and cultural activities, and in the provision of their military capabilities. This can lead to the creation of defended elite or warrior centres comprising specialised housing or settlement, training areas, armouries and storage depots. Such centres may acquire further meanings concerned with the display of status both within the tribe and to outsiders. Status tends to attract wealth which may also find its display in the form or function of elite or warrior centres, and of course the erection of a defensive centre housing such groups displays the strength of the community both to potential outside foes and to dissidents within its own ranks. It is possible to consider Iron Age hillforts in this quite complex light, as well as castles of the medieval period – as multi-functional constructions deriving their form and meaning ultimately from a military exigency, but comprising a far greater range of social and cultural meaning.

Such centres, because of their inherent function of protection, may attract many other forms of use. Distribution, production and trading activities may become centred on the site, as well as religious and ceremonial practices and the practices of administration, justice and governance. They can begin to assume an urban status.

Towns and cities have further implications for defence. They typically acquire larger populations than other forms of settlement, and store larger amounts of wealth and commodities in proportion to their populations and area. They also acquire different social and cultural imperatives, status and levels of meaning. Towns become more than just centres for the land around them – they transform into spatial and social entities with significant differences from their hinterlands. They may be regarded as foci of particular significance for defence and attack. For the Romans, an attack on any Italian city was seen as disastrous, but an attack on Rome itself was cataclysmic. Such an event was regarded as a blow to their whole identity and view of the world.

Greater than individual towns and cities is the idea of state, again exemplified by the Romans in their mission of bringing 'Romanitas' to their provinces. A state may be defined as a more or less cohesive large-scale geographic territory linked together by commonalities such as ethnicity, language, political complexion, religion and culture. To defend a state is to defend a notion of sovereignty over a particular way of life regarded as valuable and significantly different from that of neighbouring states. Two particular features of the protection of states are the notions of defence-in-depth and of linear defence, especially along frontiers and major arterial routes important for communications and the supply of individual elements within the territory.

There are other forms of and reasons for defence not immediately concerned with the protection of communities. Defence of resources at a local or state level necessary for the long-term survival or prosperity of the community may be regarded at least as equally important as the defence of lives in the short term. Defence of religious or cultural sites can be a vital part of the protection of a way of life or the manner in which a society achieves and maintains its identity. Such sites may also be given defences as a means of stressing their importance within a society; it may be that only certain members or groups can be permitted to enter the precincts of these places, either to preserve their sanctity, or to avoid dissipation of their power, or to protect lesser people from the effects of the power enclosed, or to underline their communal centrality.

An important group of defences, and often one of the most visible, is the construction of fortifications by attackers and invaders, built to protect their personnel during the aggressive action, to serve as bases for forward campaigning, and to provide safe refuges for conquerors among a defeated, hostile, population. [illegible] fortifications can include siegeworks, beachheads, marching camps and depots [illegible] as forts and castles.

There are also many types of defensive or aggressive construction intended to be of a more temporary nature, used only while a war is being waged. From slit trenches and foxholes to underground tunnel systems and bunkers, there is a great range of construction forms that were designed to be ephemeral and often invisible, quick, cheap and easy to construct and capable of being abandoned without significant loss of time or effort.

All these forms of and reasons for defence recur throughout mankind's history in many guises; waves of military technological change periodically race across most societies. It is useful to consider a number of different examples from different periods at each level of what is to be defended, and also to examine the role of landscape in relation to these imperatives rather than to specific responses and sites.

The following discussion concentrates on built defences both for protection of various forms of population and as part of aggressive actions.

Defending the family

The immediate necessity of defending a family unit has been approached in different ways by various communities. Small-scale perimeter barriers such as ditches and banks, sometimes surmounted by palisades or hedges, were constructed at least from the Chalcolithic and Early Bronze Ages onwards in many parts of Europe. Late Únětice settlements in east central Europe have these types of defences, as do numerous examples in Britain from the Bronze Age right through the Iron Age and into the early period of the Roman occupation.

A few examples will suffice to demonstrate this form of defence; at Vinor to the north of Prague, excavations revealed part of a house within an enclosure surrounded by a ditch and traces interpreted as a palisade. At the site of Staple Howe, Yorkshire, which dates to the middle of the first millennium BC, two successive palisades surrounded first one then two roundhouses and granaries.[2] At Broxmouth, near Dunbar in East Lothian, a large wooden roundhouse was enclosed by a strong fence and was probably guarded by dogs. On the South Downs, a number of family farms have been investigated with similar small-scale protection around them, such as Itford Hill, in Sussex. This settlement consisted of a terrace surrounded by banks, which was occupied for perhaps three generations by an extended family, and contained, at most, two or three dwellings with associated working huts. The excavator considers it possible that the banks were topped by hedges.[3]

In the north-east of Britain, many small defended sites were constructed during the Middle Iron Age – of the approximately 1500 known, most enclose less than a hectare with one or more circuits of banks and ditches. They appear to be miniature hillforts, but are really just defended farmsteads, often sited on the remains of earlier palisaded enclosures, although some are new constructions of the Later Iron Age. Huckhoe, in Northumberland, was an earthwork enclosure built very soon after the preceding palisade-enclosed settlement was burned in the sixth century BC. Cunliffe suggests that the building of defended farmsteads in the Late Bronze Age was related to a change in social attitude, which regarded the farmstead as a symbol of territorial dominance on a small scale. He predicates that

> the 'monumentalizing' of (the homestead) with ditches and earthworks may have represented another stage in the same general process which linked the control of the land to status and used the settlement as the outward and visible sign of this. It may even be that size and complexity of the enclosing earthworks and the elaboration of the entrances directly reflected status and was rigorously controlled by social convention.[4]

If this is true, then an obvious comparison could be made between these farmsteads and the smaller range of moated manors of the fourteenth and fifteenth centuries. It has been generally maintained that providing a moat and bridge around the dwelling offers little in the way of military protection (moats generally being only a few metres wide and of no great depth), and that their popularity was much more to do with a desire to demonstrate wealth and status within the landscape. Moated sites vary enormously in their size, complexity, distribution and date, but

> it would appear to be a reasonable working hypothesis to suggest that moated sites first emerged as a fashion amongst the aristocratic elements of society and that the diffusion was not only temporal and spatial but also had a social component, extending downward through society until a cost threshold was met which inhibited further multiplication.[5]

Is such a comparison valid? In some ways it may well be, but it would be unsafe to make any assumptions without a consideration of the social structure of the periods. The period of the Middle or Late Bronze Age through to the Roman invasion lacked the national social perspectives and infrastructures of the later medieval centuries. Development of defended homesteads in prehistory must be seen in a much more parochial light, related to more limited territorial and social perceptions. Their builders' relationships with tribal aristocracies and the role of material wealth may have been much less clear cut than the hierarchies of the Middle Ages. Whilst there are many undefended settlements in both eras, the fact is that during later prehistory, there was a very widespread occurrence of a variety of forms of defended small settlement in Northern Europe, and they are generally designed in more militarily viable styles than moated houses. A better comparison must be between more truly defensive building styles such as the tower houses and bastles previously mentioned. Status building seems unlikely to be the only explanation for the appearance of so many forms of small-scale defences in the later prehistoric centuries.

Another way to provide defence for a family unit is to isolate the dwelling within the landscape in some way. A typical stratagem in Britain and Ireland was to build a crannog, or artificial island. These structures happily combine the defensive imperative with the opportunity to exploit an extra resource – the fish and waterbirds of the lake itself. Traces of crannogs are sometimes well preserved in the peat deposits of the lake edges, and a number have been excavated, such as Knocknalappa in Co. Clare and Ballinderry in Co. Offaly, Ireland. The former site consists of an artificial island composed on peat and stone, some 60 x 30m, revetted by short timber piles. Occupation debris was identified on the platform.[6] At Ballinderry 2, a slightly smaller island (50 x 28m) was surmounted by a surface of parallel laid oak planks over an area of about 120m^2, considered to be, possibly, the raised floor of a dwelling, and in another area by a layer of brushwood and a small structure made out of woven light timbers, perhaps a working or storage building.[7] These sites also date to the Middle or Later Bronze Age.

A third strategy for family defence is to use the architecture of the home itself to provide a barrier. Across much of the north European plain and the Low Countries, farmsteads of the medieval period and later were constructed in the form of quadrangles, with a central open courtyard surrounded by ranges of buildings facing inward. The external elevations of these farms present a single continuous blank wall, broken only by a strong gate. Many also have a tower structure incorporated into one of the building ranges, to provide a look-out point and early warning system. For the people of these regions, dwelling in a landscape essentially unprovided with natural defensive locations, and equally well-suited for large military campaigns, the only safety lay in providing their own strongholds and viewpoints. A typical defended farmstead of this type is La Haye Sainte, on the battlefield of Waterloo, in Belgium. In other locations, there has always been a tendency to move uphill in times of trouble, so that access for enemies is more difficult, and the inhabitants have more chance of spotting trouble coming early, giving them a chance to hide stores and the weaker members of the family, bar their gates and arm themselves.

A way to combine the advantages of strong architectural barriers and the early warning given by height is to build a tower house. Many of these were constructed on the Scottish borders and in Ireland in the later Middle Ages and Tudor period.

22 *Artramon, County Wexford. Early Irish tower house. These simple square towers have a vaulted ground floor for protection against fire. Their origins are disputed with some favouring a native development from Irish Hall houses, whilst other eastern towers may have sprung directly from a £10 grant offered by Henry VI in 1429*

Tower houses, pele towers and bastles

A feature of the troubles along the Anglo-Scottish border in the fourteenth century was the building of small fortified towers. Following the Battle of Bannockburn in 1314, when the forces of Robert the Bruce defeated the English, Scottish reivers began to raid south, attacking any settlement that offered a quick and easy profit. In retaliation, English border families mounted their own offensives, led by the Marcher lords Percy, Neville and others. Such raids included assaults on churches, manors and farms. A response was to erect defensive pele towers (as the small structures on the English side of the border are known). Some of these apparently date from a little earlier than 1314, reflecting the unsettled times leading up to Bruce's campaign. The Vicar's Pele at Corbridge seems to date from 1300 and consists, like others, of a three-storey tower. Other forms soon followed, but none were large and defences were fairly basic: stone vaulted ground floors, a sturdy door protected by an iron grille or 'yett', first-floor entry achieved by means of a ladder, narrow windows and thick walls. It is estimated that some 200 were built during the fourteenth and fifteenth centuries.

The small size of many of these refuges reflects the general poverty and hardship suffered by most of the less aristocratic population of the area, eking out a living on poor soils in a hard landscape constantly ravaged by the depredations of the feuding reivers from both sides of the border.

On the Scottish side, tower houses were often more complex constructions. Many were in the form of a tower with an adjoining wing, forming an L-shape, and were raised within a barmkin, or stone-walled enclosure which acted as a sort of bailey, containing stables, workshops and storage sheds, often larger and more complex than the simple barmkins attached to English pele towers. The L shape provided a rather more commodious residence than the limited accommodation of a pele tower, which might only have a single room on each storey, and it also was sited to provide flanking fire for the tower's entrance. Like castles, tower houses underwent a continuous process of development and innovation; turrets, gun platforms and gun loops were common additions.

23 Derrhivenny, County Galway. Late Tower House and bawn, an annexe used for storage and workshops. Similar towers constructed of timber have failed to survive

Later Scottish tower houses became even more developed and strongly defended with the addition of extra full-height wings forming a stepped L-shaped castle, or a Z-plan house consisting of extra towers built at opposing diagonal angles; corbelled bartizans in the French style at the upper corners of the structures, and increased numbers of gun loops and artillery embrasures were often added. Noltland Castle in Orkney was built in the 1560s and has 71 gun-loops arranged in tiers. Eventually, the trend moved away from stark defence towards palatial comfort, typified by such castles as Glamis and Balmoral.

The origin of the tower house in Ireland has been the subject of some dispute. Some writers claim that they were a natural development from earlier hall houses or solar-towers attached to manor houses. Sweetman[8] believes that most of the earlier, more easterly examples sprang from a grant of £10 offered by Henry VI in 1429 for the building of towers 'within the Pale', a partially demarcated territory protecting the western edge of the area around Dublin, the main foothold of the English in Eire. These early towers are of a simple rectangular design (**22**), such as the examples at Artramon in Wexford, Roodstown and Kilincoole, both in Louth. They generally have a vaulted ground floor, as a protection against fire, very similar to those of Scotland, but they also often have one or more angle towers, frequently on opposing diagonal corners, which contained spiral stairs or garderobes.

> The main element of such a dwelling was a single tower which was the most cost-effective form of defence for an individual of fairly limited means who needed such a fortified structure to protect himself and his family against raiding or the minor outbreaks of warfare which seem to have been such a common occurrence in late medieval Irish society.[9]

Tower houses were usually accompanied by small bawns (**23**), similar to barmkins, to contain stores, stock and workshops. Surviving examples are built of masonry, but there are records of timber, wattle and earth defences. Later more westerly examples are larger and more complex; some have upper vaulted floors,

24 *Blarney Castle, Cork, built 1446. A developed form of defensive tower, which operated as a statement of the power of the MacCarthy clan*

bartizans, machiolations and gun loops and they could rise to six storeys, as at Clonea. They lacked angle towers but were generally bigger, and some were provided with a high standard of accommodation, including fine windows and large fireplaces. These were built by wealthy landowners, and functioned not just as defensive refuges, but as centres of power and control, like Blarney (**24**) in Cork, a strong statement of the might of the MacCarthy clan, or Barryscourt, also in Cork, chief seat of the Barry family. It is perhaps hardly surprising that the greater proportion of these tower houses in Ireland are sited in areas of fertile agricultural land, rather than with an eye to wider strategic considerations, although the Cork examples tend to be sited close to rivers or the sea on prominent headlands.

Estimates suggest that some 1057 definite Irish tower houses have been identified, with a possible original maximum number in the region of about 3800. Some were being built as late as the first quarter of the seventeenth century, especially in the midland counties of Laois and Offaly.

Contemporary with many Irish tower houses, but of a more humble form than earlier or contemporary strongholds along the Scottish borders (**25**), are bastles. These are two-storey stone structures, and their role as defensive structures has been questioned, but there is no doubt that their strong walls would have provided an important refuge in times of need.

> Tynedale, in the words of a visitation report of 1828, 'is full of uncouth but curious old houses which betoken a state of constant insecurity and of dubious defence, in which the inhabitants of the Border were so long accustomed to live'.[10]

Like earlier Norman stone manor houses, bastles often have a ground floor without external windows and just one stoutly defended door; stock could be herded into the base of the building, which sometimes had a stone vaulted ceiling in case of fire. The

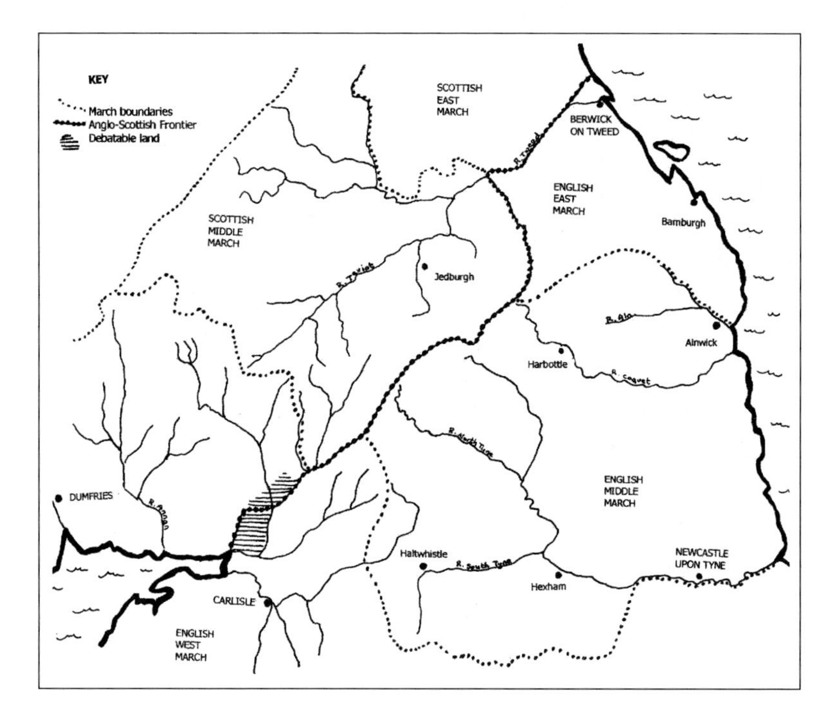

25 The Anglo-Scottish Marches – a disputed region notorious for its rievers and lawlessness in the sixteenth century

main entrance was at first-floor level, reached by a timber ladder or steps that could be drawn up when danger threatened. Windows are few and small even on the first floor, and some bastles have small openings at either side of the door perhaps allowing the defenders to aim missiles from them. The several hundred bastles known were constructed for the most part in the latter half of the sixteenth century. It was a period of continuing political instability in Scotland and there were constant scuffles and raids on both sides of the border. Small farmers were under continual threat.

> It is easy to dismiss bastles as hardly deserving the title stronghold, but it all depends on the circumstances. That so many were built in so short a time suggests that there was not only a need for them, but that they were reasonably successful. Reivers were likely to strike quickly, plunder and be off again into the night. If one was able to herd one's stock safely behind barred doors, Reivers would not hang about too long.[11]

The defence of small settlements

The difference between defending one's family and defending one's hamlet or village is often only one of scale. The Bronze Age defended farms discussed above were precursors of, or contemporary with, larger defensive settlements. These became more numerous towards the end of the second millennium BC and into the period of the Bronze-Iron Age transition.

The evidence from many sites suggests that this was a period of climatic change, possibly linked to events such as an explosion of Mount Hekla, in Iceland, which around 1159 BC sent so much volcanic dust into the atmosphere that succeeding years saw abnormal low pressure and temperature conditions, leading to unusually high rainfall and cold weather. This incident may be connected to the development of peat in areas hitherto intensively farmed, such as Bodmin Moor and Dartmoor. People displaced from these regions would pose a threat to the inhabitants of more fortunate regions, as they tried to find immediate support for their families and new land to farm in the future. At around the same time, major changes occurred in the Mediterranean with the decline of the Hittite Empire and Greek city states such as Mycenae, Tiryns, Pylos and others, whose centres become deserted in the century between 1200 and 1100 BC; there is some evidence to suggest a major population decline in the area at this time. Many causes for this have been suggested: over-exploitation of the arable resources of the region, raiding by the 'Sea Peoples' or climatic deterioration and drought. In south-eastern Europe at the beginning of the first millennium BC, changes in artefact and settlement types may reflect the westward movements of large population groups such as the Scythians and Cimmerians mentioned by Herodotus; similar disruptions of older patterns occur in central Europe in the Lausitz cultural zone and beyond. In many areas, there is evidence for a proliferation of weapons and armour, and for the building of a variety of forms of settlement with overt defensive characteristics. Many such settlements seem to develop into the familiar hillforts of the Iron Age. It is important to note that despite the increased size and number of defensive settlements across Europe, there are many undefended settlements to be found in the same areas.

In Britain at the end of the Bronze Age there was an increase in the size of some settlements, and there seems to have been a tendency to occupy more defensive locations from the Middle Bronze Age onwards. Excavations at sites such as Ram's Hill in Berkshire and Mam Tor in Derbyshire suggest that they acquired ditches and ramparts enclosing settlements during this period.

These defences were by no means slight – at Ram's Hill the enclosure ditch had steep sides and varied between 3-3.75m wide and 0.9-1.24m deep. Many sites begin to show an emphasis on defence, if less impressive than sites like Ram's Hill. There are also one or two apparently high-status sites which acquire defences, such as Thwing, Yorkshire. Here, a massive outer ditch, over 100m in diameter and some 3m deep, was backed by a rampart made of chalk and a timber box-form rampart. The defences enclosed a massive timber building around 28m in diameter, in the centre of which was an inurned cremation. The recovered artefactual material suggested domestic occupation.[12]

Early defended hilltop sites also appeared in Wales – the first phases of the hillfort at Dinorben, Clwyd and that at Breiddin, Powys, have produced Late Bronze Age occupation material. In Ireland too, radiocarbon dates are suggesting a similar date for the beginnings of several sites such as Haughey's Fort in Ulster.[13]

Similar sites in France appear around the same time. The reasons for the appearance of such a wide range of defended sites, large and small, hilltop and lowland, seem to be complex in western Europe. Many of the larger hilltop sites, which later developed into hillforts, are apparently sited to control rivers and passes – important trade routes, especially with the developing markets of the Greeks and early Italian cultures as well as the possible rise of tribal aristocracies in the north. Other sites appear to dominate rich agricultural areas or the sources of valued raw materials such as metal ores. The smaller sites, especially those in lowland areas lacking more obvious defensive potential, are perhaps more problematic.

> One could perhaps make a case for a 'ritual' motive behind certain elements of construction, demarcating important spaces and routes of passage. Some sites may have been given banks and ditches to contain or keep out animals. In addition, some structures could have been established for pure bravado, and to reflect prestige upon the builder. However, the Late Bronze Age competition for land must have been equally significant on these lowland sites too, with people becoming less mobile than before, and some authors have suggested that food supplies were now being controlled in a more centralised fashion. Defences at these sites were created for similar reasons as the hilltop sites, and reflect increased raiding for land, food and/or prestige goods.[14]

A particular feature of small local defences in the north and west of Britain and in Ireland was the development of a range of settlement types offering protection by means of towers or strong stone walls: the brochs and duns. Other forms of defended settlement more or less contemporary with these sites abound: the raths of Ireland and Wales, lake villages such as Glastonbury and Meare, larger crannogs and the blockhouses of the northern isles among others. Their relationship with the equally various number of forms of undefended settlements remains unclear. Nevertheless, there can be little doubt that many small communities recognised a sufficient degree of threat to their existence to be prepared to expend a fair amount of effort and resources in the construction of defences, whether or not the desire to display status was also a factor in their thinking.

The brochs and duns of Britain and Ireland

There are many different forms of these settlements and, confusingly, their nomenclature is often used interchangeably. However, certain features of each form can be regarded as classic of the type. Duns, which seem to date from towards the beginning of the Iron Age, are often found in coastal locations. They comprise thick solid stone walls enclosing a courtyard area, with a defensible entrance and, in many cases, traces of intramural stairs to a wall walk. The walls of duns can be variable in their thickness around the circuit, varying between 1.6-4m, and were anything from 3-6m high. Entrances were often narrow and there is evidence for strong bars that could have been drawn across in times of need. Some have 'guard chambers' and 'murder holes' built into the entrance passage. Within the defences which could enclose up to 375m^2 were

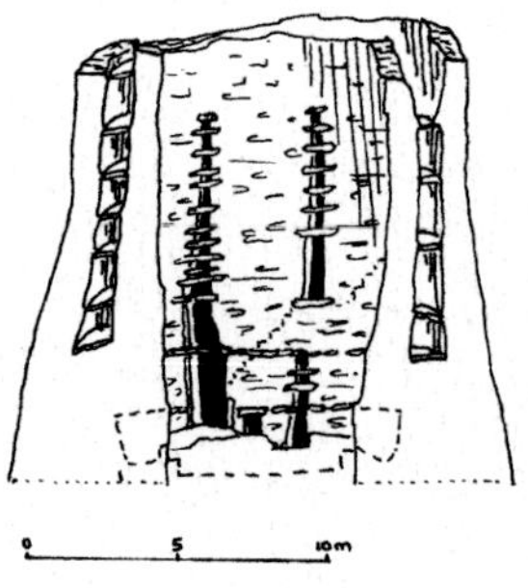

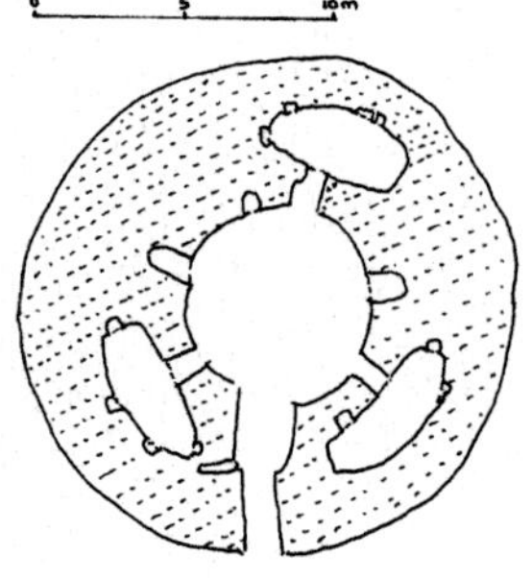

26 A typical large broch comprised a tapering dry stone tower, accessed by a narrow entrance passage. A spiral stair ran up between the thickness of the walls, lit by voids opening into the central well. Stone ledges on the inner face may have supported wooden galleries

small huts or lean-to shelters for domestic habitation. The Loch Varavat dun is one of a number built on a small island in a loch, connected to the shore by a causeway. Dates for its construction and usage seem to lie between about 600 bc and 100 bc. Evidence suggests duns remained in occupation as late as the third century AD, although there are few dates to indicate when they were first constructed. The dun at Rahoy has been dated to the fourth century BC by the presence of a La Tène IC brooch, but elsewhere dates in the first century BC are suggested. Some evidence for the development of these sites comes from work at Dun Skeig, in Kintyre, where a stone-walled fort-like structure was succeeded by a dun created initially with timber-laced walling, and then finally with solid stone walling. It has been suggested that duns may be viewed as 'proto-brochs', but in the absence of a secure series of dating, this must remain conjectural. Recent evidence tends, in fact, to suggest that duns may be more contemporary with brochs, and that both forms owe their origins to a series of development from stone-built roundhouses and other forms. On the whole, the distribution of duns tends to be a little more southerly than that of the brochs.

Brochs (**26**) (**colour plate 11**) may be properly defined as dry-stone tower-like structures usually surrounded by stone-built villages. The towers may have stood up to 13m or more in height and have walls 5m thick at the base. They seem to have originated as an architectural form in the second or first centuries BC; radiocarbon dates of 55 ± 105 (115 BC) were obtained from Dun Ardtreck on Skye, a 'semi-broch'. Excavations at a number of sites have demonstrated a sequence of occupation over some time, which eventually culminated in broch-building, such as Dun Mor, Vaul (Argyll), Dun Lagaidh (Ross & Cromarty) and Clickhimin (Shetland). The latter site began as a settlement in the late Bronze Age; during the Iron Age it changed its shape and began to acquire defences. Like the dun in Loch Varavat, Clickhimin is also built on an island in a loch, with a causeway to shore. Around AD 200 a broch was

27 *Interior staircase of a Broch, showing how such staircases were built into the thickness of the outer walls.* Photograph: Sue Walker

built – it was about 19.8m in diameter, and between 12-15 m tall. Towards the latter part of its use, its height was reduced and the interior rearranged into something more closely resembling a wheelhouse. Broch walls usually enclose fairly small areas – the example at Mousa, Shetland, is only about 6m in diameter. A spiral staircase (**27**) wound up through the thickness of the outer wall, lit by vertical voids and leading to internal timber galleries or internal floors supported on scarcement ledges integral to the inner wall structure. The outer wall is unbroken except for the narrow entrance. A feature of some late examples of brochs is the insertion of a single or double guard chamber within the entrance passage. In the Caithness region, where the countryside is more open, double doors were introduced as an additional defensive feature. The brochs of the north are not always in as strong a defensive location as more westerly examples, and there seems to have been a move towards greater defensive sophistication over the period of their use. The central area was probably unroofed, although the lower galleries may well have had partial roofing. The tower sometimes stood in the centre of a settlement of small stone houses, the whole village being enclosed by a stone wall in a number of cases. The broch at Gurness in Orkney stood in a village that could have been home to up to 40 families and which was enclosed by three stone-faced ramparts and ditches, and that at Howe, also in Orkney, was large enough to provide a home for 250 people.[15] The form of broch settlements brings to mind the *nuraghi* villages of Late Bronze Age Sardinia[16] and the *torri* of Corsica, although in the case of the former it is suggested that villages were a later accretion to isolated buildings, and a ritual purpose has been ascribed to the latter.

Many of the 500 or so known brochs are sited in places where the height of the tower would have given a useful advantage for early warning of trouble – on islands in lochs, on coastal headlands and at the heads of glens – and often close to or within the relatively small and scarce (and thus probably highly valued) areas of reasonable arable in the region. It is generally thought that their function was either as a chieftain's stronghold, or a communal refuge, or most likely both. The coastal location of a large number of brochs and duns has led to the suggestion that the main threat to these communities came from the sea, in the form of raiders seeking cattle, portable wealth and slaves. Contact between the communities in these settlements may also have been largely seaborne, and the general westerly distribution of these settlements suggests possible cultural or trade connections with Ireland and perhaps other cultures facing the Atlantic seaways.

Defences of larger settlements

The fully fledged Iron Age hillforts combined a number of functions. They acted as a focus for territories (**28**) and for settlement as well as for defence. The Heuneberg, Baden-Wurttemberg, like many other sites, is associated with nearby concentrations of rich graves. Unlike any other hillfort in Europe at the time, the Heuneberg's Phase III included a rampart of adobe bricks on a limestone foundation, and square projecting towers provided the defenders with the ability to crossfire against attackers.[17] Perhaps surprisingly, given the European climate, the adobe wall lasted longer than any of the other more usual rampart phases. Like many other hillforts, the Heuneberg overlooks a trade route, in this case the river Danube. It is an imposing spur with a relatively flat summit, of which about 3.2ha is enclosed. Excavations have revealed an area of workshops, adding confirmation to the proposition that such sites were centres of production as well as trade and distribution.

Hillforts are found, of course, in topography other than hills – they occur on slopes, in river meanders and in valley bottoms. Their siting seems to be related as much to their proximity to that which was to be defended or overseen as to any consideration of natural defensibility. Rampart building varied in its style from place to place and over time; it has been pointed out that soil geology was an important consideration in the choice of building technique.[18] The chalk soils of southern England and northern France are easy to dig and can form a bank that survives fairly well in a damp temperate climate, while in the more extreme climates of central Europe or where soils are less stable, vertically fronted timber-laced box ramparts were more popular.[19] In regions where free stone is available, of course, stone-built or stone-faced ramparts appear – in Scotland, Saxony and Provence, for example.

The construction of hillforts reflects a development in military organisation and strategy. In recent years there has been a reluctance to accept the warlike character of these constructions. Their functions as economic centres, as aristocratic holdings or as ritual foci have been stressed over their military rationales. However, a proper analysis of their features and the archaeological and historical evidence from their

28 Hod Hill ramparts with Hambledon Hill settlement in the distance, southern England. There are a number of examples of neighbouring hillforts where one seems to become dominant and others were abandoned. Photograph: Jez Smith

29 The entrance to the hillfort at Danebury, Hants., southern England. The complex hornworks here are associated with the discovery of 6000 slingshots

investigation will readily show not only the extremely sophisticated military design of their structures, but also the actual evidence of violence associated with many of them. The complex design of hornworks and gateways is not a function of economy or status – it is a result of very practical defensive planning. Hornworks such as those at Danebury (**29**) or Maiden Castle (**30**) overawe attackers, confuse and congest their assaults, and provide a range of attack and command positions.

They could be designed to force attackers to approach the entrance with their right, unshielded sides exposed to the defenders on the ramparts. At Danebury,

30 *The impressive ramparts of Maiden Castle, Dorset. Despite its awesome defences it was no match for a properly equipped Roman army, led by the future emperor Vespasian*

31 *Reconstructed murus gallicus at Péran, France. This Celtic walled defence system attracted the admiration of Caesar himself*

'thousands of sling stones found on and around the inner hornwork and the dump of 6000 or so in a pit just inside the gate' demonstrated the very real preparations for warfare made by the inhabitants.[20] Gateways could be equally complex – at Seuftenberg in Germany the narrow entrance passage was lined and floored with timbers. The passage is over 15m long, with two sharp opposing turns. It is considered probable, at several sites, that a continuous structure ran over the top of the gateway, providing a fighting platform, or even perhaps a tower, over the entrance.

Julius Caesar described the way in which hillforts were attacked by other Gauls:

> They begin by surrounding the whole circuit of the wall with a large number of men and showering stones at it from all sides; when they have cleared it of defenders, they lock their shields over their heads, advance close up, and undermine it.[21]

This tactic must have been employed against vertical box-ramparts or gate structures, rather than the sloping glacis-style ramparts of southern Britain and northern France.

A further rampart style is also mentioned with some degree of admiration by Caesar: the murus gallicus (**31**). This comprises a wall of stone facing a cross-laced timber rubble-filled rampart. He notes how the timber lacing allows an even, strong construction in which 'the masonry protects it from fire, the timber from destruction by the battering-ram, which cannot either pierce or knock to pieces a structure braced internally by beams running generally to a length of forty feet in one piece.'[22] It is clear that Gaulish defences presented the Romans with some severe problems on a number of occasions, and that they had to respond with new tactical developments of their own.

A further development in larger-scale fortification occurred in Britain, although we may see some traces of its development in the tactics of the Belgae against Caesar's invasion. The Nervii developed a means of defence against cavalry; they created laid hedges interplanted with briers and thorns, creating impenetrable barriers too thick to even see through, much less clamber through.[23] Survey and excavation in a few British sites have revealed a very different form of aristocratic and economic centre, provided with defences that depended on strategic use of topography and other natural features, among which hedges of the type created by the Nervii probably played a part. These are the territorial oppida, built at tribal centres such as Chichester, capital of the Regni tribe, and Camulodunum, modern Colchester, a major centre of the Catuvellauni.

The earthworks associated with the oppidum at Camulodunum cover some 16km^2. A massive system of dykes, sometimes in multiple groups, sometimes single, stretch across the countryside, creating a defensive frontier and utilising rivers and streams and other landscape features to enclose an area within which were a number of distinct and separated areas of use or settlement: industrial centres, aristocratic settlement, cemeteries and ritual areas, divided from each other by woods and fields. Although very different from the Graeco-Roman form of town development, it is thought that these places do actually represent the beginnings of urban life in Britain. All the functions of an early town are enclosed within the boundaries, including mints and, by extension, governance. It is intriguing to wonder how these oppida may have developed, had their growth not been cut short by the Roman Conquest. It is notable that of all provinces of the Roman Empire, Britain was the least inclined to adopt large scale urbanisation; all its towns remained small and failed to evolve into any but the most lowly classifications of Roman urban status, and it appears that urban life was quite quickly abandoned once the Roman administration broke down. Even in the medieval period, few towns in Britain began to approach the size and population of many European examples. It would appear that the British were at heart a rural people until the massive urbanisation created by the Industrial Revolution, and even today many people mark their success in life by the acquisition of a second home in the country. We have also developed the concept of garden cities; the spatial organisation of Milton Keynes reflects, to some degree, the separation of sectors of building both by function and by physical divisions of countryside – a city made up of distinct villages – that might have been the logical progression of the territorial oppida. As defensive structures, they certainly gave the Romans a headache. The apparently random stretches of banks, the woods, the confusing complexity of the layout of these sites meant that the British could harry the heavily burdened Roman troops, using their light, fast chariots or the deep cover of the forests to strike quickly and then disappear before the Romans could organise a counter-attack. When, with the use of a two-sided attack, Caesar succeeded in capturing one of these strongholds, he found that the British had escaped from the rear of the defences, and he only succeeded in capturing some cattle, although he claimed that many of the fugitives were captured or killed. It was certainly not the kind of decisive victory that he probably envisaged at the start of his campaign.

Later town defences have much more in common with the classical city pattern. Roman provincial towns eventually acquired walls, as did medieval towns and cities. In many cases, the construction of these was driven rather more by the desire to display civic wealth and status than for real defence. In both periods, imposing gates on the major roads into the town were often the first features to be erected, and the linking walls did not appear until much later, if at all.

Southampton's walls and towers

The medieval city of Southampton grew up on rising ground to the west of the middle Saxon trading port of Hamwih, which had no particular defences to speak of, except for a small ditch running across the north of the peninsular joining its two flanking rivers, the Test and Itchen. The port's main function was to provide for the royal centre in its hinterland, which in Hamwih's case was Winchester. The settlement was clearly an attraction to the raiding Vikings of the age, as had been so many other trading 'wics' across the coastal shores of northern Europe. In 842, it fell prey to an attack from which it does not seem to have fully recovered. The trading port's vulnerability lay in the way in which it did its business. It had no conventional quays as such. Instead, it relied upon a sloping beach on which visiting merchant vessels would be drawn up. Some ninth-century coins point to limited activity on this low-lying site, and it appears that a ditched enclosure on higher ground to the west by the river Test came into use in the Later Saxon period, forming the nucleus of medieval Southampton.[24] The burghal defences of Hamwih seem to have reutilised the old Roman Fort at Clausentum, apart from both the trading wic and the site of later Southampton.[25]

This important medieval port began to grow in wealth and importance in the twelfth century AD and marked its increasing status with the erection of an imposing stone gate, the Bargate (**32**), at its northern entrance on the road leading to London and Winchester. Built around 1180, and much altered and extended since, an original arch from the first structure still survives within the gate. However, this

32 *The late twelfth-century Bargate of Southampton survives in the form of an arch incorporated into later material. The Bargate was not attached to a wall, but was part of an earth bank and ditch defence system on the town's landward sides*

statement of the town's self-importance and confidence was not attached to a wall. Instead, the town's defences consisted of an earth bank and ditch on its northern and eastern landward sides, which was completed around 1220. Later, a further outer ditch was added to part of the system.

The seaward sides of the town were undefended; instead, the quays were lined with grand masonry merchants' houses and warehouses. At this period, a merchant's home also served as his trading office, store and salesroom. It was only after a disastrous raid in 1338 by a French and Genoese piratical armada, when substantial parts of the town were destroyed, that opinion began to shift towards building more effective defences. The earth walls to the north and east were rebuilt in stone. Excavations in the north-east sector have shown that in places the foundations of this wall consisted of no more than three courses; the wall they supported was very thin, but even so had to be supported by a bank of earth. The section excavated dated to the late fourteenth century, showing the slow process of the wall building despite the salutary lesson of the earlier raid.

Work on defending the western and southern sides of the town did not, in fact, even begin until after the resumption of raids by the French in the 1370s. The important merchants continued to resist efforts to build the walls, which might protect their homes and families, but would impede their commercial activities by reducing their free access to the quays, adversely affecting the rapid and large-scale movement of goods on which their prosperity depended. In the event, the wall was built to incorporate the walls of

33 Arcades at Southampton. This odd part of the seaward wall was built incorporating the mercantile houses lining the west quay

34 Catchcold Tower, Southampton, built in 1418. The larger diameter of the gun loops compare with the ones of the western wall of the town and demonstrate the rapid development of gunpowder weapons

35 God's House Tower, Southampton, extended in 1417 to house guns and a gunner. The roof was strengthened to support a cannon and it is hailed as the first English residential gun tower

some of the mercantile residences (**33**). The wall also utilised the stone arches of the bailey wall of the motte and bailey castle, as well as the castle's quay and Watergate. Southampton's walls are extraordinarily thin as a result of these factors – 0.76m compared with 1.9m at Bath, 2.1m at Newcastle and 1.5-2.5m at Bristol. However, by 1385 the city was at last enclosed by stone walls, with 29 towers and seven main gates.

Southampton was later able to boast of its up-to-date state-of-the-art defensive system. Some features pre-dated the wall building, the Bargate for example, and the late thirteenth-century Polymond Tower at the north-east corner, where the structure is not bonded into the later masonry wall. The wall's fragility was addressed at later periods; during the fifteenth century a trench was excavated into the rampart immediately behind the wall and backfilled with masonry in order to strengthen the construction in part of the north-east sector.[26]

Other features, such as the incorporated walls of the merchants' houses, the Half Round Tower created from the eastern half of a pre-existing dovecote, and the piercing of the walls for such reasons as the postern gate created by the Franciscan friars to connect their convent with its gardens, seem to indicate a lack of total commitment to the process of defence.

However, the gunloops added to the western wall are considered to be among the earliest in Britain; their size compared to those in the Catchcold Tower (**34**) built in 1418 demonstrates the development of gunpowder weapons over the period. The earlier examples have a diameter of 12.7-15.2cm, with the length of the slit being about 1.12m; the later ones average 27.9cm in diameter, showing how much larger were the guns then in use.

The Westgate and other features are well equipped with machicolations, and by 1417 the God's House Tower (**35**) was extended to house the town's guns and its gunner, forming the first residential gun tower in England. Gun loops were incorporated into the first floor, and the roof was strengthened to support a platform for a roof-mounted cannon. By this time Southampton's defences were probably as fine and modern as any port in the country.[27] Despite its poor start, about 75 per cent of the wall circuit survives in Southampton, and God's House Tower now houses the archaeological museum.

The earliest ditch around the Roman town of Verulamium (St Albans) possibly dates from around AD 50. It surrounded three sides of the town, enclosing just over 48ha. It is hard to know whether this was intended as a defence, or as a definition of territory confirming the status of the new town as a municipium. If in existence by that time, it certainly did nothing to stop Boudicca's army some 10 years later, and was filled in around AD 125. It has been suggested that the devastating fire which destroyed the town again around AD 155 may have been deliberate. Certainly, part of the rebuilding programme seems to have included the erection of defences; a bank and ditch system, the Fosse earthwork, was constructed, with a ditch over 15m wide and 5.5m deep and a bank of similar width and over 2m high; incorporated into the circuit were two gates built in masonry. These are of a similar plan to a gate at Corinium (Cirencester), which also acquired earth defences at this time. At Corinium, stone towers seem to have been built into the earth rampart. The Fosse earthwork seems never to have been completed, and enclosed a large area of land (93.6ha) that does not appear to have been very much developed. Similar defensive enceintes around Wroxeter and Canterbury, as well as Corinium, were equally ambitious but underused.

Verulamium's defences were revised again in the early third century AD, when a system of ditches with a wall of flint and tile backed by an earthern bank was erected to enclose about 81ha. This wall, just over 3.5km in length, had a number of internal towers and three gates. Projecting bastions were added in the fourth century AD. Two of the gates were the earlier ones mentioned above, and were not bonded into the wall. This smaller defensive circuit abandoned areas in the west of the town within the earthwork that had not been developed. Extramural suburbs, however, did exist outside the walled area in the north-east sector and on the approach to the London Gate.

Defence building around towns in Britain in the Roman period was rare in the first century, but a number of these settlements built walls or ramparts in the second century.

> Earthwork defences imply either economy or emergency. In so far as economy is concerned, the period in question was a time when the imperial administration was certainly trying to limit the financial excesses of some urban communities, but it is not possible to say whether this was being tried or even needed in Britain. As for emergency, there were more than enough episodes to account for it being the initiating factor.[28]

Wacher goes on to consider whether the earthwork defences of these towns were a response to a growing sense of insecurity culminating in the usurpation of power by Clodius Albinus, forcing those towns which had commenced building in masonry, perhaps starting with specialist structures such as gates and towers, to complete their works more rapidly than intended using earthworks and timber, a solution to urban defence unique to Britain at this time. This form of defence was, of course, related to earlier hillfort defences and would reappear in Wessex and Mercia after the Roman occupation ceased; it is hardly possible that late second-century Britons would remember the techniques of their distant forefathers, of course, but it is interesting to speculate about whether the example of surviving Iron Age sites held more force in Britain than it did in Gaul.

The masonry replacements for the earthwork defences were generally begun, so far as dating can be ascertained, in the early AD 200s, and continued for perhaps half a century with many stops, starts and changes of design. The reasons for all this effort are not clear – immediate threat, however, does not appear to have been one of them. During the later third and the fourth centuries, the addition of bastions and towers may represent a reaction to changes in military strategy and technology, particularly the increased use of artillery. Alternatively, they may be related to changes in the way defence of provincial towns was undertaken, perhaps implying that local militia used these platforms as points of concentration to bring conventional projectile weapons to bear in order to prevent attempts at scaling the walls.

Was the enclosure of excessive amounts of land an expression of the ambition of the city fathers, or does it represent a desire to enclose urban farm land, either for the security of supply it might represent, or for the amount of profit to be expected from it by important landowners who could influence the route and extent of the defence building? In other smaller towns, and in northern Gaul, a very different strategy was being adopted in the later AD 200s. Here, strong fortifications were created that in fact defended only very small areas of the inhabited area, examples including the castella or citadels such as those of Amiens, Neumagen or Junkerath. The areas enclosed by these defences were tiny – 1.52ha at Junkerath, 1.28ha at Neumagen – and the fortifications were very strong. The castellum at Bitburg was surrounded by a ditch, within which was a strong wall punctuated by 13 round towers enclosing just 2ha.[29]

Defences of territory

The demands of larger scale territorial or national defence will be examined in more detail in the next chapter in terms of the ideas, successes and failures of linear systems and those which depend upon a philosophy of defence-in-depth. However, territorial defence need not be restricted to frontiers alone. Sometimes entire kingdoms and counties can be provided for by a system of defended places. Among the most famous responses to a national emergency in the archaeological record is the arrangement of fortified places instigated by Alfred the Great, king of Wessex (AD 871-99) which is discussed below.

Anglo-Saxon burhs

One of the most notable episodes of territorial defensive building in English history was the creation by Alfred the Great of a system of burhs, or fortified places, throughout the kingdom of Wessex, built to counter the threat of incursion by the Danish Great Army and its descendants in the late ninth century. Here, the idea of

ÆLFRED REX HA
NC URBEM FE**CIT**·
ANNO DOMI**NIC**
AE INCARN**ATIO**
NIS DCCCLXXX
REGNI SUI VIII

36 Drawing of a rubbing of a plaque fragment from Shaftesbury once seen by William of Malmesbury in the twelfth century. The original plaque, now lost, stated that king Alfred had built the town in 880

defence-in-depth was employed to a demonstrably successful effect. The philosophy behind the establishment of the Anglo-Saxon burghal system was perfectly simple, as too was the organisation of manpower required to achieve it. The kingdom of Wessex was the only remaining kingdom of middle Anglo-Saxon England not to fall political and military victim to the desires of the Danish forces occupying the country. It also had the most resources at its disposal of all the kingdoms of the heptarchy as is evidenced by its rating, measured in hides (a taxable unit based on land productivity), in the tribal hideage document. The document, thought to be an eighth-century tribute list compiled by officials of the kingdom of Mercia, assesses Wessex at 100,000 hides, which differs markedly from its neighbour Sussex at just 7000.

With such resources at his disposal, Alfred established defended strongholds in his kingdom, some of which went on to qualify as towns in their own right by 1086. All of them, whether large re-fortified Roman towns such as Winchester (rated at 2400 hides) or small geographical 'gap-filling' fortifications such as Chisbury (700 hides) and Eashing (600 hides), are to be considered as walled settlements of both a temporary and permanent nature. The system, with its royal or state patronage and conception, has recently been compared to the military arrangements in fourth-century Britain with both periods being described as wearing 'the aspect of an embattled military monarchy'.[30] Alfred's achievement was in the way in which he assigned his men to a tripartite rotation system of duties, so that at any one stage there would be burghal garrisons, field forces and farmers serving in his kingdom.

Listed in a document known as the Burghal Hideage, a sixteenth-century transcript of an eleventh-century Winchester document, are 33 strongholds with a note of how many hides are attributable to each place. Cornwall, Kent and London are conspicuously absent from the list probably because at the time of its original compilation, these areas were under semi-independent jurisdiction, like Kent and Cornwall, or controlled by the remnants of the English Kingdom of Mercia, like London. It is not too difficult for us to see how the system of defences might have extended into these other areas. Exeter, Bath, Winchester, Portchester, Chichester, Rochester and Canterbury form an obvious network of nodal points. The list is a simple clockwise run around the kingdom of Wessex, but importantly, shows that the burhs were not merely concentrated on the frontiers of the kingdom, but were carefully placed within the kingdom so that no burh would be more than a day's march from another, a distance generally taken to be about 20 miles. The defences worked not only as places of refuge for the local population during times of Danish incursion, but as bases from which to dominate a territory under hostile attack. The strongholds were close enough together for each of the garrisons to support each other in the event of combined military action. The estimated garrison strength of all the burhs of Wessex was around 27,000 men. The calculation of this figure is arrived at by a remarkable piece of good fortune. A footnote on the manuscript states that

> If every hide is represented by one man, then every pole [16 feet] of wall can be manned by four men. Then, for the maintenance of 20 poles of wall, 80 hides are required and for a furlong, 160 hides are required by the same reckoning.

This formula works remarkably well and ties-in with the archaeological evidence for most burhs with the peculiar exceptions of Exeter and Chichester.[31]

The fact that the burghal system could be used offensively on a grand scale, by providing strong points for co-operating garrisons, is evidenced by the extension of the system into Danish Mercia in the years after the reign of Alfred when his son Eadweard the Elder and Aethelflead, Lady of the Mercians used burhs as the foundation for their reconquest of the Danelaw between 900 and 924. The inclusion of Buckingham, Worcester and Warwick in the list hints at this policy and suggests a date for compilation of the Burghal Hideage in the Edwardian and not Alfredian period. Eight new burhs were added to the system between 907 and 913. The burhs of North West Mercia, which included Chester (907), Eddisbury (914), Runcorn (915), Thelwall (919), Manchester (919) and Cledmutha (Rhuddlan) built in 921, have all had their function variously interpreted. Certainly, it is true that there was a need to defend north-west Mercia from the Norse-Irish threat which had resulted from the Irish expulsion of the Vikings from Dublin in 902, and there are some compelling accounts of Viking attempts to take Chester in a remarkable siege. However, the continuing Welsh threat may have played just as an important part in their construction. Some have sought to point out that there is more than just a defensive and militaristic aspect to the burhs and that this can be gleaned from the nature of their placement in the landscape. In north-west Mercia for example, Thelwall, Cledmutha and Runcorn are low lying in river valleys, crossings or road intersections. It is argued that this may be linked to the increasing importance of such settlements as places of trade and economic power. Whilst it is still true that the economic side of the argument is part and parcel of a policy of territorial annexation and control, this multiple role aspect of the Anglo-Saxon burh in an expanding urban landscape cannot be underestimated.[32]

The capability of burghal garrisons can be seen from the misfortune which befell the only invading force to make a serious attempt on Wessex after the construction of the burhs. When, in 893, a new Viking army entered the Wessex heartland intent

37 *Aerial view of the Town of Wallingford, one of the largest West Saxon frontier forts. The Anglo-Saxon burghal defences are still clearly visible in the top left of the picture.* © Crown Copyright 1951/MOD. Reproduced with the permission of the Controller of Her Majesty's Stationery Office

on wreaking the kind of damage its predecessor had done, the burghal system displayed two different aspects of its usefulness. Exeter (rated at 734 hides) successfully withstood a siege and in the same year Alfred instigated a burghal garrison call-out of troops from all burhs east of the River Parret, which succeeded in tracking and defeating the invading force outside of the kingdom.

The form which the burhs took varied in many ways, but all had the same protective reasoning behind their construction. In some cases, their perimeters were refortified Roman stone defences surrounding an existing urban settlement such as at Winchester and Chichester, whilst in other smaller forts the construction was entirely new from the start and consisted of earthen bank, ditch, rampart and timber palisade, such as at Wallingford (**37**). In other places like Chisbury, Pilton and Halwell, the defensive banks of Iron Age hillforts were once again pressed into service. In the case of Sceaftesege, or Sashes, an island in the Thames near Cookham, natural geography provided an ideal

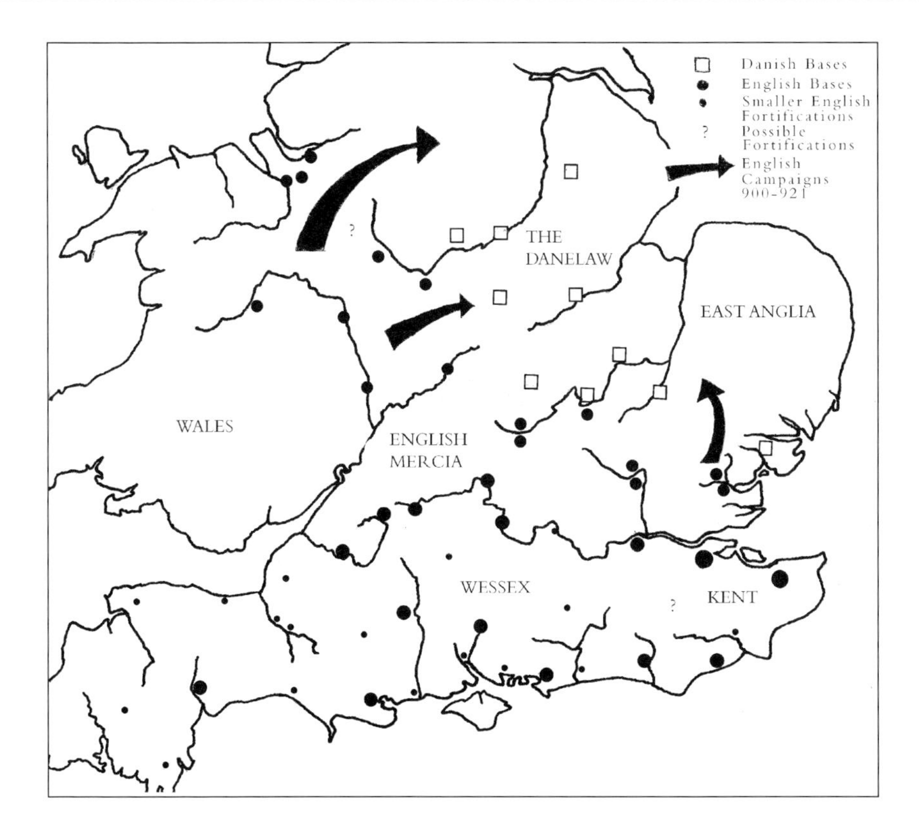

38 Map showing the Anglo-Saxon burghal system of Wessex and its extended usage into Mercia under Edweard the Elder (900-924). These fortified strongholds were used as bases during the re-conquest of the Danelaw

refuge in the river itself. What unites all the sites in the system, regardless of which ones went on to become towns, is their role in mutual support and population protection. Those burhs which did achieve borough status by the post-conquest period did so on the basis of their size and on the deliberate policies of successive monarchs who encouraged economic, legal and ecclesiastical activity in these places.

British home defences

During the First World War, most defensive arrangements inland were related to impairment of mobile enemy advances using the horse. Simple stop-lines were created in East Anglia and across Kent and the south-east of England. They were formed using a combination of ditches and banks, barbed wire and scattered strong points formed by pillboxes and batteries. Some refurbishment of the London Defence Positions was undertaken. These were a series of small strong points begun in 1889 as a result of media alarm over the undefended state of the capital, despite the absence of any real threat at that time. Two lines of these positions were created, one protecting the approaches to London from any invasion via the Essex coastline,

39 *Second World War Pillbox at Pevensey Castle East Sussex, built into a Roman Bastion of the late third century AD.* Photograph: Sandra Luff

and the other south of the city along the North Downs from the Thames Estuary across to Guildford. These sites had been abandoned or not completed but where they did exist in 1914, they were brought into the stop-line system.

The situation in 1939 was somewhat different. A mobile invasion threat was a distinct possibility; this time it was not horses but mechanised vehicles that would have to be stopped. Additionally, there were now inland sites of extreme strategic importance in the prosecution of the war which were highly vulnerable to attack from within the territorial boundary – the development of aerial warfare had created a whole new set of problems for defensive architects. The sheer size of airfields, their visibility and the mobility of an airborne foe made them something of a defence headache. The Luftwaffe could also easily attack and destroy a whole range of other installations and centres of population, or drop parachute troops near these targets which therefore also required defence from a completely new angle.

The first response at the start of the Second World War was to create a new system of stop-lines, employing a wide range of techniques.

> These comprised a mixture of natural barriers, particularly rivers, backed by fixed defences consisting of thousands of miles of anti-tank ditches, often supported by pillboxes and other obstacles. It was the greatest system of defensive earthworks ever built in Britain, and was probably the shortest-lived.[33]

The principal stop-line, the General Headquarters Line, ran from Musselburgh near Edinburgh along the eastern side of the country through Yorkshire, Cambridgeshire and East Anglia to London and then from the Medway across Kent, Surrey, Berkshire and Hampshire, ending at the Bristol Channel. Secondary stop-lines protected the Firth of Forth, the manufacturing centres around Derby, the territory bordering the Solent, and the hinterlands of the important ports of Plymouth and Dover. They were

40 *Pillbox in a Wiltshire field.* Photograph: Sandra Luff

designed to be manned by volunteer troops and the Home Guard, supported by local efforts to block routes with dragon's teeth, barbed wire and other obstacles. A massive programme of pillbox building was commenced, and great ingenuity was displayed in camouflaging these – notably as part of a Roman bastion at Pevensey Castle (**39**). Other disguises included a tea kiosk near Newlands Corner in Surrey, railway coal heaps and even chicken sheds. Perhaps the most frustrating disguise for many would have been the pillbox camouflaged as a public convenience.

About 18,000 pillboxes were built (**40**), using poured concrete and scrap iron reinforcement within wooden shutters, or brick permanent shuttering as wood became scarce. A number of designs were produced, of various sizes and providing shelter for varying numbers of troops and sizes of weapon.

> It was the coming of the machine gun to the battlefield which caused the development of the pillbox. The weapon, needing a good field of fire to be effective, would in a built-up area be sited in a house with a commanding position. Such a position would be strengthened by the use of concrete to thicken the inner walls, providing extra protection for the machine gun and crew. From such an emplacement, it was a short step to the purpose-designed pillbox, especially in open country where there would be no convenient house at the best fire position.[34]

Smaller versions housed riflemen, larger ones held Bren guns, sometimes so designed as to allow anti-aircraft fire. These were particularly concentrated around airfields. The largest pillboxes were designed to house the two-pounder anti-tank gun. Some special types included the Pickett-Hamilton retractable pillbox which could be raised or lowered into the ground by means of a winding mechanism. The Tett Turret was a concrete turret set over a concrete shaft sunk into the ground, with a 360° field of fire. Much ingenuity was applied to these structures; by mid-1941, however, the whole programme was abandoned. The new concentration of defensive building was aimed at coastal emplacements. The possibility for national defence based on local militia had always been questioned – in the early months of the war, however, the unpreparedness of the country meant that this solution had been accepted as the best that could be managed in the time available.

The danger from parachute landings and from bombing raids was seen as acute. Airfields were heavily defended with trench systems, pillboxes, machine gun emplacements and subterranean command posts. Dummy air strips and hangers were created to confuse enemy bombers, and anti-aircraft guns were concentrated around the Royal Air Force's vital bases. Barrage balloons were designed to force enemy planes into the path of the anti-aircraft batteries and to spoil their bombing aim. Starfish sites, sited near to major strategic targets, were remote-controlled networks intended to set off explosions, which took the attention of enemy bombers away from the real installations and encouraged them to waste their payloads of explosive on empty locations.

Some major underground structures were developed – the strategic military command centre housed in tunnels below Dover Castle is well known, as are the Cabinet War Rooms in London. At Corsham, Wiltshire, a project was begun in 1928 as a result of growing concern over future danger from aerial warfare. Set in old stone quarries, it grew from a six acre secure storage depot holding 12,000 tons of ammunition and costing £100,000 until

> by 1943 it became a complete underground town covering 125 acres, housing 300,000 tons of explosives and costing over four and a half million pounds. "Many thousands of lights burn continuously in this land of hidden cities", wrote a journalist in the Daily Express . . . "Here, carved from the living rock, is a great bomb-proof cloister hundreds of feet long, supported by square thirty-foot columns hewn out of stone."[35]

Defence of the civilian population also became a crucial issue because of the threat from the air. In a single day, 15 September 1940, over 1700 German aircraft attacked London, and hundreds of people were killed. In all, the Blitz accounted for over 43,000 civilian deaths. London Underground stations were used as shelters and public shelters were erected in major population centres, but many people obeyed government advice to build an Anderson Shelter in their gardens – a corrugated iron shed which was partially buried into the soil, and covered with a thick layer of earth. Despite their unpopularity because of their dampness and cramped conditions, there is little doubt that these simple structures saved the lives of countless thousands. They were little protection, however, against the V-1 and V-2 rockets which started to hammer London and the surrounding area late in 1944.

It is sobering to consider the helplessness of civilian populations in the nuclear age. Massive shelters exist for specialist sections of the government and armed forces, at places such as Burlington at Corsham, below Brunel's Box railway tunnel and the £126 million installation completed in 1992 under Whitehall. For the rest of us, the choices of running away, hiding or striking back would be equally impossible. We must place our trust for defence in the hands of our politicians.

Defences of invading forces

Britain has seen two major invasions which have entailed the construction of these forms of defences: the Romans in AD 43 and the Normans in 1066. In addition, parts of the British Isles have been invaded by various monarchs; Wales saw the construction of a major series of castles under Edward I. Abroad, the British were responsible for several phases of defensive building, as were many other colonial powers, in Africa, India and the Americas.

The Roman legions which invaded Britain under the emperor Claudius numbered some 40,000 men, who intended to defeat and hold in perpetuity a land inhabitated by perhaps 4 million people. Confident though they undoubtedly were of Rome's ability to achieve this stupendous task, based on their experiences across most of Western Europe and the Mediterranean, they needed to be able to defend themselves while the process of turning Britain into a Roman province was under way. No army can march forever without rest, resupply and consolidation. Each soldier would have been trained in the art of fortification building, and each legion carried with it the tools and expertise to construct everything from a temporary overnight shelter to a permanent base.

Roman fortifications in Gaul and Britain in the first century AD were constructed in a variety of forms – from the vast legionary fortresses to marching camps, however, they conformed to a more or less standard layout. They were generally of a 'playing card' shape, rectangular with rounded corners. There are a number of sources which tell us how the defences of these fortifications were undertaken, one of the most important being Trajan's Column, erected to commemorate the emperor's victories in Dacia, modern Romania. Surveyors laid out the lines of the exterior and marked out the line of the enclosing V-shaped ditch, which provided spoil for the construction of a rampart surmounted by a palisade, or a masonry wall.

The ditches average between 2.4 and 6.1m wide and between 1.2 and 2.7m in depth at the earlier forts. Over time, a number of different profiles developed, later ditches often being much wider, or part of a system of multiple ditches. Ramparts were consolidated by the addition of various local materials to the ditch spoil: rough stone, clay blocks and turves have all been noted. They varied in width from about 4.5m to just over 9m during the first century AD. Each of the four sides had a central entrance. The wisdom of this has been questioned – after all, an entrance to a fortification is its most vulnerable spot.

> The answer is probably that the Roman army was an offensive, not a defensive, force. If attacked, whether in an overnight camp, a fort or even a legionary fortress, the troops would quickly muster to meet the enemy in the open, attack being the best form of defence.[36]

Towers were inserted into the wall defences; in Britain they frequently occur at the gateways, at the corners and spaced out along the wall. Both timber and stone examples are known: timber at such sites as Lincoln and York and stone in London at the Cripplegate fort, Caerleon, York and Chester.

It is presumed that one of the most important uses of towers was for the siting of artillery, although sources make it clear that ballistae and other artillery could be placed in other locations round the fort as well. Caesar mentions (*BG* VIII,I:239)

> The Roman camp had a twelve-foot rampart with a breastwork of proportionate height, two trenches fifteen feet wide with perpendicular sides, and three-storeyed towers at frequent intervals, joined together by floored galleries protected on the outside by wicker breastworks. Thus, in addition to the double trench, it could be guarded by two rows of defenders – one on the galleries, where they were less exposed on account of the height, and could therefore hurl their missiles with greater confidence and make them carry farther; the other on the actual rampart, where, although nearer the enemy, they were protected by the galleries from falling missiles . . . These elaborate defences had two purposes. Caesar hoped they would make the Gauls imagine that he was afraid, and so give them greater confidence. At the same time they would make the camp so strong that it could be defended by a small force, while the rest scoured the country in search of forage and corn.

This quotation amply illuminates both the thinking behind the defence design, and the needs of an army in hostile territory, especially where they are potentially badly outnumbered. Important aspects of the siting of forts or marching camps would include the availability of water and forage, and in cases where a longer stay was envisaged, of timber. The site should be free of the risk of flooding. Preferably, it should utilise any natural defensive features of the location. A document, called *de munitionibus castrorum*, lists the kind of sites preferred, best of which was 'a slight prominence on gently sloping land'.[37] Care to avoid giving advantage to enemies was also to be taken; the fort or camp was to be sited away from places where a foe may lie concealed, or where the interior could be overlooked from a nearby hill.

> The abundant evidence from archaeological discoveries of sites in Britain . . . reflects much of this advice . . . But other factors, including the relationship of the respective fort to the communications-system, and good visibility, had obviously to be taken into account. Consequently, fort-sites were often strategic points in the road system. And, since in the so-called 'Highland Zone' of Britain, many bases were continuously occupied in hilly country, where the roads followed the river-valleys, there was a high incidence of forts situated at river confluences.[38]

Navigable rivers could carry supplies and troops, and rivers were also a significant factor in defence of a site. Of course, geography alone did not define the siting of a camp or fort – proximity of valuable resources or centres of population were vital considerations, but the Romans had a highly successful military culture and knew all about how to take advantage of the landscape. The siting of the legionary fortress at Colchester is a good example of the considerations necessary before building could commence:

> It had to be inside Camulodunum's defences, but on unoccupied land to minimise the disruption. It had to be near the river to use water-borne transport and yet be high enough to command a good view of the surrounding area. It had to guard the main river crossings into the native settlement, and it had to be close to a good supply of water.
>
> The site which met all of these requirements was a spur of land immediately downstream from the Sheepen site . . . The longitudinal axis of the fortress was placed on an east-west ridge formed by the steep slope down to the river Colne on the north and a more gentle slope to the south. The fortress was deliberately aligned on true north so that it faced east with the principal gate . . . facing seaward.[39]

At this site, as perhaps at others once the Conquest itself had reached a certain stage, defensibility has to be combined with a certain degree of diplomacy. The more permanent fortresses built in the first century needed not only to enforce Roman control, but also to be part of the process of Romanisation. The native population had to be overseen, the tribute and plunder had to be collected, protected and transshipped, and revolts had to be guarded against while the troops were themselves protected – but in such a way that the process of winning over the nobility to the imperial cause was not endangered. A complex challenge for the military, and one that for the most part they succeeded in meeting with great success.

The central part of the interior was occupied by the *principia*, the headquarters building. Near this would be the commander's billet, with the other officers quartered close by. Rows of tents, wooden or masonry barracks housed the troops. In a short-lived marching camp, each infantry century of about 80 men was divided into ten eight-man tent-parties, with a larger tent set at the end of the row for the centurion and his supported non-commissioned officers. The same layout is reflected in the more substantial wooden winter camps: most barrack blocks seem to have been divided into ten parallel pairs of rooms with a number of rooms at the end for the centurion's party. Barrack blocks of this type have been excavated at the legionary fortress at Colchester, where Legio XX was apparently based for several years immediately after AD 43. Each block was about 69m long, and some rooms had hearths.[40]

A legion was supplied with a great many specialists from within its ranks. A list of the second century AD includes those concerned with building: surveyors, architects, tilemakers, stone cutters, plumbers and the like. There were also various artisans concerned with ordnance and transport: helmet and sword makers, arrowsmiths, and other metal workers, farriers and stablemen, wagon-makers and shipwrights; and of course, there were those concerned with basic supply and support trades such as butchers and cooks, woodcutters and charcoal makers, and medical staff. Within a fortress there were a number of workshops and storerooms for these trades, as well as amenities such as an infirmary, latrines and bathhouses. In this way, each fortress was a more or less self-contained township, providing everything necessary for the survival of the legion whatever the situation in the surrounding territory. Less official needs were met by the growth of a *vicus* outside the gates – an unofficial settlement of camp followers and traders which provided entertainment and local goods to the troops when they were off duty. The interaction in these settlements would also, over time, have contributed towards an acceptance of the Roman presence, especially when the soldiers had just been paid! Garrison towns of the Roman period are unlikely to have been of a substantially different character to garrison towns of any other era in respect of the pleasures on offer and the rapacity of those providing them.

Early fortifications in the American colonies were on the whole much less sophisticated than the Roman fortresses. Interpretation of a sketch on a map of 1546 of the Quebec region suggests that Cartier's fort, one of the earliest British or French installations, was sited on the edge of the great bluff. It seems to have taken the form of a half-moon-shaped enclosure protected by a palisade with a single entrance, and embrasures for four pieces of field artillery. Some 70 years later, Quebec was still protected by a timber fort, but had acquired several large buildings protected by a solid parapet, a ditch and drawbridge, and external earth triangle bastions for heavier artillery. The fort had acquired an external garden and an internal protected dovecote.

Earth and timber were also used during the eighteenth century in the northern parts of the American colonies, even when the design of the fortifications copied European stone models. Further to the south, the Spanish did use stone when they could. When this was not available, they either imported stone from Spain, or utilised adobe blocks. Supporting the colonial forts and stockades were blockhouses, which were also used in more far-flung locations. Capable of holding up to 120 men, they were often sited at river or road crossings to protect the routes. Timber walls were built of thick logs laid horizontally enclosing a square or rectangular area of 6-10m in length. The upper floor was accessed from within by a trapdoor with a removable ladder, like a bastle. The walls were pierced by loopholes and gunports, as was the upper floor, so that if the ground floor was taken, defenders above could fire down on the intruders. Steeply pitched roofs deflected fire and protected the building from the weather, and a stone-built fireplace and chimney provided for cooking and warmth.

Fort Phil Kearny, Wyoming

By the nineteenth century, expansion into the Indian Territories of the West led to periods of general war between the Plains tribes and the US cavalry supporting the settlers, gold diggers and traders who were setting out to exploit what they saw as virgin territory. The forts 'served as refuges for those same civilian pioneers, and inevitably became centres of government administration'.[41] These forts included storehouses, stables, barracks, offices, magazines, and even bandstands within a strong timber palisade and corner blockhouses, and averaged about 180m x 210m. Howitzers were provided, though never in great numbers at these forts, and it is rare that the building design accommodates artillery embrasures – usually, they just fired out of the gates. The isolation of these frontier stockades was their weakest point, especially facing a particularly mobile foe highly skilled at rapid assaults, and who could survive off the land much better than the colonials.

Fort Phil Kearny in Wyoming (**41**) was built in 1866.

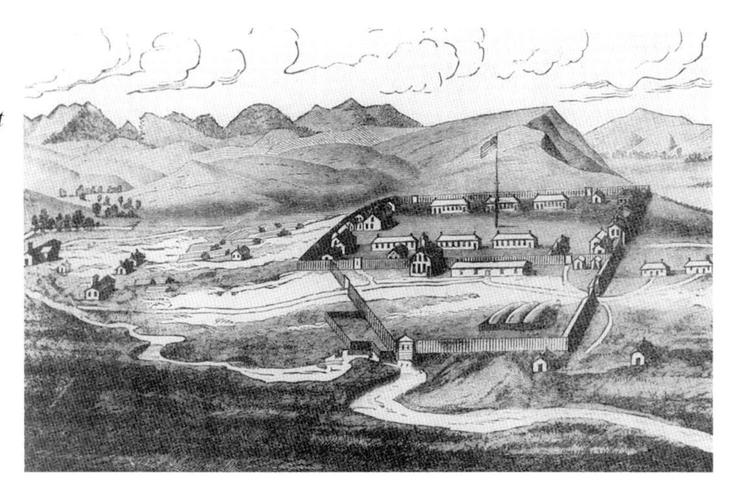

41 *Fort Phil Kearny. An example of the citing of a frontier fort in hostile territory whose isolation proved to be its downfall.* Photograph: Courtesy of the Western History Department, Denver Public Library

> It had a good supply of water and forage, and two neighbouring hillocks for lookout posts. There was plenty of timber, but not immediately around the fort. That was a good point because it meant there was no cover for Indians; it was also a bad point because soldiers had to be sent out to cut wood – and might well be cut off themselves, as happened on a number of occasions.[42]

Some 12,000 timbers were required in the building of the fort, all of which had to be cut and hauled in under fairly constant hit-and-run Indian attacks. There were two large warehouses, a sutler's store, a laundry, officers' quarters – for both married and single men, a headquarters building, a bandstand, a magazine sunk more than 2m into the ground, and two massive blockhouses, as well as civilian quarters, a smithy, a wagon shop, various other workshops and stables. In October 1866 the complement was 360 soldiers and several families as well as the civilian employees. The weak point of such a fort is its isolation and the ease with which it may be denied support and supplies from established settlements. The disruption to travel caused by Indian raids along the trail, together with the difficulties of transporting supplies or maintaining communications over poor roads in severe weather conditions, left Fort Phil Kearny in a dangerously weakened condition.

During the winter, food supplies ran very short and temperatures down to 40° below zero were recorded at the fort. The mules starved and began to eat the logs of their stables. Fuel supplies were quickly exhausted in the bitter cold. Red Cloud's Sioux blockaded the fort; there were a number of skirmishes including the famous Fetterman incident (**42**). There was much suffering on both sides, resulting in the troops' inability to carry out their duties of protecting the Bozeman Trail. The route consequently went out of use and in August 1868 the soldiers were withdrawn. Red Cloud may have then entered the fort and burned it down. Alternatively, it may have been burned by the US Army engineers to prevent its use by hostiles. The total American losses were five officers, 91 enlisted men and 58 civilians, with a number of deserters unaccounted for, plus those lost as the Sioux attacked every white traveller on the trail.[43] Despite its technological superiority, the US army's relatively tiny numbers

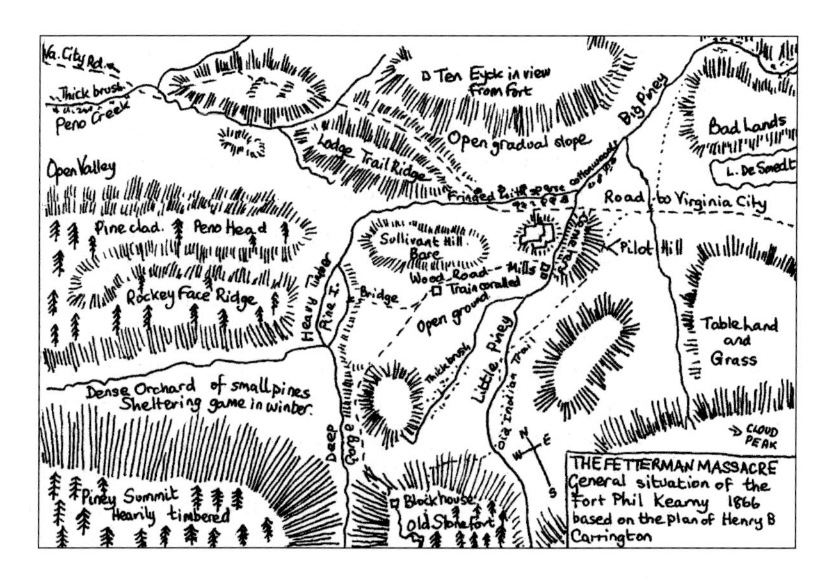

42 *The Fetterman Massacre, 21 December 1866. Map showing the nature of the landscape surrounding fort Phil Kearny based on Henry B. Carrington, 1866*

in a vast landscape created a situation where it was highly vulnerable. The problems faced by the troops at fort Phil Kearny were potentially similar to those which could have faced the Romans or the Normans as they attempted to gain footholds in Britain.

Norman Castles

When the Normans invaded Britain in 1066, they lacked the support of a regular trained army with specialist personnel and organised supply lines. They were relatively few in number at first and their strategy of conquest and domination has been compared to that of Hitler's blitzkrieg in Poland in 1939. Much of William's army probably consisted of landless men, younger sons without patrimony, and adventurers motivated by greed for plunder. England was not a potential province, to be 'civilised' and brought into the family of provinces of a great empire; it was a land that could be grabbed, parcelled up and crushed under the heels of men bent on carving out their own personal fiefs under the patronage of a man intent on making himself a king. William's control of his followers was based on his claim to the ownership of all the land he had conquered. It did not extend to control of their actions towards the people living in the territories he shared out as rewards to his supporters. William's strategy has been the subject of much argument: how clearly had he planned his actions following on from his success at Senlac Hill? To what extent were his plans dictated by his expectations of the Norwegian invasion? How much resistance did he expect to encounter? That he recognised he was going to need defences is clear if it is true that prefabricated dismantled wooden towers were among the supplies brought by the invasion fleet.

The building of castles was an essential part of the Norman strategy: 'In William's camp there were men who believed that, no matter how brave its soldiers, a land without castles was virtually indefensible.'[44] There has been much argument about the nature and status of late Saxon defensible residences, but it seems clear that they were not what the invaders wanted or needed, and they were relatively few in number, although evidence for more such sites is constantly being found. It is unlikely that they functioned in precisely the same way as Norman castles, which had a duel role where the functions of the castle and its garrison were entirely separate, the garrison being described as a field-force and the castle as its depot.[45]

Early Norman defences come in several forms: the motte and bailey castles, the ringwork castles, lookout towers and the stone keeps. One of the invaders' first actions was to dragoon English peasants and prisoners into the building of motte and bailey and ringwork defences. Motte and bailey castles are characterised by a mound formed either completely artificially by piling up stone, earth, clay, turves or other materials, or by utilising a natural mound which was levelled; whichever way the motte was formed, it supported a timber or stone lookout tower or keep surrounded by a palisade. Access to the motte was protected by a ditch crossed by a removable bridge structure and perhaps by another palisade, and access to the summit was by a stair or ladder. To one side of the motte, beyond its bridge, lay the bailey (or sometimes two baileys as at Windsor), a larger flat area, protected by its own ditch, rampart and palisade, and with a defended entrance. The bailey held a number of buildings for shelter, stables and stores. The surviving heights of mottes vary between 1 and 20m, with base diameters from 50 to 150m and summit diameters of 5 to 10m. The encircling ditches were between 10 and 20m wide and 3 to 6m deep. Ringwork castles are generally similar to the baileys, having ditch, rampart and palisade defences; the major defensive structure is often a gatehouse, or a free-standing keep or tower erected on the ground surface.

The reason for the two contemporary forms is unclear; suggestions include individual responses to local topography, simple expediency and economy and different ethnic or experiential preferences amongst the varied groups of William's followers. There are about four times as many motte castles as there are ringworks. Mottes give the obvious advantage of height: the artificial or natural eminence dominates the surrounding landscape and provides a defensible base for security and surveillance. On the other hand, a ringwork would be easier and quicker to construct. In some cases,

> . . . the geology seems to have influenced the distribution of ringworks . . . in the Vale of Glamorgan, which lies to the south of the drift deposits of the southern limit of glaciation, the shallow layer of soil above the natural rock was more conducive to the construction of ringworks than of mottes. As the mottes required a greater quantity of soil to form the castle mounds, it is not surprising that mottes in Glamorgan are found in the north of the county, on the drift deposits.[46]

Spurgeon notes, however, that ringworks appear at eight sites in the county on the drift deposits.[47] There must be reasons other than the geological at work here. It has been suggested that ringworks were primarily a campaign form of construction, because of the speed with which they could be built. They are also found at pre-existing settlements, often reusing earlier fortifications. Places like Carisbrooke, Pevensey and the Tower of London all began as ringwork-style castles, reusing Roman defences or the earthworks of Anglo-Saxon burhs.

> It cannot be a coincidence that when the Normans were endeavouring to extend their hold on south Wales in the early twelfth century, many of the castles were ringworks . . . Here the Normans, during their advance and occupation, were deliberately constructing what they considered to be a quick and effective form of castle.[48]

The identification of ringwork castles is complicated by the later addition of mottes or keeps such as those at Castle Neroche and at Carisbrooke, and in a few cases, the removal of mottes giving an impression of a ringwork. Dating is also problematic at many sites, as is the identity and origin of the builder. William's followers came from a variety of places with their own building traditions, such as Britanny, Anjou, Flanders and Germany.[49] These areas had their own histories and traditions of defensive building which may well have contributed to the final decisions and forms of castles in Britain.

Early castles were sited at centres of population like Winchester, on important frontiers (such as Chepstow on the Welsh border) and at strategic places such as river crossings and passes, as for example Rochester on the Medway. A number of fortifications were built along the south coast, including Hastings and within the Roman fort at Pevensey. Another series appears along the Thames, and a third lies between these two, along the greensand ridge from Kent to the borders of Hampshire. Many of these sites are substantially unexcavated and their origins are obscure. It is worth considering whether there is a possibility of strategic planning here. Defences of coastal sites would have been important – if the invasion had gone wrong, these strong points would have provided bases for retreat, and in the event of success, they protected communication with Normandy. The castles along the Thames similarly safeguarded an important line of communication, and may also have been utilised as a forward line. That the Normans were familiar with and well-informed about affairs in southern England is certain. How good their knowledge of the rest of England was, and how much opposition they might have met as they advanced out of more familiar territory, must have been at best a matter of educated guesswork.

A line of strong points along the Thames would have enabled them to consolidate their hold on the south, with its important centres such as Winchester and London, while providing a physical barrier between their forces and any concerted counter-attacks from the north. The centre line protects a number of important routes – the Medway valley, the Mole valley and the Wey, as well as an ancient east-west route. The castles are also sited close to important resources for the Normans, especially timber, building stone and iron. They are spaced approximately evenly apart and may have been connected by a system of lookout posts or beacons. It is possible to interpret the small motte at Abinger in this light, linking the castles at Guildford and Betchworth. Reigate and Bletchingly were ringwork castles,

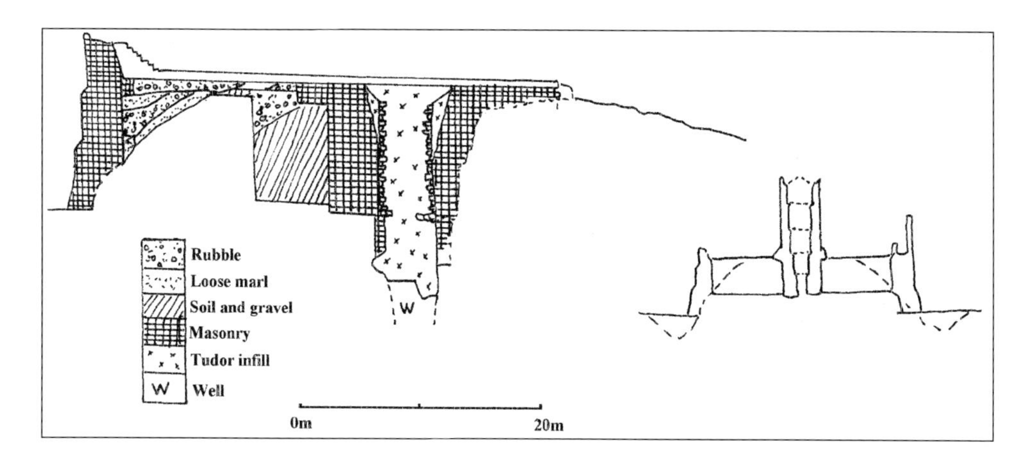

*43 Farnham Castle, Surrey. An example of a keep encased entirely with masonry. Section after M.W. Thompson (*Med. Arch. *Vol. IV, 1960). Showing on right outline conjectural reconstruction of the keep and motte, with the original line of the earthen motte and ditches shown as a dashed line*

Guildford, Walton on the Hill and Farnham were of the motte and bailey type. A castle at Lingfield was destroyed during the Anarchy. Further uninvestigated possible sites have been noted at Godstone, Ockley and south of the Hogsback between Guildford and Farnham.[50] If these castles were conceived as a strategic unit, they could also provide a stop line between the Thames and the sea to protect either a retreat or to facilitate communications. This is all highly conjectural due to the lack of firm evidence, but it may be worth noting that the line of castles through Kent and Surrey is very similar to the stop line constructed during the Second World War.

Stone keep castles were constructed in major centres of population and had a number of functions. They were military bases, to control the inhabitants and to overawe them with the might of the conquerors. They were also conceived as major residences for important lords, and as such had a great deal of domestic sophistication and comfort, and they were intended additionally as administration centres from which to rule. For this reason, an important castle was constructed in virtually every county centre, in addition to those baronial castles erected to control the lands with which William rewarded his followers.

> Ease of defence was a significant factor, but possibly not one of overwhelming importance . . . the vast majority of English and Welsh castles were established on lowland or valley sites, even though they might take what advantage they could from the terrain. The reasons are clear. Most of the population and much of the cultivable land were to be found in the valleys, where the yielding soil of river terrace and flood plain facilitated the construction of earthworks. A statistical study of the sites of early castles suggests that a lowland or valley site was a matter of deliberate choice.[51]

It may therefore seem odd that it is on such lowland sites that some of the largest early stone tower keeps were constructed. Soft lowland soils do not lend themselves to supporting massive blocks of masonry. For this reason, some keeps were enclosed within a supporting mound of earth, as at Farnham (**43**), or provided with battered plinths and buttresses. The plinths also helped to impede attempts to undermine the walls. A vital consideration was the availability of water – this may be the reason why Windsor Castle was sited as it was, and not on the higher, firmer but waterless Cooper's Hill a couple of miles south on the other bank of the Thames. Most tower keeps have a well in the basement. The ground floor had no external openings, and was used for storage, to house soldiers and to keep prisoners. The entrance was at first-floor level, accessed by a removable stair, and was sometimes protected by a strong forebuilding. There were one or two residential floors, which might be divided by a cross wall to add strength to the structure, as can be seen at Rochester. A chapel was often incorporated, in some cases in the upper storey of the forebuilding. Stairs, passages and latrines were incorporated into the thicknesses of the walls.

There would have been access to a roof walk for sentinels, and roof structures may have been covered with lead as a protection against fire. Windows, even on the residential floors, were not usually large, but were splayed inwards to allow as much light as possible into the interior. Pre-existing structures were sometimes used as foundations for these keeps – at Colchester, the massive rectangular structure stands on the remains of the Temple of Claudius built in the early years of the Roman occupation, and it has been suggested that the Tower of London may overlie a late Roman castellum built into the south-east corner of the London Wall.

Keep walls could be up to 5m thick, and the interior dimensions varied between about 25 square metres (Totnes, Devon; Goodrich, Herefordshire) and nearly 600 square metres (Tower of London). The majority range between 80 and 140 square metres. Some were provided with slightly projecting corner towers or turrets giving the opportunity to provide enfilading fire along the walls. As a structure, keeps are totally defensive. There was little that could be done against an attack if the tower was surrounded – the defenders relied totally on their inaccessibility and their ability to last out the assault. The early tower keep represented a strong point from which forward aggressive action could be mounted and political control enforced from within its protection.

Norman castles are noticeably smaller than most of the Roman forts – at Portchester and at Pevensey, Norman castles sit within small corners of the Roman enclosures. They have more in common in some ways with colonial forts, but unlike those which were temporary installations to protect an eventual large-scale colonisation, castles were also designed as aristocratic centres for more or less permanent dominance of a subject territory by a small foreign community.

The castles of Edward I in Wales

Edward I undertook two major campaigns in 1277 and 1282 in north Wales. The Prince of Gwynedd, Llewelyn ap Gruffydd, had formed an alliance with the powerful baron Simon de Montfort against royal authority, and the first campaign

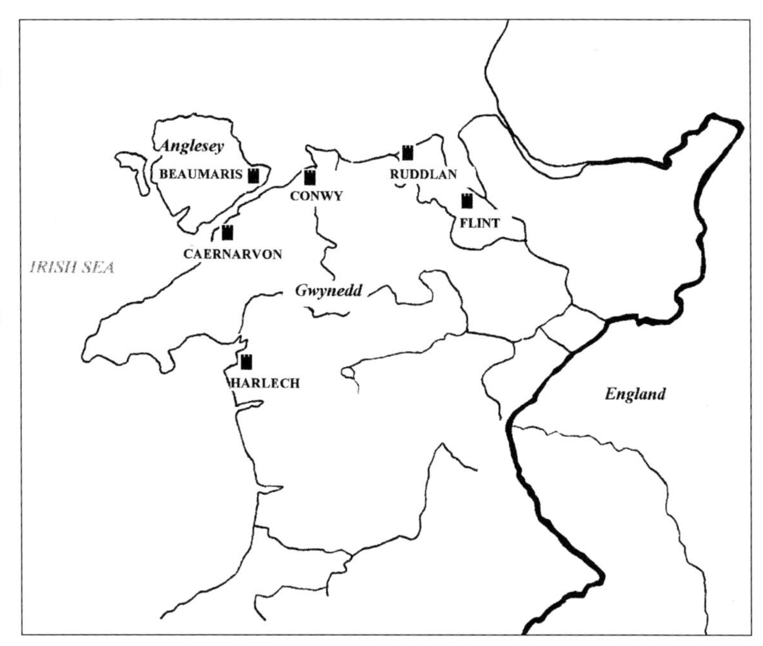

44 Map of Edward I's castle building in Wales. These castles were begun between 1277-95 and were designed to surround and control the region

was designed to force Llewelyn back into his own territory so that the English could establish their control over east and south Wales. The second campaign was originally a reaction to actions by Llewelyn's younger brother David, but Llewelyn's death opened the way for a seizure of north Wales by the English.

Edward's castle building (**44**) began in 1277 with the apparent intention of surrounding Gwynedd with a series of strongholds; it developed into a strategy for the holding and long-term control of a captured territory. Alongside the castles were fortified towns, to be settled by English colonists attracted by favourable financial terms, who were intended to provide civilizing and 'colonial' influence in the area. Finance and professional help were also provided to a number of barons for the building or refurbishment of a number of seigneurial castles along the Welsh Marches.

The ground plans of several castles were being laid out from 1277; in 1278 a new architect was appointed to take charge of the rest of the programme, Master James of St George. Edward had fought in the Holy Land; he had visited Cyprus, the great fortified town of Carcassonne, and in Savoy had seen examples of the latest designs of castle construction; indeed Master James is thought to have been a Savoyard.

Each of the six royal castles is different. The first to be started was Flint, and within a few weeks work also began at Rhuddlan. A purpose-built town accompanied the castle at Flint, and the local settlement was replanned at Rhuddlan. Both towns were surrounded by earthwork defences.

Work at Flint went on from 1277 to about 1285, and cost £7,022. The castle was designed as a more or less square enclosure with three-quarter round towers at the angles, and a strong, detached circular keep with a surrounding circular curtain. It was sited alongside the River Dee with its exposed southern side protected by an outer ward and moat.

45 Flint Castle in 1742 after a sketch by the brothers Buck

Rhuddlan was placed on the high east bank of the River Clwyd. It cost some £9,506 and work continued from 1277 to 1282. On the landward sides of the castle, a dry moat revetted in stone provides an outer defence. The river, which was canalised for over 2 miles so that shipping could be brought up river to supply the castle directly, formed the western defence, and the dock gates were protected by a strong tower. The design of this castle as a base for aggressive action as well as for defence is clear: each of the mural towers on the outer curtain wall surrounding the diamond-shaped bailey is provided with a flight of steps down into the moat with a sally port. The inner curtain wall, higher and thicker than the outer, is well provided with arrow slits backed by embrasures, and includes drum towers, two double-towered gatehouses, and central turrets on the wall walks.

Records indicate that between them, Flint and Rhuddlan required the services of 1845 labourers, 320 masons and 790 woodworkers. To meet the vast expense of the building, the issues of the sees of York and Winchester were diverted to the building programme in the years 1279 and 1290-2 respectively.[52]

In 1283 work began on three more major strongholds: Conwy, Harlech and Caernarvon. Harlech was originally protected by the sea on two sides, although it is now further inland. It was completed in seven years. On the seaward side, the combination of cliff and curtain wall reach a height of 85m. The landward side was protected by a rock-cut ditch. The inner bailey has four projecting angle towers and a massive twin-towered gatehouse in the inner curtain on the east side. Here, the most vulnerable face of the castle, the wall is specially thick – up to 3.6m. The entrance passage of the gatehouse, over 15m long, is equipped with three portcullises, two sets of doors and a number of murder-holes. The middle bailey consists of a narrow terrace, and the outer bailey is irregular in shape, incorporating the rocky slopes on the seaward side. Like the other castles, Harlech was designed to be defended by a very small garrison. In 1294 a mere 37 men defended the castle against the entire Welsh army, and in the early 1400s just 40 'men of Harlech' held out against the forces of Owen Glendower until French naval action cut off their supplies.

Conwy has been described as the definitive medieval fortress town. The eight towers of the castle connect with the town defences and the whole was built as a unit between 1283 and 1289. The town wall contains three gates and 21 towers, each of which was crossed by a wooden bridge that could be removed or destroyed to isolate each section. The town really forms the outer bailey of the castle, which contains two inner wards divided by a massive wall which originally had a simple gate protected by a drawbridge. The innermost ward has four massive angle towers, each with its own bartizan, and a barbican leading to a watergate. The outer ward also has four drum towers and a barbican protecting the western entrance. All the towers on this irregular site are carefully placed to ensure complete crossfire coverage. The castle is placed at the juncture of the Conwy estuary and the River Gyffin, and the town wall was extended out to form a protected dock. The town, roughly triangular in shape, is surrounded by 1100m of walls with three gatehouses. A simple town plan was laid out. Costing £13,670 (and perhaps as much as £19,000), Conwy was immensely strong. Again, it was designed to be defended by a tiny garrison – records show this consisted of 15 crossbowmen, one chaplain, one artificer, one carpenter, one mason, one smith and ten others, including watchmen.

Caernarvon also utilised an irregular site, but is a very different structure. It was commenced shortly after Conwy but clearly intentions here were different. The enclosed area for the town is only just over half the size of that at Conwy, and the town wall circuit of 700m is supplemented by just eight plain, widely-spaced round towers. The town was laid out with a High Street separating the area into two, each sector further subdivided by three streets running from the High Street at 90°. The rivers Seiont and Cadnant were utilised in the design of the defences, which were partly predetermined by the existence of the eleventh-century motte and bailey castle of the earl of Chester. The architectural treatment of Caernarvon was quite different from the other castles. It has 13 towers, no two exactly alike, and unlike Conwy has a keep. The towers are polygonal, and constructed in coloured bands of masonry, an apparent reference to Byzantine style. Other Byzantine features have been identified, including the construction of the scaffolding during the building. The massive Eagle Tower is surmounted by three individual turrets and, originally, by stone eagles which may have been a reference to the finding near the site, as work began in 1283, of bones believed to be those of Magnus Maximus, thought at that time to have been the father of the Emperor Constantine. The aim appears to have been to develop Caernarvon as a provincial capital, a symbol of control of north Wales, and so it was designed to have a most extraordinary and impressive appearance.

Nevertheless, practical defensive considerations were paramount. The walls were crenellated and the placing of the towers was very skilful. The walls contained shooting galleries in their thicknesses – two superimposed in the south wall, one elsewhere, which with the wall tops gave two or three platforms for archers all round the circuit. The placement of arrow slits could give a single bowman up to three different defensive angles. Again, a small garrison of just 40 or so could have held the castle. Platt suggests that the design for defence became almost overdone – the King's Gate built during 1294-5 following a further revolt includes a drawbridge, five doors, and six portcullises, with each section of the entrance corridor covered by arrow loops and murder-holes.[53]

The last of Edward's castles was begun in 1295, and work continued intermittently until 1330 when it was abandoned, unfinished. Beaumaris has often been called the perfect concentric castle. It had a defended town, its own dock and a fortified mill, but it is the almost perfect design of the castle itself that demands attention. The moat enclosed an outer curtain wall with 12 evenly-spaced round towers and two outer entrances, to the north and south. These were placed off centre, to force attackers to expose their undefended right sides to the defenders. Each tower in the outer curtain was carefully placed to be further protected by those of the inner curtain, which was higher. The inner curtain had four round angle towers, with a D-shaped tower midway along the east and west walls. The walls were over 10.5m high and 4.5m thick, and traces of an intramural shooting gallery survive. In the centre of the north and south walls were massive gatehouse keeps, which projected into the inner bailey. The northern gatehouse survives in a better state than the southern and includes three doors and portcullises, supplemented by arrow loops and murder-holes. The gatehouses were designed to function as stand-alone independent strongholds if the rest of the castle fell. The overall design is square, with the outer curtain about 103.5m a side, and the inner (measured to the outer edge of its projecting towers) just over 91m a side. Beaumaris employed some 2000 labourers, 400 masons and 30 smiths and carpenters.

The logistics of the building of these castles were staggering. Vast sums of money were drained from the Exchequer, and labour was levied from all over England. The workmen had to be fed and housed for years, and also protected and controlled. At times it took 500 soldiers to protect less than 1000 workers from Welsh attacks and to prevent them from absconding because of the poor conditions and lack of pay. A major supply base was built at Chester, and long lines of wagons and fleets of boats were employed to move men and supplies to the castle sites. Initially, the small garrisons and the effect of the new English colonies made them cost-effective. However, Beaumaris was already redundant before it was half-built. The technology of warfare had moved on too rapidly for the castle builders, and new theatres of action had taken over.

Of all the types of site we have considered, no two are exactly alike in any period or place. The scale, design, materials and role of defences vary according to situation, society and need, but within general broad outlines, certain patterns can be made out. There are several recurrent themes, of which some of the more obvious are strongholds, perimeters, strategic siting and the willingness to expend a great deal of effort in construction. Different solutions to the provision of these imperatives may be applied according to what is available to hand, and the demands of the technology of warfare prevalent at the time. The same imperatives apply to wider scale defences, those of nations and states, which we will consider later. It will also be useful to look more closely at the technology of war; mankind has infinite resourcefulness in creating weapons of destruction and ways to counter their effects. This chapter has not really been about battles and armies, but battles and armies could not occur or continue in existence for any length of time without fortifications.

3 Frontiers

> It is necessary to determine the perception on the utility of fortified cities. There are fortified cities that defend a gorge and which, by that fact alone, have a fixed character. There are fortified cities that can contain large garrisons and resist for a long time, providing an inferior army has the means of being reinforced, reorganizing itself, and attempting new risks. In the first instance a fort or small town could be mentioned; in the second, a large fortified city, where one must spare neither money nor fortified works, is appropriate.
>
> In addition to these two cases there is a third – the fortification of an entire frontier. Thus the frontier from Dunkerque to Maubeuge presents a large number of fortified towns of different sizes and importance, placed en echiquier in three lines so that it is physically impossible to pass on without having captured several of them. In this case a small fortified town has for its objective to support the flooding that runs from one city to the next, or to create a bottleneck. Then there is established, in the midst of all these fortified cities, a different kind of war. The capture of a convoy or the surprise of a magazine gives the advantage to a greatly inferior army without measuring swords or running any risk of having a siege raised or an operation fail . . .
>
> Napoleon to General Dejean, 27 June 1806[1]

What characterises a frontier? Are they places of exclusion and separation, or areas where different people come together? In many instances where natural features form barriers dividing nations, the differences between those nations may have come to exist because they were separated by this very barrier. An obstacle like a mountain range can create the conditions whereby societies develop facing in opposite directions, either towards or away from the barrier depending upon their sources for trade, production and subsistence. The societies of prehistoric Greece and Italy developed in the context of Mediterranean contact, being influenced by other cultures around its shores in such realms as settlement form, architecture, ideas and customs, rather than by any strong contacts with 'barbarian' Europe beyond their northern mountain ranges.

Major natural barriers, such as the Alps, can act as environmental frontiers as well as symbolic ones, with a markedly different ecology and climate on either side which can contribute towards diverging social developments. Few frontiers are as profoundly divisive as that created by geography between Italy and the rest of Europe, however. Despite the apparent intransigence of the English Channel as a frontier, prehistoric British cultures seem to have maintained relatively close contact with the European mainland for much of the time. Indeed, there is often more apparent similarity between European and southern British cultures than between southern Britain and the rest of the island. Despite local anomalies (such as the British preference for round houses), the Channel only seems to have become a truly significant frontier after Gaul fell to Julius Caesar.

The whole issue of frontiers is extraordinarily complex. We can look at them in terms of scale, of military design, of psychology, of contact and cross-fertilisation and of separateness and rejection, and in terms of economic, demographic and political control. If we approach them in terms of scale as we did for defences in chapter 2, we could see a complementary pattern emerging. For the individual, we accept the notion of 'personal space' as important (perhaps rather more in the modern period than in the past), and we can relate the frontier of a person to expressions in common use like 'at arm's length', or 'as far as you can reach with a ten foot pole'. In other words, a personal frontier is tacitly recognised as that area within reach of a man and his hand-held weapon. Families have frontiers too – from the much disputed garden fence to the medieval moat or the Iron Age enclosing palisade. From here on we can readily see the development of the frontier through all the other stages of forms: from walls, earthworks, ditches, gatehouses, forts, stop lines and satellite early warning systems to star wars.

Clearly not all these frontiers are primarily military. There are many other factors at work: issues of ownership and trespass, privilege zones, exploitation frontiers (like the use of coal tax posts exemplified by medieval towns such as London), ecological frontiers and protective barriers (such as Australia's rabbit fences). Frontiers as points of trade control (and taxation), or demographic or ideological control (the Berlin Wall) may be more overtly military in form, but do not necessarily imply warfare. This dichotomy is easily expressed, again, by reference to common expressions: we may 'build bridges' or 'tear down barriers' between peoples, but good neighbours take care to 'mend their fences'.

Human responses to neighbouring groups may be modified by the landscape and its resources. They may lead to the creation of barriers for both practical and psychological reasons. We have noted that natural features can act as divisions between peoples – seas and rivers, mountains, marshes and wastes have inhibited contact and cultural influence. However, frontiers between people often grow up in areas of natural wealth and usefulness. Neighbouring groups may wish to exploit the same water resources or arable potential, mineral sources, hunting grounds or communication routes. The form of contact and the nature of the frontier are then often related to the history of dialogue between the two sides, their perceptions of ownership and fairness, bellicosity or fear, sharing or greed, and degrees of social confidence. It is often where a frontier grows up in otherwise geographically undifferentiated territory that the greatest military presence evolves. It is entirely natural that such a great investment should occur in vulnerable terrain, but it has often been the case that military commanders in control of areas which also include natural barriers will place their weaker forces behind such features to maximise their resources in the other areas. In 1940, the Allies were surprised by German advances through the Ardennes which were designed to push through the weaker units lying behind it and completely bypass the much vaunted Maginot Line. Again, in 1944, General Bradley thinned his troops out in the Ardennes on the correct assumption that you cannot be strong everywhere, thus inviting the famous German counter-offensive of that year.

Frontiers between different traditions of land and resource exploitation also tend to be particularly fraught – the boundaries between the ranges of nomadic pastoral-

1 *Bodiam Castle, East Sussex. An idyllic looking castle, although poorly positioned in the landscape to offer good protection. A hill rises above the castle to the north. The walls, with their many windows, would not have withstood a serious siege. Note Second World War pillbox in the foreground.* Photograph: Sandra Luff

2 *Painting of the Royal Standard of Ur, War panel. This detail is found on a sound box from a lyre and shows warfare from the Sumerian period. The regular infantry each sport a soft cap and studded cape. The four-wheeled chariots had a wide turning circle and were only used to ride down enemy after the battle*

3 *Warrior Vase, Athens,* c.*1200 BC. These impressively dressed Mycenean soldiers probably date from a generation after the 'Catastrophe' and it is argued that they represent the Mycenean response to the new military threat. Note the close order of the infantrymen*

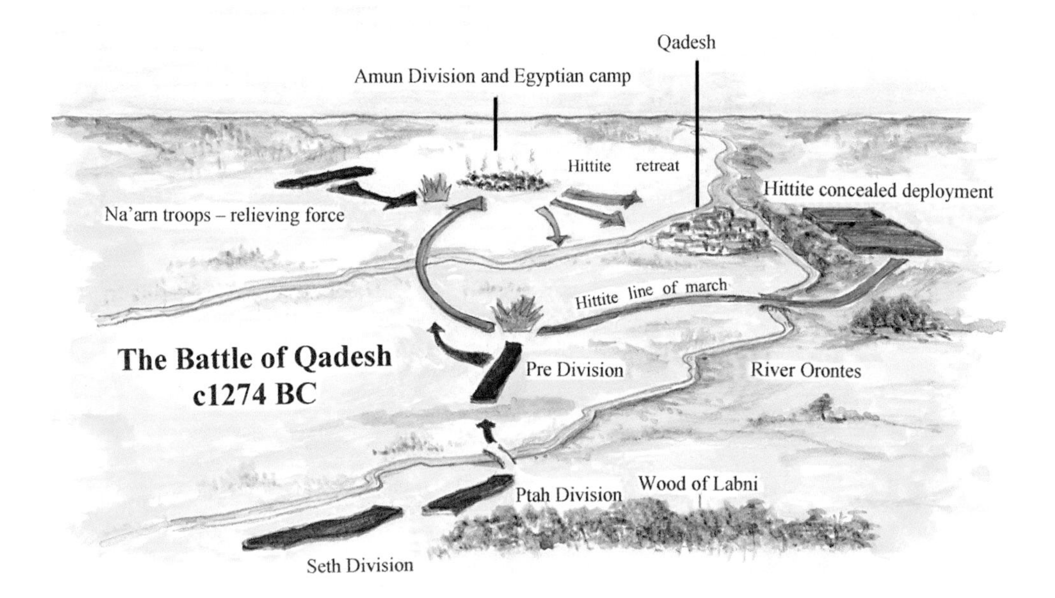

4 *The early thirteenth century BC saw a struggle for power in the Levant between Egypt and the Hittites. The Battle of Qadesh was an extraordinary affair involving the deliberate use of concealment behind a man-made topographical feature in the landscape, the town of Qadesh*

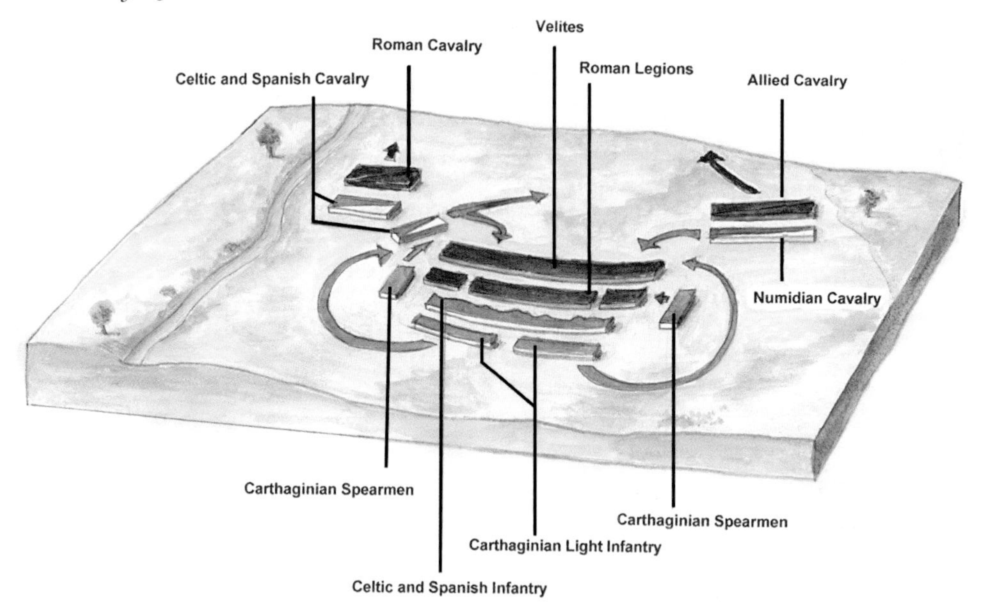

5 *The Battle of Cannae 216 BC. Hannibal the Carthaginian out-generalled his Roman opponent by forming up his Celtic and Spanish swordsmen in a crescent pointing towards the Roman legions. This allowed them to absorb an expected frontal assault. As the Carthaginians fell back, the flanks of the Roman army became exposed due to the successes of the Spanish and Numidian cavalry. The result was annihilation for the Romans*

6 *The Greek hoplite. Greek city states developed the close-order infantry phalanx which had first come to Argos via the Carians of south-west Asia Minor.* Photograph: John Eagle

7 *Spartans make their way through the trees to clearer ground.* Photograph: John Eagle

8/9 *British Camp, Herefordshire. This impressive hillfort overlooking Wales later became the site of a Norman motte and bailey castle.* Photographs: Richard Hill

10 *The Rumps Promontory Fort, Cornwall. The headland, being defended on three sides by steep cliffs down to the sea, only required ramparts across the neck of the peninsular to make it a secure fortification.* Photograph: Jeanette Hicks

11 *Dun Carloway Broch, Isle of Lewis.* Photograph: Sue Walker

12 *Many forts and passages along the Maginot Line contain paintings rendered by the waiting soldiers. This one proclaims how sweet life is and bears the legend 'Do Not Enter'*

13 *Clun Castle in Shropshire, one of the great Marcher Castles of the border between England and Wales, showing the view from the castle towards Wales.* Photograph: Richard Hill

14 *Clun Castle, despite its siting and defences, was not invulnerable to Welsh raids. It was burnt to the ground by one such raid in 1196.* Photograph: Richard Hill

15 *The Great Wall of China at Jinshangling in Ruanping county of the Hubei Province dating to c.AD 1570 and built under the Ming Emperors.* Photograph: Abigail Robertson

16 *At Simatai the original earlier medieval Qi wall was rebuilt by the Ming Dynasty and dominates the Yanshan Mountains.* Photograph: Abigail Robertson

17 *Hadrian's Wall, England.* Photograph: Jeanette Hicks

18 *Hadrian's Wall, England.* Photograph: Sandra Luff

19/20 *Offa's Dyke on Llanfair Hill. Whether an agreed boundary, or an overt statement of Mercian power, Offa's Dyke was an immense undertaking. In places, it still dominates the landscape today.* Photographs: Richard Hill

21 *South Bastion at Pevensey Castle, East Sussex. The photographer's position, in Roman times, would have been beneath the sea.* Photograph: Jeanette Hicks

22 *Portchester Castle from a print. Built in the transitional square cornered style, probably with its own dock*

23 *Late Anglo-Saxon Housecarle. In the Welsh campaigns of the 1060s, the Earl of Wessex, Harold Godwinson ordered his Housecarles to dispense with their chainmail in favour of lighter textile body armour in order to give the force more mobility in the difficult countryside.* Photograph: Martin Pegler

24 *The Spartan hoplite was the Greeks' most feared infantryman. Here Leonidas surveys the area around Thermopylae and awaits the Persian attack.* Photograph: John Eagle

25 *The battle of Thermopylae in 480 BC ended in annihilation when the small Spartan force defending the pass were trapped upon a hillock by a Persian force which had found its way through the mountains to the rear of the Spartan position. Treachery had undone Leonidas, but the defence was heroic nonetheless.* Photograph: John Eagle

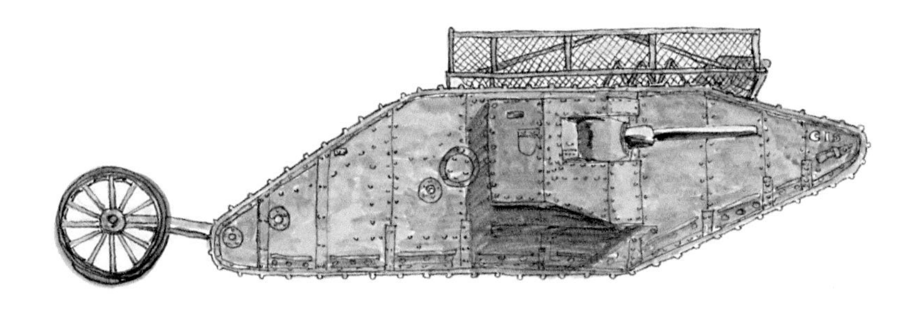

26 The tank was invented in order to bring mobility to a static battlefield. From top to bottom: Heavy Mark I (male), British; Light Renault FT, French; PzKpfwIa, German. Eventually, tanks were organised into their own divisions capable of long-range strikes, utterly transforming the nature of twentieth-century warfare

27 *Rochester Castle, Kent. After the siege of 1216 one corner turret (not visible) was rebuilt in circular form.* Photograph: Sandra Luff

ists and settled farmers, for example, or between developed and primitive social and economic systems, or hunter-gatherer and agricultural communities. Frontiers create their own cultural and social conditions, sometimes quite contradictory. The frontier community breeds the 'frontier mentality'. Separated from the cultural core of their people, sometimes by very great distances, frontier societies can be either freer in structure, with less emphasis on class or caste status, law or custom, than their cores, or more narrow and traditional, exclusive, suspicious, touchy and defensive. They may be inclined to interact with neighbouring groups, to share resources, offer support in times of crisis, accept and adapt foreign customs and practices as part of their own social identity, learn from other peoples and even intermarry. Conversely, they may make very clear distinctions about their neighbours, restrict contact, avoid any form of social interaction, combine into defensive militia-style groups, and regard their neighbours as rivals to be distrusted.

There are many questions about why such different attitudes can develop. Factors include those of race and ethnicity, political complexion and religion. Confidence is clearly important. Different conditions will exist depending on whether the frontier zone is peopled by groups indigenous to the area, or by colonists, or by a mix of the two. Often frontier territories are relatively sparsely settled with low population levels. Such communities may well feel vulnerable and isolated; they must choose either to attempt to preserve the mores and values of their core groups in order to maintain their perceptions of their own identity and history, or to abandon these to forge new self-confidence and identity in the face of alien cultures and territories. The imposition of formalised frontier demarcation by one or both of the central states can then be viewed in one of three ways by the border communities:

1 As a reassuring buffer and an affirmation of their right to exist and their value to the core.
2 As an impediment to their way of life and an attempt by the core group to dictate to what they see as their own more dynamic and independent society.
3 As an actual threat, implying that one or other side will use the line of demarcation not only as a defence but also a base of attack across the frontier line.

Circumstances along frontiers tend to be more fluid than in core areas and social and psychological factors are likely to change more rapidly. This can be due to the psychology of the groups involved, especially where there is strong rivalry for resources: fierce competition or group insecurity, to natural stresses being less easy to absorb by small isolated communities, and to the effects of changes in the opposing core being outside the control of each frontier group. The human factors relating to frontier zones may be partially summarised as opposing continuums (**46**).

Recognition of frontier zones, especially in prehistory, can be quite difficult. The main problems relate to sparsity of settlement, the possibility of trade and cultural exchange, and the similarities likely between settlements in similar landscapes. As a result, archaeological awareness of such boundaries tends to be both geographically and chronologically vague, based on observations of cultural assemblages, settlement types,

FRONTIER STRENGTHS
Exploitation of new territories and resources
Open dynamic social systems
Points of trade and exchange
Self-reliant, independent societies

DIVISIVE POTENTIALS	CONNECTIVE POTENTIALS
Rivalry and competition	Exchange of ideas
Political/ideological incompatibility	Cultural exchange
Issues of ownership	Shared experience and support
Language	Information sharing
Prejudice/racial separateness	Intermarriage

FRONTIER WEAKNESSES
Isolation from social/ political core group
Sparsity of settlement
Vulnerability to raids and attacks, intrusion and trespass
Self-defensive, touchy, nervous societies

46 Diagram explaining the dynamics of frontiers

ritual practice and changes of land use that can only rarely be assessed in relation to each other. Where a frontier has been delineated by structures, or fortified in some way, the recognition of the location of the frontier is, of course, much more simple. Understanding its purpose is less clear cut. Defence is only one reason for creating a physical barrier; at the same time, or at different periods, a defended frontier may have a primary role that is basically economic, ideological or demographic. Strongly defended frontiers can be envisaged as preventative of conflict – the precursors of Cold War nuclear deterrent philosophies. They may be designed to keep a population in, and under ideological control, rather than to exclude a military foe. They may also be intended to restrict colonisation or penetration by migrant workers or refugees. In many cases, frontiers are designed to control and to levy tax on imports; protection of valuable resources is another common intention. Another function which occurs frequently is the design of frontiers to support policing of a remote or disputed sector. Police action does not necessarily imply conflict on any significant scale, but is typically supported by the appearance and implicit threat of physical aggression or control, even in the most enlightened regimes. If the landscape does not provide enough features upon which to place a system of fortifications, then sometimes a deliberate depopulation of a border area takes place. The Assyrian Empire operated under this ideology to a powerful and lasting effect. As the empire expanded, it came more into contact with potential enemies, who sooner or later, feeling themselves threatened, became real enemies. A policy was put into practice in the border areas of this vast empire to deliberately deport people from chosen zones. The words of Sargon II sum up the divine inspiration of this philosophy, but it clearly had a practical benefit:

> Ashur, father of the gods, empowered me to depopulate and repopulate,
> to make broad the boundary of the land of Assyria.

The lack of natural boundaries to provide defensible frontiers in Assyria may account for the form of militarism that we come across there – the lands were rich and fertile and vulnerable to threats from all sorts, notably the nomads and mountain peoples as well as the more organised political enemies of the Assyrian city states such as the Mitanni. The response, it seems at least in the Assyrian period, was to keep a powerful and active army to hand for offensive as well as defensive operations. The absence of natural boundaries seems to create a more active and aggressive style of militarism.

Defence-in-depth and defence along a broad front

The manner in which land frontiers are defended varies throughout history. There are two opposite schools of thought which in practice are sometimes used in isolation and other times together. The first is a very simple concept indeed – defence over a broad front. This term implies the imposition of a barrier, such as a wall or other form of linear fortification system. Hadrian's Wall in England and the Limes of Germany and Raetia serve as good examples of the Roman Empire's adoption of this method of protection in the second century AD before it was forced, perhaps more by circumstance than choice, to opt for the second of our frontier defending methods. The Great Wall of China, with its long history and vast scale, is a testimony to the practice in the Far East, although the idea that there was only ever one Great Wall designed solely to keep out invaders is somewhat misleading.

Defending a broad front in the form of the imposition of walls, garrisons, watch-towers and fortifications has been termed 'Preclusive Security'. On the face of it, the idea seems to be to keep people out of a given area. There may well be portals, passes and passageways through such linear barriers, but these will be carefully managed and protected for the purposes of trade and communication either side of the frontier (**47**). The system depends upon the strength of the defences and the management of the garrisons along it. Genghis Khan is supposed to have observed of the Great Wall of China that its strength depended upon the 'courage' of its defenders. In many cases where the approach has been employed, there has not been further military provision in the hinterland of the defending state or kingdom. This displays an obvious weakness. Any linear obstacle is only as strong as its weakest part. Once breached, the entire monument is rendered at least temporarily redundant as the enemy will be behind it and active in the soft interior of the defending power. The linear barriers that we have chosen below to serve as examples of this approach to frontier management demonstrate that there were many aspects to these systems over and above the simple exclusion of outside forces.

One of the problems with such defences is their inevitable construction costs in terms of manpower resources. However, once erected, it is argued, the cost of upkeep may be relatively cheap.[2] Also, if the barriers do not stretch from coast to

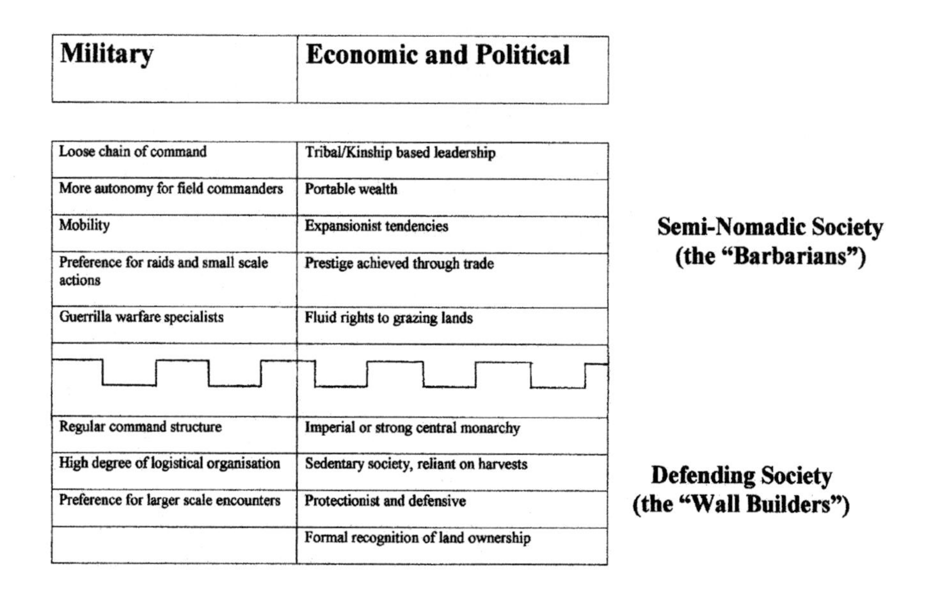

47 Diagram showing typical societies on both sides of a linear boundary

coast, have flanks simply hanging in the landscape, or are simply too short, sooner or later the enemy will go around them, as they did with the Great Wall of China and most famously with the Maginot Line in 1940.

The Maginot Line

The Maginot Line serves as a good example of the things that can go wrong with the broad front approach. It was an immensely expensive undertaking. André Maginot, war hero and one-time War Minister, died eight years before he could see his line of high-tech fortifications bypassed in 1940. It was a monument to a defensive ideology in France which existed between the wars. France had no desire to see a repeat of the carnage of the First World War. When it came to making a choice as to how to build up its forces, France opted for the defensive and chose linear fortifications over tanks and planes (despite the latter approach being favoured by de Gaulle). There was still a belief in France at the time that military technology favoured the defender and it was this mentality that was behind the great project.

Built between 1929-40, the system of fortifications stretches from Switzerland to the Ardennes in the north and from the Alps to the Mediterranean in the south. It was a masterpiece of engineering, with retractable gun turrets, lateral underground communication systems and a garrison that lived, ate and slept beneath its strongly reinforced turrets and forts. The inspiration had come from the fortifications at Verdun constructed after the Franco-Prussian war. These fortifications had had a notable subterranean element to them. The many miles of supply and communication tunnels along the Maginot Line were sometimes decorated with paintings (**colour plate 12**). However, there were fundamental flaws in the philosophy of the Maginot Line itself. It was too

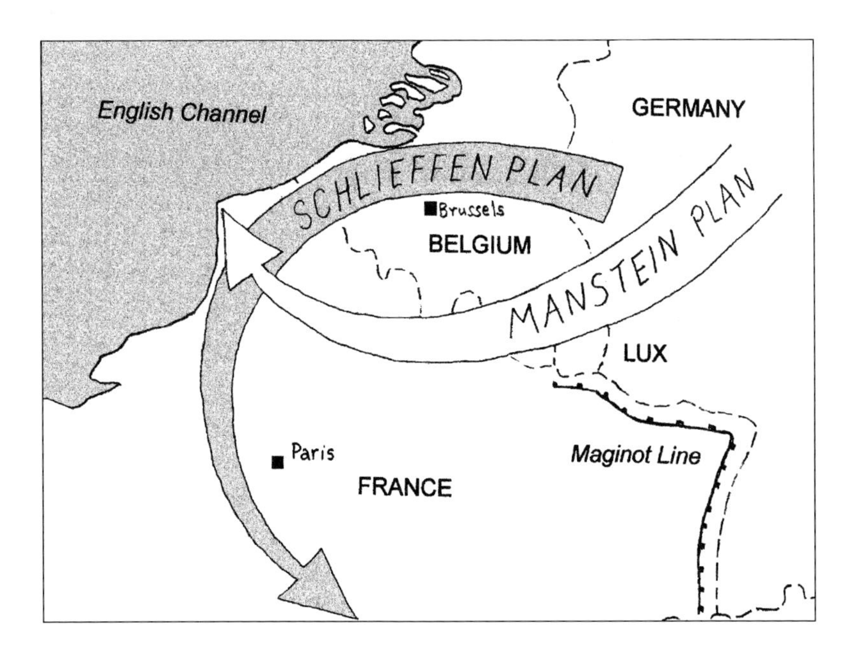

48 The Schlieffen Plan was heavily adapted by Manstein and involved pushing through the 'impenetrable' Ardennes and driving to the Channel coast. Compare the wide arc of the 1914 plan with Manstein's direct approach

short. After Belgium revoked the Franco-Belgian Alliance of 1920, the line was extended along the Belgian frontier, but was nothing like as strong as its counterpart south of the Ardennes, and it was this 'impenetrable' terrain which proved not to be so impenetrable after all. Manstein's clever adaptation of the Schlieffen Plan (**48**) of 1914 (a plan which in reality over-stretched a German army fighting on two fronts at the time of its execution) saw the Germans push through the Ardennes and sweep to the coast, cutting off the British in the process. By June of 1940 the Maginot Line had become entirely redundant. There was no great reserve force held back for the defence of France in 1940. Manstein's plan had worked (**49**). The words of Carl Von Clausewitz, writing in 1832 still echo down military history, but are particularly relevant to this episode:

> If you entrench yourself behind strong fortifications, you compel the enemy to seek a solution elsewhere . . . while states that have many fortresses will be correct in locating most of them on the frontiers, it would still be a great mistake to leave the interior completely unfortified. In France for example, this mistake is in our opinion, astonishingly common.

In a way, the Maginot Line was a success in that it discouraged the Germans from attacking across France's eastern border and gave some time for the French to deploy other forces. There was, however, too much reliance on its capability to keep France protected. The Maginot Line saw very little action again in the war,

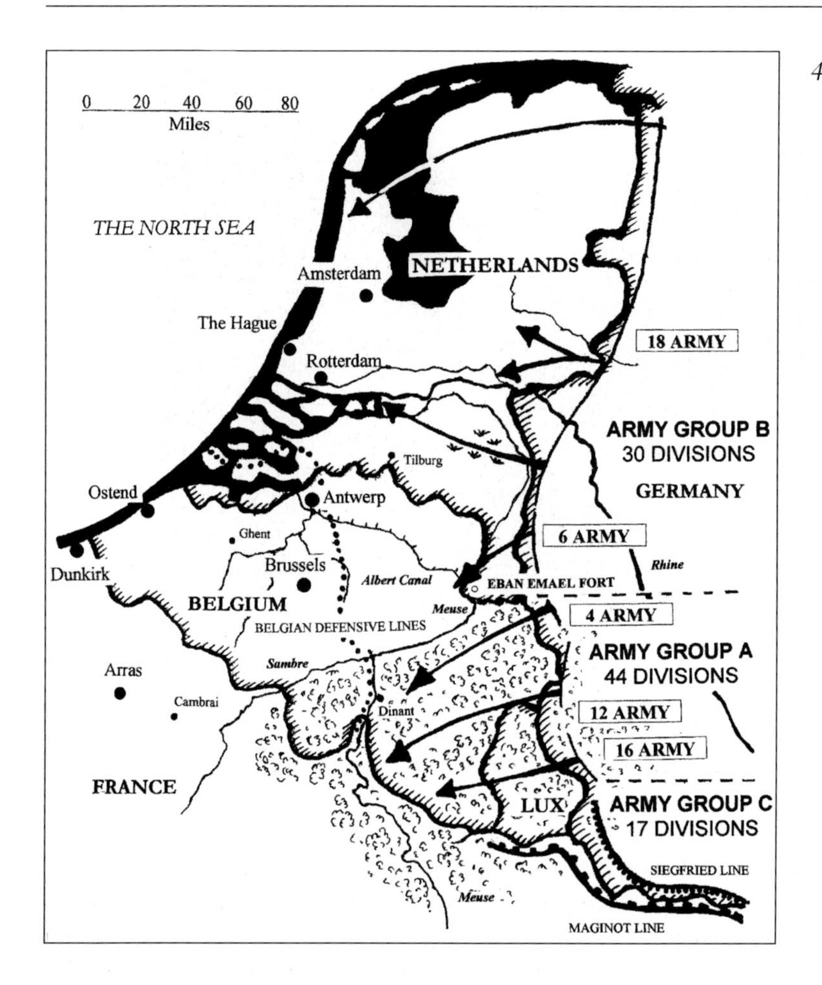

49 Map showing how the Maginot Line was bypassed in 1940 during the German attack on France via Belgium. Army Group B held allied attention in the north, whilst Army Group A reached the Meuse with little resistance

although the Allies fought through a part of it at Metz in the autumn of 1944. For the most part, it was used as storage by the Germans (**50**). Although manned once again by French troops in the 1950s and 1960s, the nuclear age brought with it a new form of national security and the lines were finally abandoned.

Another way to hold or defend a territory is with the practically applied concept of defence-in-depth. Here the philosophy is different. Enemies have no linear obstacle to breach or to go out of their way to bypass. Instead, there may be a carefully planned system of fortifications, with each supporting the other, stretching far back into the defending territory resulting in the exertion of zones of influence over vast stretches of surrounding territory. The fortifications may very well be set out in a linear form, but are not designed to be impregnable linear barriers. The system of fortifications of Sebastien Le Prestre, Seigneur de Vauban (1633-1707) situated in the low-lying area of the north-east French frontier with Belgium serves as an example of a deeply defended frontier designed to slow up an enemy. The Marshall Vauban was France's foremost military engineer during the reign of Louis XIV. Not only did he build new fortresses and refurbish old ones to a grand strategic plan, but he also directed 47 sieges during that period against enemy fortifications.

50 *German soldiers inspect a Maginot Line defensive position a few years after its abandonment. An MG Turret is in the foreground and an artillery casemate can be seen to the right of the picture. The Germans used the fortifications largely for storage during the occupation of France.* Photograph: Julie Wileman's collection

The north-east French frontier in Vauban's era became known as Le Pré Carré, or the 'Square' or 'Duelling' Field (**51**). Although fortifications in this area were hardly new, this was the first real attempt at a comprehensive frontier plan. This area of north-east France on the Belgian frontier would be fought over on and off for another 300 years or so and probably constitutes one of the most persistently disputed areas of Europe. The main reason for this is its geographical weakness. Vauban's answer to the problem was to construct a double line of mutually supporting fortified places stretching from the Channel coast to the river Meuse near the Ardennes. They operated not only as a great delaying factor in any enemy effort to invade France, but when used in conjunction with a field army, they could be the launch pad for offensive operations, as they were to prove to be under Louis XIV. The words of Napoleon sum-up the usefulness of Vauban's creations:

> Vauban has organized entire districts into entrenched camps covered by streams, inundations, fortified towns, and forests, but he never contended that the fortified cities alone could close the frontier. He intended that this frontier, thus fortified, would provide protection for an inferior army against a superior one, that it would give him a field of operations favourable for maintaining his army and preventing the enemy army from advancing; that it would offer occasions for attacking with advantage; and, finally, that it would provide the means for gaining time to enable help to arrive.

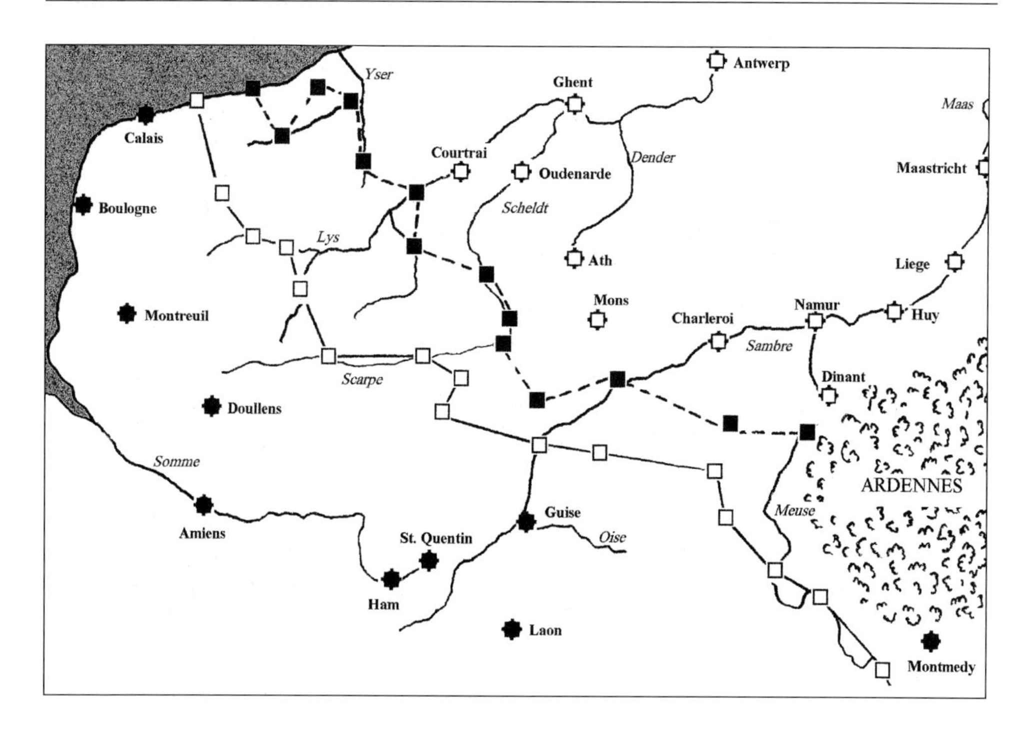

51 Marshal Vauban (1633-1707) was France's foremost military engineer. His two lines of forts in the north-east frontier of the country were built with depth in mind. The interior of France, however, was not catered for in this way

> During the reverses of Louis XIV this system of fortified towns saved the capital. Prince Eugene of Savoy lost an entire campaign season in order to take Lille. The siege of Landrecies offered Villars the chance to change his fortune. A hundred years later, in 1793, during the treason of Dumouriez, the fortified towns of Flanders saved Paris. The enemy coalition lost an entire campaign before taking Conde, Valenciennes, Le Quesnoy, and Landrecies. This line of fortresses was equally useful in 1814. The allies violated Swiss territory and became entangled in the defiles of Jura trying to avoid the fortresses, and in this outflanking movement they were forced to commit a larger number of troops than the total size of the French garrisons . . .
> Notes sur l'art de la guerre' *Corres.*, XXXI pp.335-6, Luvaas p.100-101

Another example of how defence-in-depth can work to the advantage of the defending group is shown by the lines of the Torres Vedras (**52**), where the ultimate benefit of the arrangements to defend Lisbon from the north was in the spread of manpower resources that the fortifications allowed in order to hold the frontier. Wellington's vision of two lines of defences which would capitalise on the virtues of the natural features of the landscape 20 miles to the north of Lisbon became a reality after work commenced in 1809. Each redoubt and gun emplacement in the system

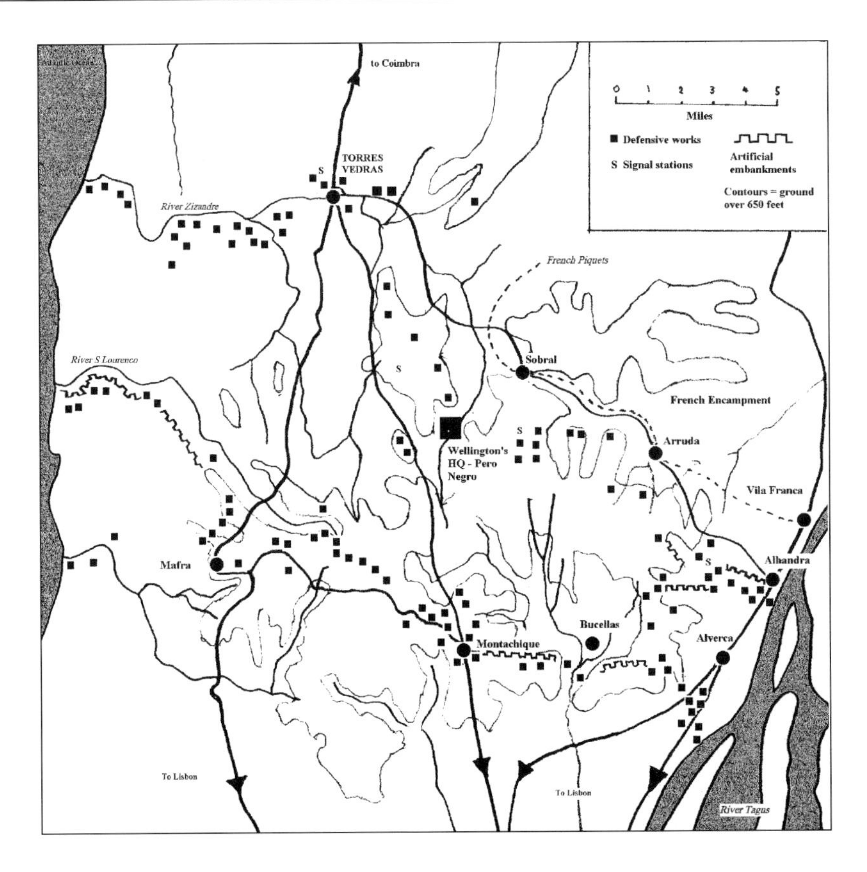

52 Map of the Lines of the Torres Vedras. Portugal. Two lines of fortifications situated 20 miles to the north of Lisbon protected British interest at that vital port. A clear example of defence-in-depth in practice

was conceived so that it supported another. The garrison on the lines consisted of a defence force of 25,000 Portuguese militia, 8000 Spanish regulars and 2500 British marines and artillery (the idea being to limit the amount of British troops in the system, since manpower resources were a pressing issue), and with the sea flank guarded by the Royal Navy; these were Wellington's stop lines.

The system comprised 152 mainly small forts – one of the smallest being Fort No. 37 which could hold just 50 men and 3 nine-pounder guns. With ditches 16ft wide and 12ft deep, each installation was built to a plan with abattis structures of twisted and interlaced olive trees placed 30 yards in front of the forts to provide difficult ground and create a killing zone. It is one of the constants of military history that such fortification systems can be manned by comparatively poor quality troops. This is due to the structures themselves which invariably enhance the defensive capabilities of such troops.[3]

Entire communities can be incorporated into the defence-in-depth system, which in the case of Alfred the Great's burhs of the kingdom of Wessex (*c.*AD 880) acted as a refuge for the population during times of Viking incursion. In that particular case, the whole kingdom could have been considered a frontier. However, these particular fortified places were manned by a specifically calculated garrison, who could be called out to act as a field army to chase away aggressors. It is little wonder that the system was extended into the midland kingdom of Mercia during the succeeding generation under Edward the Elder, since mobile armies, when used in conjunction with garrison towns, are excellent ways of taking and holding territory.

Defence-in-depth does not necessarily have to rely upon fortification systems alone. In the Later Roman Empire, for example, the great mobile armies of Constantine were used to prosecute this policy in preference to the broad front linear defensive policy of earlier Emperors. Fortifications would be strategically scattered around the frontiers and deeper into Imperial territory and during an invasion would act as supply depots and strong points. The mobile reserve would co-ordinate its campaign with these supply points. Arther Ferrill sees their usage as important in the whole concept of Late Roman Imperial frontier policy:

> When situated at strategic points such forts might also hold river crossings and passes thereby impeding the enemy's movements. From them it was easier to maintain intelligence operations, and in emergencies they offered temporary protection for the mobile army.[4]

It is possible, however, that good generalship can undo such a posture. An example of this is shown in what happened after the Normandy landings in 1944. The British role in the grand strategy of the operation was to pin the Germans down with a decoy mission on the east flank of the beachhead, while the Americans under Bradley would swing round on the westside flank. The Germans believed that Caen was a viable objective for the British and committed what little mobile Panzer reserves they had to the Caen sector, hoping to thwart the British or possibly drive them back to the sea. The committed divisions were now part of the front line and no longer performing the role of a reserve and this played into the Allies hands.[5] The art of pulling apart a mobile reserve, it seems, is to make your threat to a particular sector or objective seem real, even if you intend to do something different.

Fortifications, whether a castle, fortress, or fortified city, exert an influence in the landscape preventing or slowing enemy incursion. Suger claimed of the medieval castle at Le Puiset in France that 'when it was in hostile hands, one dared not approach within 8 or 10 miles of it'.[6] If we take this as a general statement of the effect of a medieval castle in the landscape when under the control of an active force (as they almost always were), then it is not too hard to see how a network of castles, such as the marcher castles of England, might secure a frontier (**53**; **colour plates 13 & 14**).

Carl Von Clausewitz stated that although the operations which a fortress garrison could undertake were fairly limited, even in the case of strong garrisons, the small active elements in the form of detachments and sorties were enough to exert an influence in the surrounding landscape to a distance of at least a few marches. When combined with an independent field corps which need not fall back to a fortress, the zone of influence of the fortress is greatly extended. Fortresses, according to Clausewitz, constitute the first and foremost support of defence in 11 different ways:

53 *Clun Castle, Shropshire, in its landscape. Showing the view from the angle of approach via Wales. Clun was one of the main marcher castles in a network of strong points on the borders between England and Wales.* Photograph: Richard Hill

1. As secure depots
2. As protection for large and prosperous towns
3. As real barriers
4. As tactical points of support
5. As a staging post
6. As a refuge for weak or defeated units
7. As an actual shield against enemy attack
8. As protection for existing camps
9. As cover for an unoccupied province
10. As the focal point of a general insurrection
11. As a defence of rivers and mountainous areas[7]

Linear barriers

The Great Wall of China

If there has been a tradition of linear frontier building anywhere, then it is surely in China. Hundreds of years of wall building have given the impression of a continuity of approach to the concept of keeping out invaders, but the complex history of the Wall shows a discontinuity in both space and time and indicates that there was more to the Great Wall of China than merely keeping people out (**54**). Most of the monument that we see surviving today is largely, but not exclusively, the work of the emperors of the Ming Dynasty *c.*AD 1366-1644 (**colour plates 15 & 16**). However, the origins of wall building go back to at least the era known as the Spring and Autumn Period (770-476 BC) and that of the subsequent Warring States (475-221 BC), long before the Great Wall's recognised founder Qin Shi Huangdi united the Chinese states.

There really is no truth in the myth that the Great Wall of China is the only man-made structure visible from space, but the fact that the myth exists at all is testimony to the tremendous symbolic power that this linear frontier still exerts over the minds of people from all over the world. Today, there are no nomadic tribes threatening to breach the wall and few people are under its direct influence, save those involved in its upkeep and promotion. It remains today a breathtaking sight, and certainly as far as the Ming wall is concerned it seems to have been designed to be seen from both inside and outside the frontier.

The Great Wall of China began as a defence project against northern tribes by the Zhou dynasty in the Spring and Autumn Period, with more walls being built during the Warring States Period to protect one ducal state from another, and connections to the previous structures being made. It is, however, with the Qin Dynasty (221-207 BC) and its ruthlessly centralising Emperor Qin Shi Huangdi, that the wall took on its vast multi-state form.

Qin Shi Huangdi's newly united Empire was no more safe from Hun incursions in the north than any of its constituent states had been in earlier centuries. He undertook, at the cost of many thousands of lives and with a workforce of 300,000 troops, to join-up the northern walls of the Qin, Zhao and Yan states, whilst extending the structure a further 5000km. The principal fear, it seems, was the threat from the Xiongnu tribes. The easternmost section of Qin Shi Huangdi's wall was built on the wall of the Yan State starting from Huade County in Inner Mongolia, running to Fuxin City, Liaoning Province through Hebei Province. The next definable section, the Middle section, which included beacon towers, started in Xhinghe County, Inner Mongolia and stretched across the desert. The westernmost section, incorporating some of the walls of the Warring States period, followed the line of the Yellow River from Min County, Gansu Province and ran to Yuzhong.

The next significant phase of construction came under the Han Dynasty (206 BC - AD 220), this being a period of the strengthening of the unification of the country and the amplification of an exchange programme with the western provinces. The wall along the Yellow River was greatly renovated and extended westwards to the effect that Western Gansu and other provinces were protected. Beacon towers were placed along the Han wall at 5km intervals. It is to the Han Dynasty that we must attribute the first real signs of an economic function to the wall. Trade from the west could not help passing through the wall which cut across the Silk Road. Traders from Mesopotamia, Italy and Syria passed through it bearing goods such as gold, spices and gems and came to town gates where much business was done. Two types of troops were stationed on the frontier in the Han period: farmer soldiers (concerned with irrigation and granary produce) and garrison soldiers. Also from the Han period, as early as 166 BC, an intricate system of signals using flags was in place, and to make it easier for garrison troops to see passing nomads, large sections of land on the frontier were levelled into wide strips.

There are references to constructions which help us plug the gap a little between the Han Dynasty constructions and the huge works of the Ming Period. For example, texts record walls being built in the Northern Wei (AD 386-534) and Sui

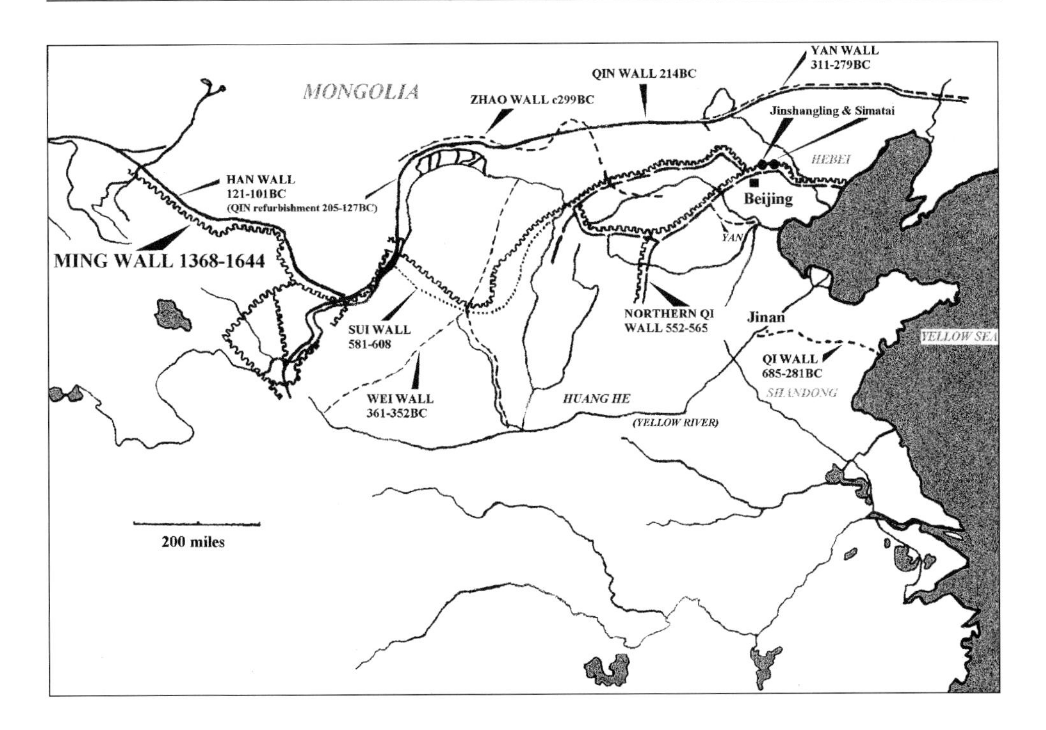

54 The Great Wall of China is, in fact, many walls spanning thousands of years. This map shows the main sequences culminating in the Great Wall of the Ming Dynasty (1368-1644)

(AD 581-618) periods. The Northern Wei, Qi (who evidently 'enlisted' 1.8 million people for the task) and Zhou Dynasties were responsible for a further 650, 1000 and 1500km of constructions respectively. In the twelfth century, the Jin Dynasty (AD 1115-1234) built a further 4000km of works, mainly characterised by ditches.

The effort that went into the construction of the Great Wall of the Ming Dynasty (**55**) was colossal. It stretched over 7000km from the Yalu River in the east to Jiayu Pass in the west. The preceding Dynasty of the Yuan (AD 1271-1368) had been built up by nomadic tribes of Mongolians and it was these people that the new emperor of the Ming Dynasty, Zhu Yuanzhang, a career politician, greatly feared. Walls were to be the answer once again, not just around the country, but around towns, too, marking a further shift to the defensive. Between 1438-49 there was a series of successful Mongol attacks from the north, culminating in the capture and imprisonment of the emperor himself.

The whole effort was an integrated one, with garrison towns, beacon towers, blockhouses, passes and garrison posts. The Ming wall functioned on many levels. It was clearly symbolic in the sense that it had to command a good view over the territory which it was supposed to be dominating, but it also had to be seen to be dominating the landscape. In a sense, it was a form of intimidation. Why else would such investment be necessary over great mountain ranges where a barbarian horseman would hardly think of threatening the structure? The answer to that question lies in logistics.

55 *The Ming wall at Simatai sits in the Yanshan mountains. A monument of great symbolism, the wall also functioned as an elevated roadway for the transportation of goods and troops.* Photograph: Abigail Robertson

The Ming wall was wide enough to accommodate traffic. It can be viewed as an elevated highway of communication and transportation of troops and goods around the borders of empire across what would ordinarily have been impassable terrain.

Methods of construction varied from period to period and from place to place. By and large, local materials were used. The Qin wall, for example, sometimes comprised local stone and earth firmed in the tamped-earth process, set within a simple wooden frame with compacted layers of 4in each. The loess, a fine yellow sand which was used for this, was a particularly good building material if compressed to the right consistency. These constructions were the work of the 'Children of the Yellow Earth'. Different techniques were required for different terrain, and this is especially true of the Han period wall. The arid Gobi Desert forced the adoption of a more traditional method of construction involving the laying of a bed of red willow reeds and branches at the base of a wooden frame, this being filled with water and gravel and tamped into solidity. Once dry, the frame would be removed.

The Ming wall, however, was a masterpiece of construction, involving stone and brick (massive kilns were constructed near to the wall), and in places the wall rose over rocky terrain at an angle of *c.*70°. Also, where the structure crossed a river, water gates were incorporated to allow the river to flow. The gaps between the bricks were filled with lime mortar and the structure included a drainage channel on the walkway. Not every part of the even the Ming wall was identical. The attractiveness of loess as a building material is evidenced by the fact that the Jiayuguan section in Gansu comprised imported loess from Heisham Hill 12km west of the pass.

There are many good surviving sections of the wall; among them are the dramatic views which can be seen at Simatai and Jinshanling. Simatai shows the Ming wall in its unrestored, yet authentic state and has a certain atmosphere to it. It is uncertain how long it will remain this way.

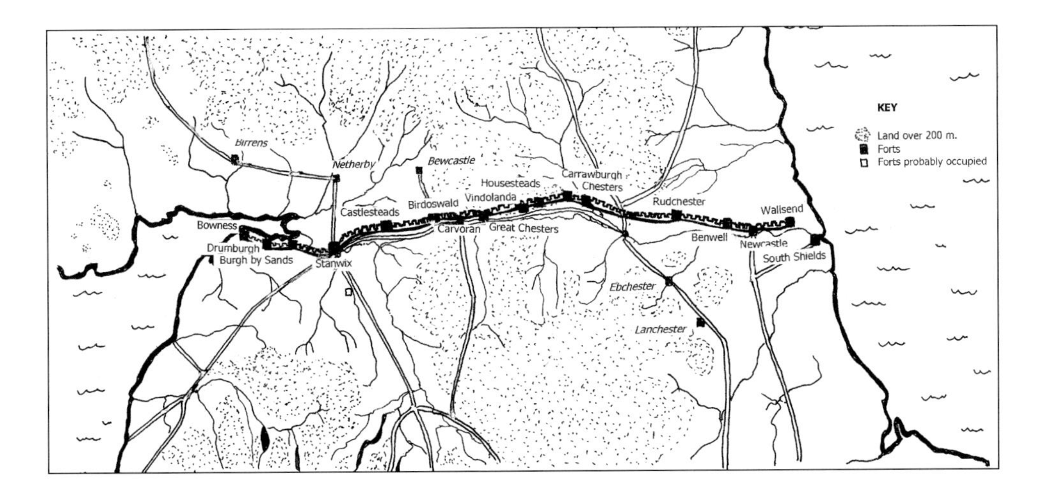

56 Map of Hadrian's Wall, England

Hadrian's Wall

One of the best known British examples of a linear frontier is the complex of turrets, fortlets, bridges, ditches, fortresses and walls built during the reign of the Emperor Hadrian in northern Britain (**56**; **colour plates 17 & 18**).

> The idea of a linear frontier was a recent development in Roman planning. The early Empire had depended for its frontiers on rivers or deserts or fortified zones.[8]

Why was it necessary to build this barrier? The conquest of Britain had been a relatively slow process that in fact was never completely successful. Several attempts to invade and Romanise Scotland were doomed to failure, both before and after construction of the Wall. The doubtful commercial gains to be made by completing the northern conquest, together with pressure on military capabilities caused by troubles on the Danube and in the East, eventually led the Romans to abandon the attempt. A defence line of forts from the Tyne to the Solway Firth was begun in the AD 80s and 90s, along the line that has come to be known as the Stanegate, including those at Corbridge, Chesterholme, Nether Denton and Old Church. Corbridge lay on the most direct of the major routes into Scotland. A tombstone found at the site demonstrates the presence of mobile mounted troops among the garrison in the first century AD. Around AD 105, evidence suggests that the fort at Corbridge may have been destroyed during a major raid, along with a number of other sites.

The situation along the line that was to become the Wall was volatile, and remained so for much of the period of the Roman occupation. It lay in the territory of the Brigantes. Control of these people and their allies, the Selgovae and Novantae of southern Scotland, could well have been one of the aims behind Hadrian's decision to demarcate the frontier zone with a static barrier.

> It could rely on no peaceful hinterland. While one of its purposes was to define the frontier of the province and debar raids from the north, and in the long run to provide peaceful conditions for economic development in the region behind it, another was quite certainly to prevent the joint planning between northerners and Brigantians which had been a fruitful source of trouble in the past.[9]

Hadrian's biographer claimed that the aim of the Wall was to separate Romans from the barbarians (*Romanos barbarosque dividere*). It has been argued that the frontier was more of an administrative and cultural delineation than a military one.

> The whole thrust of Hadrian's frontier policy was to define those inside the empire. This would enable those inside to feel they belonged to a social and economic framework which was increasingly able to spread its benefits beyond the narrow framework of Rome, Italy and the Mediterranean fringe. For the empire to thrive, its provincials must be given a sense of belonging, to be made to feel secure, and encouraged to turn their thoughts inward.[10]

The Wall was intended as a statement of power and control, a symbol of security, a useful task for occupying the energy of the troops, and a barrier to activities such as mounted cattle raiding. It could also serve as a customs and taxation point.

In support of this view are cited facts such as the length of the frontier (which could make it impossible to man continuously in any numbers); the relatively low height of the barrier, and recent evidence of an apparently well-settled and farmed landscape on either side of the structure.[11] Others are much more convinced of the primacy of the Wall's military role. One of the wooden tablets discovered at the Vindolanda fort reported that '. . . the Britons are unprotected by armour. There are very many cavalry. The cavalry do not use swords nor do the wretched Britons take up fixed positions in order to throw their javelins.'[12] This is eyewitness evidence – even if many tribespeople in the area were peaceful farmers, there were a goodly number of more belligerent Britons in the region.

The original plan for the Wall was laid out a little to the north of the Stanegate, making use of higher, more defensible land. It was to stretch 76 Roman miles (111km) from the gentle rolling slopes of the Tyne valley, over the steep rugged granite of the Whin Sill, down to the sandstone ridges towards Carlisle and ending in the flatter, softer ground of the Solway Firth. Bridges carried the structure over three major rivers. The eastern section was built of stone, on a 3m wide foundation, although many sections as actually built were narrower, as little as 1.6m wide. Well-cut stones were set as facings to a core of stone set in clay. The wall may have been between 4-4.5m high and could have been crenellated. A section excavated at Denton, near Newcastle, had a rendered mortar face, and the outer facing stones found in the Castle Nick area had been whitewashed. The Wall must thus have presented a striking and dominant appearance to the British tribes.

Small fortlets, called milecastles (**57**), were built abutting the south side of the barrier every Roman mile or so; these averaged about 18m square internally. Most of these seem to have had gates through the Wall. Between each of these, more or less evenly spaced, were two watchtowers or turrets. The western section of the Wall was built, more traditionally, of turf and was also supplied with milecastles (here built of earth and timber) and watchtowers of stone. There are three types each of milecastles and turrets, possibly a result of slightly different blueprints followed by the three legions involved in the building: the II Augusta, XX Valeria Victrix and VI Victrix. On the north side of the Wall, various sections were further protected by a ditch. The work seems to have begun in or soon after AD 122, the year in which Hadrian visited Britain, and continued until the end of AD 124 when there was a major change in the plan.

Certainly by AD 126 a decision had been made to add a series of forts to the system, some at milecastle points, others strategically placed to cover river crossings (Chesters on the Tyne, Birdoswald on the Irthing and Stanwix on the Eden). In addition to these dozen or so forts, an extension 6.5km eastwards from Newcastle to Wallsend may have been decided upon at the same time. Some of the forts were designed to straddle the Wall, projecting north of the linear barrier for about one third of their area. Further forts were added later.

Contemporary with the fort-building, or very soon after, the Vallum was added to the system, south of the Wall. Probably known to the Romans as the Fossatum, this consists of a broad flat-bottomed ditch, flanked by two banks, which stretched from Newcastle to the western end of the Wall. In places this was laboriously cut through living rock – a major undertaking. It shadows the Wall quite closely for much of its length, although topography occasionally forces it up to 1km southwards.

Why were the plans changed, and what was the Vallum for? 'Excavation on the line of the Wall has shown that the earliest plan for the system gravely underestimated the opposition it would arouse.'[13] It has been suggested that the Vallum served multiple purposes – a track along its bank served as a fast military communication route between the forts, but more importantly, it demarcated a zone of military control. Tacitus tells us that regulations in force somewhat earlier on the Rhine and Danube frontiers included payment of tolls, surrendering of arms and movement supervised by military escorts for those wishing to enter Roman territory. Perhaps the area delimited by the Vallum was such a control zone. The only easy crossing points were at the forts, and these were guarded by gates. It may also have been felt that whilst the Wall created an effective barrier against tribespeople pushing southwards, it also formed an impediment for Roman troop deployment northwards. The forts provided defended access points for more aggressive action.

> Although it began as a control across the frontier zone to ensure that access by barbarians or other undesirables was limited, the barrier had clearly evolved into something rather different, perhaps within ten years. Pressures from the south, not the north, were now firmly held in check by the vallum, not itself a defended barrier, but a marker which delimited

> military territory. At the same time, the war footing for troops on the Wall line was made more positive; they clearly faced forwards . . . if the vallum cut off access from the south, it also cut off retreat in that direction too . . . tactically speaking, if the Romans were under positive or unremitting threat from the north, the vallum was a mistake.[14]

The completion of the system may not have been total for up to 80 years after its commencement, when the Wall was reoccupied and refurbished under Severus. In the interim, it had been at least partially abandoned during the northward advances in the reign of Antoninus Pius, and in AD 180, during the reign of Commodus, a major raid across the Wall had resulted in some destruction and the killing of a Roman general.

Many changes and phases of rebuilding have been traced for the lifetime of Hadrian's Wall until its eventual abandonment in the fifth century AD (by which time it may have been garrisoned by local militias or even mercenary client groups). Later garrisons were clearly very different from the more professional legions of the Hadrianic period. Substantial *vici* grew up at many of the forts, and there is evidence of manning by troops who were recruited from within the local communities and whose wives and children resided alongside them. These units, stationed in the same area for generations, were not trained or ready for anything other than sedentary defensive actions. It has been suggested that they became more farmers than soldiers by the end of the period.

Hadrian's Wall has been regarded variously as a failure, a success, and an impediment to Roman Britain. A success, because for nearly 300 years it protected (or seemed to protect) the feeling of security of those who lived behind it, accepting the benefits of romanitas and, generally, peace. An impediment because it had the effect of 'crystallising expectations' – it encouraged the failure of the Romans to complete the job of conquest beyond its line. This meant that a permanent garrison had to be maintained along it, costly both financially and politically, as later events amply demonstrated; in addition, the freedom of the tribes beyond (and in Ireland) created recurrent trouble and possibly destabilisation of the Romanisation of the north of England.

The Wall was a failure because

> The frontier remained turbulent, the hostility of the north Britons perhaps increased because of the construction of the Wall and tighter Roman control were disrupting traditional patterns of transhumant pastoralism, commercial exchange and social intercourse in the border region.[15]

One writer[16] has likened the gates at the milecastles to

> . . . dykes, built to defend low-lying land against the tides of the sea, with frequent sluices and culverts which in quiet seasons can be left open to direct the ebb and flow of the waters into the proper channels, but which in time of storm and stress need to be completely shut.

57 *Milecastle at Housesteads, on Hadrian's Wall.* Photograph: Sandra Luff

What Faulkner and some others seem to suggest for the early period of the Wall's existence, and other commentators see as later consequences, is that it acted more like flotsam piled up in a water course, creating a dam behind it that must, inevitably, burst. This occurred not only in instances such as the overrunning of the frontier by a barbarian confederation in AD 367, but also in terms of the financial and political burden, the psychological and symbolic effects and the effects on economies both north and south of the line. The pressures eventually became too great for the survival of such an arbitrary, ambitious frontier.

Linear earthworks of the post-Roman period

The building of linear earthworks in Britain during the post-Roman period and possibly as late as the ninth century AD or beyond presents us with a number of questions which cannot, in almost all cases, be answered successfully without a great deal more research than has so far been carried out. Among the monuments created or adapted during this period are well-known features such as Offa's Dyke (**59**; **colour plates 19 & 20**) and Wat's Dyke, along the borders of the kingdom of Mercia and the lands of the Welsh; the Cambridgeshire series of earthworks along Mercia's eastern borders; the various sections of Wansdyke and the earlier Bokerly dyke along the northern borders of Wessex; and a series of lesser-known banks and ditches in Surrey and West Kent (**58a**). Few of these are well-dated, little excavation has so far been carried out on them, and most have suffered mutilation or destruction along at least part of their lengths.

The questions that we have to ask of linear earthworks are numerous. If they were intended as military works, it is hard to understand how they could have functioned effectively. If they are simply boundary markers, it is equally hard to appreciate why such an enormous amount of laborious effort was felt necessary; some dykes still stand 3m high or more, and can be miles long.

58a Map of Dark Age linear dykes and boundaries in southern England

We can consider their military possibilities by studying how they are sited in the landscape in terms of strategic prerequisites. Who was being protected from whom? Do they separate clearly different cultural regions? What kinds of tactics would be employed in defensive use of the dykes? Is it likely that the many gaps contained gates or guard posts? Were the banks surmounted by walls or palisades? Which way do they face (and how can we tell)? Were they built over a long or a short period of time? For how long might they have been expected to remain effective?

If they are boundary markers, this would suggest their commissioning by a reasonably strong centralised authority, in order to mobilise and organise the necessary labour; it would also imply the existence of some sort of diplomatic debate between kingdoms or communities. Were they also intended to act as trade barriers or customs barriers, perhaps with taxation points in the gaps? Perhaps, like Hadrian's Wall, they could have acted as a barrier to limit cattle rustling or mounted raiding parties (as opposed to organised military attacks).

We do not know if any of the series of earthworks of this type are actually contemporary with each other, nor if various sections within any one group were built at the same time or in succession. What may be important to ascertain, whatever the original intentions of each feature, is how that feature was adapted, altered or recognised at different periods of its life – something that starts out as a simple land marker could later become the basis for a defensive line, and then revert to the status of an ordinary field boundary. We cannot presently say if any or all of the sections of a particular group were ever actively in use at the same time for a similar purpose, let alone identify any large-scale design in their inception.

The practice of using linear earthworks to demarcate territory is a very old one, and there are examples in Britain from at least the Neolithic period onwards. During the

58b Map of Offa's Dyke, on the borders of England and Wales. Despite historical records mentioning that the Mercian king Offa built a great dyke from sea to sea, there are many gaps in it, which may be explained by later erosion. The northern part of the Dyke and its relationship with Wat's Dyke remain an enigma. After Hill, D. 1981, *An Atlas of Anglo-Saxon England*

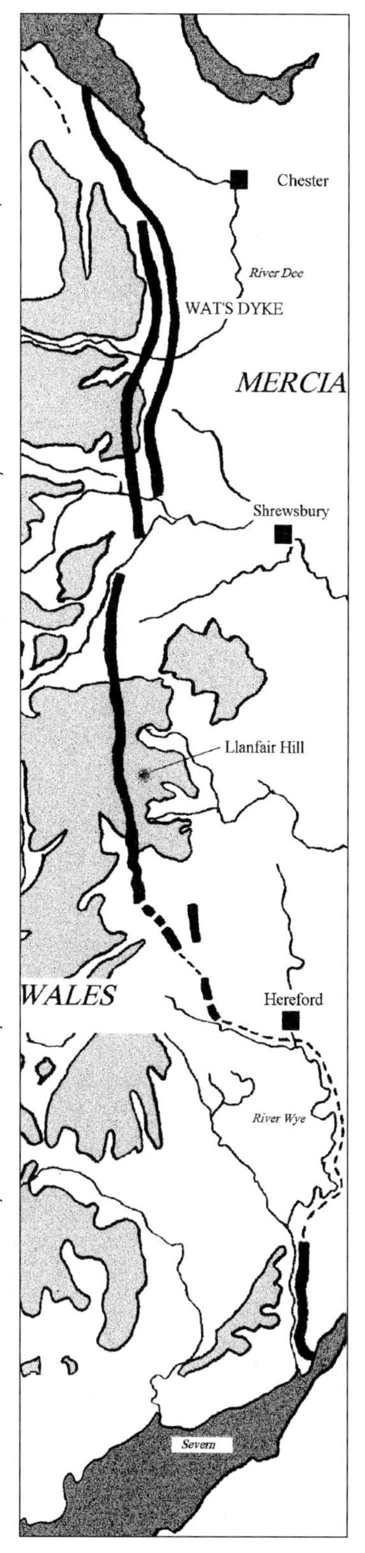

Bronze Age, a feature of the Wessex region was the long low banks known as 'ranch boundaries', apparently dividing up the land for stock management. The Iron Age has its hillfort ramparts, and the linear earthworks surrounding the so-called 'territorial oppida' of the south of England with examples at Silchester, Colchester, Chichester and elsewhere. It has been suggested that these latter dykes were possibly related to a defence strategy involving fast chariot attacks or guerrilla-style raids like those that Julius Caesar found particularly irritating.[17]

It is therefore clear that people were familiar with dykes as a way of achieving a particular territorial aim, whether this was defensive, diplomatic, commercial or political, and that for this purpose the effort in their construction was reasonable and worthwhile, however problematic this may seem to us. It makes little sense to deny their possible function as boundary markers on the basis of their size and the amount of labour involved in their construction; there are many examples of the expenditure of massive effort for non-practical purposes – Stonehenge, Silbury Hill and possibly even the Millennium Dome. There may be all sorts of other agendas involved: ritual fervour, display, the desire to put one over on the neighbours, or even the case of a good idea simply getting out of hand. It may not even have been clear to the builders at the time. In such cases, actual evidence for original function may be very hard to come by. Dating might help us to work out which leader or group would want to make such a statement about the lands they controlled or claimed, and their own puissance. Some of the apparently earlier dyke systems may relate to affairs of the later fifth century. At this time, Saxon immigration to

Britain is evident over much of the south, demonstrated especially in a number of important cemetery sites. Towards the end of the fifth century, remnants of the Romanised British may have been led by Ambrosius Aurelianus, and perhaps by the shadowy Arthur who was possibly a British war leader (*dux bellorum*).

The monk Gildas, writing in the mid-sixth century, seems to suggest that a victory by the British possibly under Arthur over the Saxons at the unidentified site of Mons Badonicus secured a period of peace between the two sides. During this period we may presume some kind of diplomatic negotiation and agreement as to territorial boundaries. This happy state of affairs lasted until some time after AD 550; during the following half-century, renewed Saxon pressure eventually succeeded in gaining for them control over most of Britain. Frere, commenting on Silchester, notes that

> Round this town the late fifth-century territorium seems to be indicated by earthworks which are best understood as boundaries rather than defences as such: they mark a state of agreement or equilibrium between the [Saxon] invaders and the Britons such as would suit the aftermath of Badon. The final stage of Bokerly Dyke is perhaps a similar phenomenon . . . now that early Saxon material is known in Hampshire and the Salisbury region, it is easier to place the dyke later in the [fifth] century than was once thought likely.[18]

Conversely, Fowler has suggested that the sections of the eastern Wansdyke he has studied may even pre-date Mons Badonicus.[19] He believes that the evidence for this area may be contemporary with that for the renewal of defensive building in Somerset at sites such as Cadbury and Congresbury hillforts, and proposes a date in the 490s for the rapid construction (over no more than one or two years) of the East Wansdyke as a defence against a Saxon invasion from the direction of the Thames valley. He further suggests that the construction came to an abrupt halt 'within hours after the battle of Badon' which he believes may have taken place at Badbury, 9 miles north-north-east of the stretch of dyke in question. One of the major difficulties of seeing the East Wansdyke as this sort of defence is that it has many gaps, particularly on routes associated with transhumance between the Vale of Pewsey and the chalk downs to the north. There is also a problem in knowing how the British population could have manned the miles of dyke effectively in any way that could have actually halted such an invasion. It may be easier to understand the gaps if we accept Frere's interpretation of this dyke as one of a number of agreed lines of demarcation post-Badon. However, other interpretations of the Wansdyke put its construction much later than this period. They might 'perhaps represent unfinished public works of Middle Anglo-Saxon date, the result of a short-lived settlement between the West Saxons and the Mercians in the late eighth or early ninth century'.[20] The only radiocarbon date, of around AD 1000, is from a later context than the building of the monument.

If the dykes were intended as trade controls, or a means to extract tolls from merchants and goods passing through them, we might expect to be able to find some confirmatory material. There could have been structures at the gaps to house officials, and it would be more likely that the top of the banks was further obstructed by a wall or palisade, to inhibit smuggling. It would also be likely that markets and emporia would have grown up near the crossing points. So far, little or no such evidence has come to light for this form of use of any of the dyke systems.

Later placing of the construction of the Wansdyke (variously mid-sixth century to early seventh, or later seventh and eighth centuries), dating for the Cambridgeshire systems (possibly early sixth century) and for some of the Surrey/Kent dykes (later sixth and seventh centuries) have all been ascribed by a variety of writers to the territorial expansion of a number of Mercian rulers (or resistance to it). The issue of who built the dykes is generally based on which side of the bank the ditch has been placed, and there is a widespread assumption that the ditch faces the enemy in the same way that a moat surrounds a house. This may be true of defensive structures; if, however, the dykes are administrative or relative to political territorial agreement, it is not clear whether the ditch could be placed inside the bank on the builders' side just as often. In common law, a garden fence shows its inside to the land of the person responsible for its maintenance; at Hadrian's Wall, the vallum was constructed inside the Roman province and seems to have been an extra element in the control system. It cannot, therefore, be easily decided whether, if the dykes were constructed as a response to Mercian expansionism, they were built by the Mercians to demarcate the land they claimed, or by their neighbours to show the Mercians where they had to stop. It also remains perfectly possible that they were built as a joint venture between both sides as part of a diplomatic treaty.

The Surrey/Kent dykes are generally little explored archaeologically. Surrey was the subject of territorial ambitions for all of the surrounding kingdoms at various times during the sixth to eighth centuries – Kent, Wessex and Mercia all laid claim to the area. Two of the earthworks run parallel to rivers and this has led to the suggestion that they are secondary defences, supporting the rivers themselves as stop-lines. The *Fullingadic*, parallel to and 5km or so east of the river Wey, is mentioned in a charter dated 672-4, where it is called an 'old ditch'. There are several interpretations of this feature.

> Already *antiquus* in the 670s, it must represent the eastern boundary of an earlier unit of which Woking hundred is surely the residue. It is a fair deduction that these two hundreds [Woking and Chertsey] formed a district identified from an early date with the tribe of the Woccingas, comparable in size and shape to the adjoining Berkshire *regiones* of the Sunningas and Readingas.[21]

So, an early tribal boundary? The '-*inga*' portion of the name may suggest a claim by an early tribal group to a demarcated area:

> Though used as a boundary mark, it seems improbable that this earthwork had been built only as a temporary division, for the River Wey itself would have served as a boundary equally well. It is likely its primary purpose was as a defence.[22]

– so, a defensive construction?

59 *Offa's Dyke at Llanfair Hill. A few miles to the north of Knighton, the earthwork is in a reasonable state of preservation. The monument measured 60ft across when first built.* Photograph: Richard Hill

On the other hand, the *Faestendic*, running along the east side of the Cray valley in West Kent, is seen more generally as a defensive line, built by Kent to protect against armies coming from the west, either across country or via the ancient line of Watling Street.

Other ditches and banks in Surrey seem placed to act as barriers across routes – the system that runs along the boundaries of the parishes between Epsom and Headley crosses Stane Street and the Portway. This dyke was originally at least 3m high, 10m wide and 2km long. Further east, a large ditch and bank lying along the present Surrey-Kent county boundary, traced for at least 300m, crosses a valley along which the present A25 runs and which has held ancient routes as well. It is believed that this was also built to impede Mercian encroachment into Kent.

Blair suggests[23] that some of these works in eastern Surrey and west Kent could date to the period in which Frithuwold, a sub-king of Wulfhere, king of Mercia, carved himself out a realm from the disputed Surrey territory; the implication is that the beleaguered Kentish men threw up a series of earthworks, one after another, in an attempt to stem the Mercian tide during the later seventh century.

Superficially, the history of Offa's Dyke is more straightforward – the chronicler Asser describes the building of a dyke 'from sea to sea' along the Welsh frontier in the late eighth century, and an entry in *Brut y Tywysogion* for AD 787 reads:

> In the summer the Welsh devastated the territory of Offa and then Offa caused a dyke to be made between him and Wales to enable him the more easily to withstand the attack and that it is called Glaawd Offa from that time to this day and it extends from one sea to the other from the south

near Bristol, to the north, above Flint, between the monastery of Basingwerk and Coleshill.

Of all the frontiers in Dark Age Europe, Offa's Dyke is by far the most impressive; it is the largest archaeological monument in Britain. Sir Cyril Fox, in 1955, was the only archaeologist to look at it closely until David Hill began a series of excavations in 1972. The frontier is about 150 miles long; about 80 miles of it survive. It has a ditch on the Welsh side about 1.75m deep and a rampart rising up to 7.5m above it to the east; the whole structure is about 18m across. It commands an impressive view to the west. There are many gaps, particularly up the Severn from Buttington to Welshpool, and in the middle section to the south of Hereford. At the northern end, Wat's Dyke runs generally parallel to Offa's Dyke on its east side for about 38 miles.

Mercian and Welsh hostilities go back at least as far as the time of the great pagan king Penda (*c*.632-55) and probably beyond. By 713 all the kingdoms of the south of England were under Mercian domination, or were strongly influenced from Mercia. Offa, who reigned from 757-96, opened up the kingdom of Mercia to continental influence and expanded its Christianity. Charlemagne regarded him as a peer and allowed his son to marry Offa's daughter. In 786 Offa welcomed legates and held an ecclesiastical council with them present, the first time this had occurred since 597 and the last until 1070, after the Norman conquest. Offa, however, failed to win over the Welsh whose frequent raids caused great damage in the English kingdoms.

Fox believed that the gaps in the dyke were original and intentional, and that the structure was an agreed frontier – the first English attempt to protect the rich lands of the Cheshire Plain. However, Welsh sources talk of almost continuous warfare in the eighth and early ninth centuries. The archaeological evidence does not help to clarify these points to any extent at the moment. Hill's excavations showed that the dyke is made up of a variety of different building techniques, and a number of mysteries. Traces of the ditch are apparently totally missing in some areas, casting doubts on its existence as a continuous feature, and some sections of the line of the dyke, where it was assumed that it had been destroyed in more recent centuries, appear to show no evidence of it ever having been built – at Tre-Abbot-Bach, for example, and at Trelaunyd, where earlier excavations by Fox had also failed to find the dyke. Fox's exploration revealed a pair of shallow ditches with a low intervening bank that was inconsistent with other sections of the dyke. Fox also failed to find evidence of the dyke in the Ysceifiog section. Hill believes that the whole northern section of Offa's Dyke is questionable. He notes that while both Offa's and Wat's Dykes make good use of ravines and rivers, there are no useful lines of these along the proposed northern line of Offa's Dyke. Instead, the more easterly Wat's Dyke uses the Alun valley and then makes a sharp turn towards Offa's Dyke, leaving only a 2.5 mile gap between the two, from Treuddyn to Alun, which suggests that Wat's Dyke is in fact the northern sector of Offa's Dyke, rather than the traditionally proposed line.[24] Hill also found traces of what he describes as a marking-out ditch, whose spoil was used to make a low bank that was probably crowned with a drystone wall; this feature has been broken down to fill the 'marking-out' ditch when the main turf bank was erected over it. This seems unlikely – what would be the point of going to the trouble of building a wall by a temporary feature? There seems to be a possibility that in this sector at least the dyke is reaffirming an earlier boundary, perhaps a feature of previous hostilities or territorial agreement. A possibly later stone wall discovered at Knighton during cleaning of the crest of the dyke may represent a medieval reaffirmation of Offa's line in the same way. Usage of boundary markers has an ever-changing pattern of need and practicality, and however frustrating changes of practice may be for the archaeologist, we should not be surprised at finding conflicting evidence of this type.

How Offa expected the Dyke to function is also problematic – the line is far too long to serve as a defensive frontier, and one imagines that small raiding parties would not have found it particularly difficult to circumvent scouting patrols, anymore than the border reivers did on the Scottish-English border in the sixteenth and seventeenth centuries. 'Linear earthworks clearly inhibited movement and, innocuous though they may seem today, that may have been their main aim: the ancient equivalent of stop-lines . . .' perhaps manned by a civilian militia until support could arrive.[25] But Offa's Dyke could also have been a grandiose statement of power and importance, signalling the self-image of a kingdom that saw itself as a part of a larger European world with a destiny that excluded the Welsh.

Objections to the Dark Age dykes as military frontiers start with the difficulty of manning and effectively protecting linear boundaries. In succeeding centuries other frontier builders faced similar problems, applying different solutions to lesser or greater effect.

Coastal defences

> Treaty engagements, political or commercial, have no doubt their value; but their efficacy in preserving peace is mightily enhanced when they are reinforced by the solid guarantees of frowning batteries and rifled cannon. Let us set what store we please upon our 'faithful allies' and diplomatic parchments, provided only we keep our powder dry.
> Editorial, *Dover Express*, 31 July 1860, approving plans to update and extend the defences of the Western Heights.

The Saxon Shore Forts

Around the east and south coasts of England there was a series of Roman forts, some now fragmentary and some still impressive, and some completely disappeared. Together they represent an enigma for archaeologists. They are mentioned as a group in a document called the *Notitia Dignitatum* which probably dates from the late fourth or early fifth century AD; the reference tells us that they are situated on the *Litus Saxonicum*, the 'Saxon Shore', under the command of the *comes* or count, which was then a military rank.

Excavations, although limited, have shown that the forts were not all built at the same time – they were part of a system that grew up between the first and third

60 Burgh Castle, one of the Saxon Shore Forts. From a 1920s illustration showing East Wall and projecting Bastions

centuries, and it is still not clear whether they ever operated as a unified system or as independent units.

Brancaster, Reculver and Caistor-on-Sea seem to be the earliest of the series, possibly dating from between AD 210-50; they are very traditional in their forms and construction. Dates between AD 230-300 are suggested for Burgh Castle (**60**), Walton Castle, Bradwell, Richborough, Dover (on the site of earlier defences), Lympne and Portchester. Also between these dates, forts were probably built at Oudenburg, Boulogne and perhaps Garrianonum in France. The forts at Clausentum and Pevensey seem to be the latest, built between AD 300-80.[26]

Certainly, the later third century was a period of unease. Towns were provided with masonry walls, and trouble erupted at a number of places across the western part of the Empire and within the political system. Between AD 259-73, Germany, Gaul, Spain and Britain seceded from the Empire entirely. Revolts broke out even after Aurelian had retaken the provinces, including one in Britain in AD 282. In 285 a Belgian, Carausius, was appointed to take charge of the fleet based at Boulogne, his job being to clear Frankish and Saxon pirates from the Channel. Accused of treachery, in 286 Carausius revolted and declared himself emperor, seizing Northern Gaul and Britain. It seems clear that he enjoyed the support of the troops in these regions (not least, perhaps, because he reformed the coinage in which they were paid to a new high standard). It has been suggested that some of the impetus for the improvement of Britain's Channel and North Sea defences came from Carausius. Conversely, it may have been part of Constantius' plan to strengthen the Roman presence in the area when he took Britain in about 296.

The architecture of the forts seems to indicate changes in military thought during the period. It has been claimed that the forts of the Saxon Shore seem to have more

61 *North perimeter wall of Pevensey Castle. The bonded wall shows a clear leaning towards the fort's use as a strong point as opposed to the role of secure barrack compound. Subsequent reuse of the fort as a Norman Castle and Second World War defence serves to prove the point.* Photograph: Jeanette Hicks

in common with contemporary continental building styles rather than British construction methods utilised in town defences. The early forts were 'more like secure barrack-compounds than defensible strong points; the idea was that the army went out to fight. Now, though, a new defence-minded military architecture was coming in.'[27]

The new forts, from early changes at Burgh Castle to more cohesive designs at Richborough, Dover and Portchester, had square corners, strong gateways, projecting towers designed to provide enfilading fire, and high tile-bonded masonry walls. The later forts at Lympne and Pevensey moved completely away from the traditional shape, having curving walls built to follow the contours of the sites. The strength of these forts as independent strongholds is underlined by their subsequent use – Pevensey (**61**; **colour plate 21**) and Portchester (**colour plate 22**) both housed Norman castles within their boundaries, and at Pevensey there are also remains of an anti-Armada gun emplacement and twentieth-century machine-gun posts and pillboxes concealed as part of the ancient walls, within clear sight of the Napoleonic Martello towers along Pevensey Bay. The sea has changed the shape of these coasts greatly since the Roman period – the fort at Walton has disappeared into the waters, and much of Reculver and Bradwell forts have also been lost, while Pevensey and Lympne now stand much further inland than they did when built.

Taken together, the forts of the Saxon Shore represent the earliest in a long line of defences along those coasts of Britain most vulnerable to attack from the Continent (**62**). But what really was their original function? The problem of piracy and raiding was clearly a major nuisance. It has been suggested[28] that each of the forts held a combined force, part of which was a small fleet of ships such as the *classis Anderetianorum* (recorded

62 Map of the Saxon Shore Forts of Southern Britain as listed in the Notitia Dignitatum

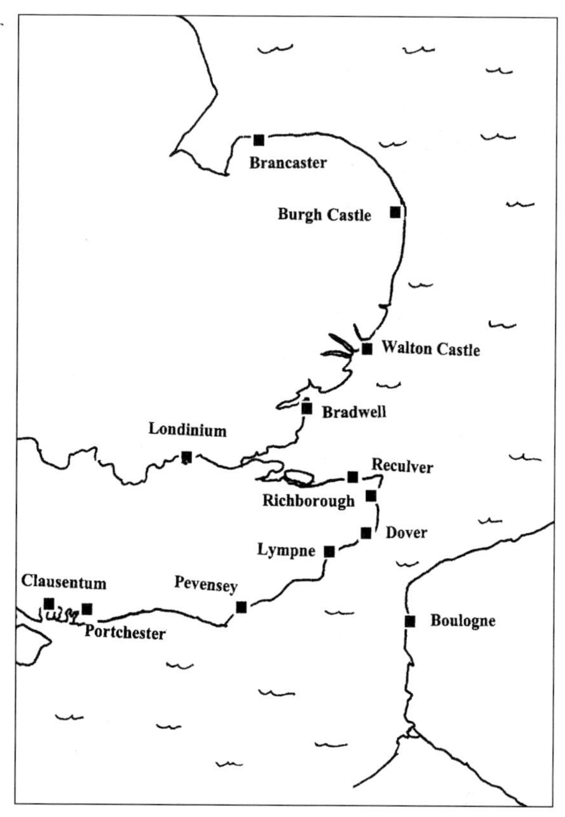

at Paris but originally from Pevensey) whose role was to head off the pirates or to catch raiding ships as they tried to slip through a defensive cordon roaming the Channel waters, perhaps combining operations with a watchtower or beacon system and rapid-response mounted shore troops from the fort garrisons.

By the fourth century AD attacks on the western Roman Empire were on a larger scale than the odd pirate raid. Large-scale Germanic incursions across the Rhine were reported between 260 and 275, and pressure on the frontiers increased from that time on. We have no historical information at all for Britain in this respect until the middle of the fourth century, when 'the barbarian conspiracy' of 367 is noted, a simultaneous attack on the province's frontiers by the Pictii from the north, the Attacotti and Scotti from the west, and Franks and Saxons in the south and east. They plundered deep into the heartland of the country and this event, however much of a true coalition it was, seems to sound the passing-bell for Romanised Britannia. Large-scale settlement by Germanic peoples is certainly attested historically and archaeologically in the fifth and sixth centuries. Were the Saxon Shore forts intended to keep these settlers out – or were they already here?

There is some evidence to indicate Saxon settlement in England well before the Romans left. There is a possibility of such a settlement at Caistor-by-Norwich from the end of the third century, although not everyone is convinced by the evidence. Roman authorities often settled barbarian groups in frontier zones:

> These barbarians accorded the special privilege of space within the Empire were required to be self-supporting by farming barren areas, to provide troops to fight for Rome where necessary, and, perhaps most important, guard their hard-won status from assaults on their territory and livestock from other barbarians still outside the Empire's borders.[29]

So, were these called forts of the Saxon Shore because they were designed to counter Saxon raids and attempts at invasion, or because they were built along the limits of land in which the Saxons *already lived*? Is it even possible that the garrisons were made up, at least in part, of Saxon settlers and their families, part of a militia defence force? Few of the sites have been excavated in any great detail so far; perhaps future research will shed light on this intriguing question.

The castles of Henry VIII

A chain of forts had existed around the south and east coasts of Britain, facing the Continent, since the 3rd century AD, but to what extent these were ever intended to form a defensive frontier is uncertain. Certainly, no system of anti-invader coastal defences was encountered by the last major invasion of Britain – that of the Normans in 1066. Sporadic, scattered works were built during the later Middle Ages, mainly to defend ports and harbours, but

> nowhere were there defences to ward off an entire fleet; partly because the need had not arisen, and partly because the increased range, accuracy and mobility of the cannon developed in the previous decades only now made such tactics possible.[30]

It was not until the first half of the sixteenth century that the defence of Britain was overhauled in an organised fashion.

The impetus came from the political situation that followed Henry VIII's divorce from Catherine of Aragon, and Henry's assumption of the title of Head of the Church of England. Catherine's kinsman, Charles V, Holy Roman Emperor, together with the Pope became determined to exact revenge for these acts. They formed a series of shifting alliances, particularly with France, that alerted Henry to the danger of a major invasion. The French were in any case less than happy that the English held Calais; they had the idea of taking the Isle of Wight, a base from which to harass English trade and contain 'perfidious Albion' within its own shores. In fact, nothing actually happened for a few years, partly because of problems with the Turkish Empire in the eastern Mediterranean, and Protestant rebellions in the Spanish Netherlands and elsewhere, but the chronicler Edward Hall records Henry's decisive approach to the threat; the king

> sent dyvers of his nobles and counsaylours to view and searche all the Ports and daungiers on the coastes where any meete or convenient landing place might be supposed . . . And in all suche doubtfull places his hyhnes caused dyvers & many Bulwarks & fortificacions to be made . . .

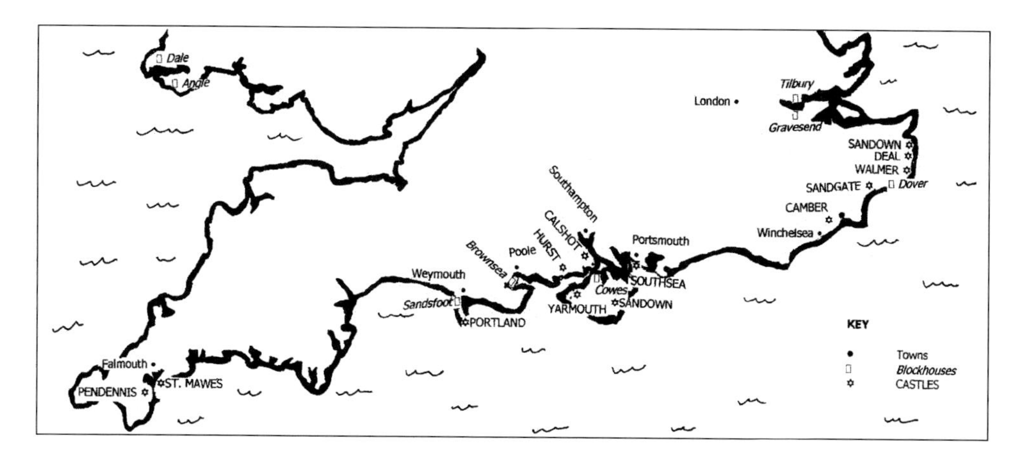

63 Map of Henry VIII's coastal defences of Southern England

Henry continued this process throughout his reign, even when the threat of invasion had faded; he also undertook campaigns in Northern France, capturing Boulogne and strengthening English control of much of the Pas de Calais.

The system of coastal defence Henry devised was innovative in many ways. It involved the protection of harbours and dockyards, the monitoring of anchorages, and the provision of safe passages for merchant vessels (**63**). Although many of the components of the system were already in existence elsewhere, it was the way in which they were combined that was new.

> Nowhere else had bastions been clustered so tightly together in such numbers, or had multiple tiers of gun positions been used to such effect. They were at once more complex and more economical in design than their continental precursors.[31]

It was the rapid developments in gunnery during the preceding 50 years that made a new approach to coastal defence necessary. Guns of the fourteenth and fifteenth centuries had mostly taken the form of heavy cast-bronze or brass bombards and mortars designed for siege warfare, or 'barrel-stave' light guns, made from tubes or bars of metal bound together to form the barrels. Most of these weapons were breech-loading, inefficient, unwieldy, and often downright dangerous – sometimes more casualties were suffered by their operators than by their intended victims. Great strides were being taken, however, in the early sixteenth century in the technology of iron-working, allowing much more reliable manufacture of artillery. Henry took a great personal interest in these developments, and in the complementary science of fortification to counter the improved artillery. In 1518 he is recorded as having observed a testing of these new guns at Southampton, and other records suggest that he may have been personally responsible for some aspects of the design of defences at Calais and in the new coastal defences. Most guns had to be imported, often from the Low Countries, so in

64 *Deal Castle, Kent. One of a series of forts built by Henry VIII to defend the south coast against the French.* Photograph: Jeanette Hicks

the 1530s Henry set up gun foundries in London and the Weald, which were actively engaged in experimental works; the investment paid off when a method of casting a safe iron cannon was achieved at one of the Sussex foundries. He also created a battle fleet, employing the latest innovations in ship design, including mounting the main armament on several decks along the sides of the ships.[32]

The new defensive system was built at great speed. The south-east coast, facing both northern France and the Spanish Netherlands, was the priority. Blockhouses were erected to defend the Thames estuary and the dockyards at Gravesend and at Tilbury (archaeological investigation suggesting that these were linked to earthwork batteries as well) and three batteries were added to the defences at Dover. A system of new, squat castles was strung along the coastline. The stretch of coast facing The Downs, a well-known sea road and anchorage with a vulnerable series of beaches, was defended by three new fortifications – Sandown, Deal (**64**) and Walmer Castles (**65**), linked together with an earthwork and trench system. A circular gun tower of 1514 at Camber protecting the entrance to Rye harbour was rebuilt with a higher tower, curtain walls and four round bastions by 1540 (and remodified and strengthened again in 1542/3). Another large castle was built at Sandgate, close to Folkestone, and Calshot and Hurst Castles protected the entrance to Southampton Water, supported by two blockhouses either side of the Cowes inlet. Portland and probably Sandsfoot Castles were erected around the same time to defend Weymouth Harbour. All these works were apparently completed and garrisoned by the end of 1540. Later defences were added to Kingston-upon-Hull, Harwich, and in the West Country, where Pendennis and St Mawes castles were added to the existing blockhouses defending the Fal estuary and Carrick Roads, and blockhouses were erected at Dale and Angle to defend Milford Haven. Further works were undertaken or supported by the Crown at Brownsea Island, near Poole, Sandown and Yarmouth, and at Southsea, guarding Portsmouth.

> It is easy to forget the serious military purpose of many medieval castles whose great halls still seem to speak of pageantry and splendour. Not so with these castles: uncompromisingly they were fortresses, packing the maximum artillery capability into the most compact structures.[33]

65 *Walmer Castle. A design which showed a shift towards accommodating new forms of artillery.* Photograph: Jeanette Hicks

There were very few frills and furbelows; the castles, all different, share a central squat keep, most circular, but 12-sided at Hurst and square at Southsea and Hull, these slightly later works demonstrating the on-going programme of experiment and innovation. The earlier castles presented no square surfaces to enemy bombardment – everything was curved and sloping, even the parapets and embrasures.

They are concentrically designed, with tiers of semi-circular bastions surrounding the tower, and in many cases an encircling dry moat and chemise, or curtain wall. Deal Castle has five gun tiers, but there are never less than three. Despite their siting to command seaways, the castles are designed to offer all round defence. The entrances contained surviving medieval features such as portcullises and murder holes, and typically the keep entrance is set facing away from the outer gateway. Embrasures in the lower parts of the keep and bastions allowed handgun fire cover of the inner courtyards and the outer dry moat. The keep basements acted as stores and magazines, lit by lanterns behind thick glass screens, with vents to allow air in and heat out, minimising the chance of accidental explosion. The ground floor usually contained casemated embrasures, and a mess hall, kitchen, and accommodation for the soldiers. On the first floor were officers' quarters, and on the roof, which was thick and cased in lead, was the highest gun tier. Internal divisions were constructed of timber-framing with wattle infill. Vents from the casemates cleared the gunsmoke from the interior. Blockhouses were simplified versions of the castle plans, consisting of a single bastion, some including accommodation for a gun crew. Later fortifications such as Hull and Southsea incorporate new Italian ideas about enfilading angle bastions.

The armament of the period included cannons capable of throwing stone or iron shot weighing up to 32lb up to 3 miles. Guns of this calibre could therefore command the seaways extremely well; low in profile, and presenting an almost invisible target to ship-borne artillery. On the other hand, ships sailing past a castle could be in range 5km offshore, and for 10km sailing distance – an hour or more sailing time. Hand weapons including arquebuses and bows and arrows. Like other castles, Deal was manned with professional soldiers – a captain and 34 other ranks (who were expected to provide their own hand weapons).

One of the things that made the hasty building of these fortifications possible was the Dissolution of the Monasteries – records for Sandgate show that in addition to Kentish ragstone and Wealden timber, good quality Caen stone was acquired from nearby monastic houses, and the roof lead came from an abandoned priory. At Yarmouth, fragments of monastic carvings are still visible in the castle structure.

Henry's system could make use of the beacon warning system to attract help from troops and naval ships to a beleaguered fortress. It could not have, in itself, stopped an invasion, but it could certainly have delayed one and made it more costly and difficult to achieve. In the event, it was never severely tested. A naval engagement in 1545 in the Solent (during which the *Mary Rose* was lost) prevented a major French effort; subsequently they achieved a landing on the Isle of Wight but were rapidly dislodged. However, the value of these installations continued for centuries to come. At Hurst, for example, batteries were sited during the Napoleonic period, and in the late nineteenth century massive casemated wings were added for the placement of 61 heavy guns; in the early twentieth century, quick-firing guns were installed, together with searchlights, to combat actions by fast torpedo boats. It held a garrison through both World Wars, and its anti-aircraft guns were only removed in 1956. Similar additions occurred at St Mawes and elsewhere.

> Henry VIII comprehensively dragged England out of the military Dark Ages. Though most of his castles and blockhouses soon became outdated, he laid the firmest of brand-new foundations, on which the defence of England was to rely for centuries ahead.[34]

Most important was the acceptance of a pragmatic, economic and systematic approach to national defence; Henry's castles were not designed to impress, but to work. They were the brainchild of a technologically informed, forward-thinking monarch who understood the practicalities involved in defending an extended frontier – despite the limitations of the period, he did so successfully, for although diplomatic and political changes removed the immediate threat of invasion, the deterrent effect of the country's preparedness was clearly an important factor in the abandonment of French and Spanish military plans for some decades.

The Napoleonic era in Britain

In 1779, Britain was facing war on two fronts: North America and Europe. The French and Spanish formed an alliance, and as occurred the best part of 200 years earlier, they decided to try to take the Isle of Wight, as a sort of Gibraltar. The majority of the British fleet was occupied in the other side of the Atlantic. An invasion force of 20,000 infantry was assembled in northern France, whose aim was to take Portsmouth after a diversionary attack on the Channel Islands. The whole thing fell apart due to general incompetence, not least because of the inability of the French and Spanish commanders to communicate, but it served to alert Britain to the possibility of invasion. However, the received wisdom of the day was that the country's most important line of defence was the navy – indeed, Admirals St Vincent and Nelson believed the first line of defence to be the enemy's coast; increased efforts were made to get new ships on the stocks and to improve dockyard facilities, but little attention was paid to shore defences.

Several further invasion scares followed, in Britain and in Ireland, which came to nothing as a result either of bad weather, or delays, or the actions of a not very numerous and sometimes mutinous British navy. The threat continued, however, and the squadrons concerned with home water defences were reorganised and strengthened; the North Sea Fleet covered the area from Selsey Bill to Scotland, with the Downs Squadron protecting the Straits of Dover and the Dungeness Squadron watching Boulogne and other ports. The Western Squadron or Channel Fleet operated from Selsey Bill westwards, with squadrons stationed at Portsmouth, Plymouth and in the Channel Islands. It was the Downs Squadron that was conceived as the main defence against invasion. Admiral Keith, in charge of the North Sea Fleet, also organised the Sea Fencibles, a volunteer organisation whose task was to operate a chain of signal stations and telegraph posts, employ their own inshore boat squadron, and man coastal defensive installations.

The man in charge of land deployment between 1803 and 1805 was General Sir David Dundas. He inherited an ageing system of coastal batteries and forts (**66**); they were supplied with an extraordinary range of different calibre guns, and most installations were simple, temporary earth ramparts with guns mounted en barbette.[35] Vulnerable locations had been identified along the south coast, although Dundas was of the opinion that the most likely invasion point would be in East Kent, with Canterbury the key to a French advance on London. Apart from the batteries, defence rested on the signalling systems, the local militia, and the belief that local populations could delay enemy advances by sabotage, including the flooding of the Romney Marshes. It was not thought possible to actually halt a serious invasion on the coast. In 1803, French plans for two massive flotillas, one each at Dunkirk and Cherbourg, and camps for about 100,000 men, were well advanced. Napoleon was prepared to launch this invasion as soon as the French navy could achieve a hold on the Straits for the few hours necessary to allow the flotillas to cross the Channel. An invasion in Ireland was planned as a feint to draw attention, and the Toulon fleet sailed for the West Indies, drawing off the blockading Royal Navy squadron and reducing the protection ability of the navy in home waters. In fact the pusillanimous conduct of Admiral Villeneuve, faced with only 17 ships guarding the Western Approaches, lost the French their best chance; Napoleon realised that the moment had gone, and concentrated efforts instead on attempting to interrupt merchant shipping and create a trade blockade to isolate Britain financially.

However, in 1803 the threat was perceived as very real, and a new strategy was devised. Now efforts would be made to oppose any French landings, while defence-in-depth would be achieved by providing defence lines on strategic points inland. The job of the new coastal installations would be to hold up the French advance at the coast until help arrived, either from land forces or from the navy. The key to this plan was the building of a series of gun towers along the threatened coasts – the Martello towers (**67**):

66 The Western Heights at Dover. Part of the nineteenth-century improvements to the south coast defences of England. Photograph: Sandra Luff

> In one respect . . . Martello Towers were innovative, in Britain at least. Designed to hinder an invasion or landing party until the navy arrived, they were an early example of combined operations.[36]

The towers were named after a sixteenth-century Genoese tower at Mortella Point, Corsica. During 1793-4 it had been captured by the British, handed over to the Corsicans who lost it to the French, and then recaptured by the British. During the second capture, 38 men with three guns held out for two days against a four-gun battery firing from just 150 yards away. The strength of the tower left a lasting impression in military minds. Similar towers were built at the Cape and in Nova Scotia. They seemed the perfect model for anti-invasion strong points – Dundas had commanded in Corsica at the time of the Mortella action. Between 1805 and 1808, 74 were built along the south coast; the intention was to site them every 457-548m (500-600 yards) so that they could provide interlocking arcs of fire, and some were placed on either side of the sluices controlling the water in the Romney Marshes. A further 29 Martellos were built along the East Anglian coast between 1808 and 1812, followed by one at Leith and two in the Orkneys to protect the assembly point of transatlantic convoys in Longhope Sound during the War of 1812-15.

Each tower, built of about half a million bricks laid in hot lime mortar to increase resistance to bombardment, and rendered with cement and sand stucco on the outside to prevent scaling, stood an average of 10m (32ft) high, and were some 19m (62ft) in diameter, tapering like brochs to 12m (49ft). They were elliptical in shape, with the thickest section of the wall facing seaward, and each initially mounted a single 18- or 24-pounder on its 3m (10ft) thick lead-covered roof; the gun was sited on a pivot allowing 360° rotation. Extra or larger guns were added to some towers later. They were to be manned by an officer and 24 men, many of whom were local auxiliary troops. The towers on the east coast tended to be larger than those on the south, with more room for accommodation, and some were equipped with carronades and 5½in howitzers. The sturdiness of their construction was demonstrated in 1860, when

67 Diagram of a Martello Tower

Martello No. 68 at Eastbourne was demolished – the job required 50 rounds each from 40-, 80- and 100-pounder rifled Armstrong guns. The towers were accessed by removable ladders at the first-floor level, or if surrounded by a ditch, then via a drawbridge. The first floor was divided by partitions to form accommodation for the garrison, with the magazine and stores in the ground floor.

In addition to the Martellos, large redoubts were also constructed at Dymchurch and Eastbourne. These large circular fortifications comprised bomb-proof barracks and casemates below a roof platform for 11 guns. Major works were undertaken at Dover: the eastern defences were strengthened with outworks, bastions and tunnels, caponiers were inserted to protect the medieval gates, and covering the approach to the redan constructed on the north side were caponier-covered ditches, and an underground system with remote-controlled or dropping doors. The great Norman keep was strengthened with brick vaulting to provide gun positions on the roof and a bomb-proof magazine. On the Western Heights, the Drop Redoubt was constructed at the eastern end of the Downs, and the Citadel at the western end, with the North Centre Bastion between, connected by realigned earthwork and masonry lines. The Archcliffe Fort was refurbished and the Grand Shaft was built to improve communications between the Heights and the harbour below: this remarkable construction contains a triple staircase to allow the rapid movement of many troops.

Defensive lines and camps were set up to protect London. A line was planned to run from Chelsea to the River Lea north of the city, and from Wandsworth to Deptford on the south, with fieldworks at Shooter's Hill and Blackheath. A floating bridge was constructed to connect Greenwich Marshes with Blackwall Stairs. South of London, the 'Chalk Ridge Communication' line ran from Guildford to Rochester along the North Downs, to be spanned by military camps which were to be built in the various river gaps.

Extra defences were built around Chatham and to seal off access to London across the river Medway. A series of detached works were built in a ring around Rochester, the largest being Fort Pitt. South of this on the Maidstone road was Fort Clarence, with two two-storey brick guardhouses between these forts. A series of forts, batteries and towers were erected in the Channel Islands, including Fort George above St Peter Port and Fort Regent above St Helier, with the addition of Military Roads to speed the provision of reinforcements to key locations.

A major south coast work remains to be mentioned – the Royal Military Canal. Great local consternation had been expressed over plans to flood the Romney Marshes in case of invasion; in 1804 an alternative scheme was developed by Lt Col. John Brown and commenced by a civil engineer, John Rennie. This was a 28-mile long canal, looping up to 10 miles inland, in an arc around Dungeness from Hythe to the river Rother at Rye, with an extension to the west to Cliff End. Specifications were for a 19m (62ft) wide canal, 2.7m (9ft) deep from the level of the Marsh. On the north side of the Canal ran a drain, rampart and Military Road, with another drain and rampart and a towpath to the south. Every 600 yards or so was an earthwork gun position. The threefold aim of the project was to create a defensible physical barrier, avoid the necessity of flooding the Marshes, and provide a means of communication for transport and troop movements. The Canal itself is some 30ft wide within its works. William Cobbett was unconvinced about the cost and usefulness of many of these defensive projects. In his *Rural Rides* he is particularly scathing about the Canal: 'Here is a canal . . . to keep out the French; for those armies that had so often crossed the Rhine and the Danube, were to be kept back by a canal, made by Pitt, thirty feet wide at the most.' The Royal Military Canal may well have been of doubtful efficacy; in any case, Dundas was convinced that an invasion would not choose this southern option, as they would then be faced with a long and difficult crossing of the South Downs, Weald and North Downs before getting to within striking distance of London. He was sure they would prefer the easy and more direct choice offered by the eastern coasts (as apparently had the Romans the best part of 18 centuries earlier). However, the overall schemes for the defence of Britain in the early nineteenth century were impressive. Many were not completed (or even really begun) until after the threat had passed, due to political and financial wrangling, but they remained important for much of the nineteenth century. Eventually, like the Henrican forts before them, they became redundant in the face of new military technology. They could not hope to stand against the kind of guns developed in the later nineteenth and twentieth centuries. By the Second World War, the uselessness of this kind of fortification was fully recognised, invasion defences now being composed of continuous barbed wire and other barricades, supplemented by mines, traps, small batteries and air cover – no one target to draw fire, but an endless series of obstacles.

The Atlantic Wall

Adolf Hitler had stated after the British evacuations at Dunkirk in 1940 that never again would an Anglo-Saxon set foot on continental Europe. It became clear, however, that sooner or later the Anglo-American invasion would come. The Allies spent years planning the largest amphibious assault in military history and by the spring of 1944 they established three factors in their favour which the Germans had not managed to do in their own proposed crossing of the channel in 1940: total air superiority, appropriate transportation and landing craft, and overwhelming naval power.

But where would the invasion come? The German belt of fortifications constructed along the coast of Western Europe between 1942-4, which became known as the Atlantic Wall, betrayed the expectations of the German High Command. It was at its strongest in the Pas-de-Calais, the narrowest stretch of the English Channel where the Germans expected the invasion to come. Surely, the Allies would need to seize a major port at the earliest opportunity, or their offensive would simply run out of supply. Indeed, in August 1942, a large-scale Allied raid was launched against the French port of Dieppe with disastrous consequences. Designed as a 'Reconnaissance in Force' to test the strength of the Atlantic Wall, the Allies found it much stronger than they had thought: 6000 troops, mainly Canadian, took part in the attack. Although some of the coastal batteries were knocked out by British commandos, the beaches were relentlessly fired upon by German guns and all 30 Churchill tanks were destroyed, being unable to traverse the shingle beach. Over 3500 men were wounded, killed or taken prisoner. It was clear to the Allies that a great deal more planning would be involved in the final breaching of Hitler's Fortress Europe. The Pas-de-Calais was too strongly defended to be the landing point for the planned invasion. The Bay of Biscay was outside the range of Allied air support, so it too had to be ruled out. Despite the Dieppe disaster, the Allies successfully managed to convince the Germans through ingenious means that they were preparing for an attack in the Pas-de-Calais region. Wireless traffic indicated the build up in England of several fictitious armies, with two in Scotland, hinting at a possible Norwegian route of invasion. The deception worked very well. The favoured place was in fact to be Normandy. The problem of there being no natural ports in that vicinity would be solved by ingenious floating Mulberry Harbours, capable (in theory) of handling 12,000 tons of supplies a day. The head of the British team in 1943, Lieutenant General Frederick Morgan, began the planning for the invasion. After many revisions, the plan – Operation Overlord – saw reality on the morning of 6 June 1944 on the beaches of Normandy.

Defending a giant coastline against invasion was no easy task. The German-occupied territories ran from the north of Norway to the French border with Spain, a total of nearly 3000 miles. In reality, the Atlantic Wall itself constituted a string of fortifications, pill-boxes, blockhouses, guns and bunkers imbedded in cliffs, or on the sea front in towns from the Netherlands to the Atlantic Coast of France. In 1942 the construction began under the auspices of Fritz Todt, the man who had designed the German West Wall along the France-Germany border. A million tonnes of steel and 13 million tonnes of concrete were used in the construction, carried by a work force of press-ganged slave labourers.[37]

As the threat of Allied invasion became more likely, Hitler appointed Field Marshal Erwin Rommel to inspect the fortifications of the Atlantic Wall. Rommel was chiefly concerned with the stretch from Denmark to Brittany and he did not like what he saw. He believed that there would be only one way to thwart the landings – by throwing the enemy back into the sea. This belief was at variance with that of Field Marshal Gerd von Rundstedt, Commander-in-Chief in the west who took the view that the Wall was too static and that by concentrating reserves inland in the most likely areas of invasion, the enemy would be beaten. Rommel sent a report to OKW dated 31 December 1943 expressing his dissatisfaction at the

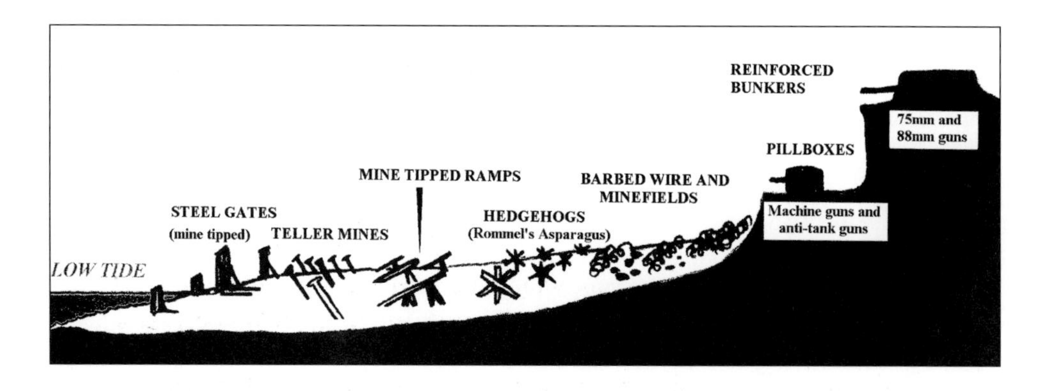

68 A stylised section of a typical Atlantic Wall series of defences. Most of the obstacles would have been covered at high tide

current arrangements. The defences were not deep enough, nor were they properly manned. The mobile reserves were too small and positioned too far inland. In any case, with overwhelming Allied air power mobile warfare was an unpalatable option.

Infantry units would now defend themselves with additional mines and wire, and armoured units were positioned nearby to help cut off enemy penetrations. Vast areas were to be flooded to prevent Allied airborne landings, particularly in the Cotentin. More building works were to be undertaken and more mines were needed for the defence of the coast. In fact, Rommel put in an extraordinary request for 50-100 million mines when only 1.7 million were available.[38] In the end, he succeeded in laying more than 4 million mines. Over 9000 fortified positions were completed by June 1944. But Rommel did not just restrict himself to land-based obstacles (**68**). On the beaches and beneath the waves at high tide were steel girders crossed over each other which became known as 'hedgehogs', poles with mines attached to them, known as 'Rommel's Asparagus', and an array of other mined obstacles.

The intention of throwing the Allies back into the sea did not work. When it came, the invasion was a success, although bought at high cost on some of the beaches of Normandy. It was not just the weakness of the Atlantic Wall at that point which contributed to the success. Hitler's insistence on retaining a great degree of command over the ten Panzer Divisions stationed in the west had something to do with it. Early release of some of these units by the Führer might well have shifted some of the balance back into the Germans' favour. But Hitler was asleep when the moment came and could not be woken. Permission for the release of the Panzers lay with him and him alone. The subsequent fighting in Normandy was hard and the countryside lent itself to the defenders more than it did to the attackers. In chapter 4 we look in detail at one of the battles in the Normandy campaign that British forces were involved with, that of the taking of Mont Pinçon, to illustrate this point.

4 Using the landscape

> I order that the map of Germany, which has been made at the Depot de la Guerre, be sent back. It is so bad that I cannot use it. I would rather have the first map captured in a library. This mixture of good and bad portions is fatal – worse than if all the parts were bad – for it serves only to jeopardise important operations. I know of nothing more dangerous . . .
> Napoleon to General Clarke, 19 December 1809

During certain periods of history, military commanders have displayed a preference for selecting battlefields that allow them to dispose their troops like miniature figures in a complex board game, making move and countermove according to foreordained rules, overseeing the action from some lofty viewpoint with an almost godlike detachment. War rooms are equipped with maps over which markers are pushed so that distant commanders can follow the progress of play. Even military historians tend to illustrate campaigns with plans on which the blocks of the forces are represented like counters moving across a two-dimensional board. If warfare is an art, however, rather than a game, it must be seen three- or even four-dimensionally. Commanders must come to terms with a field of action in which the forces of nature also play their parts.

The natural world presents many pitfalls, problems, challenges and surprises for the unwary general. He must take into account the geology and topography of the area of campaign, its drainage patterns, settlement and land use forms, its potential for communications and supply, its flora and fauna, and the most unpredictable aspect of all – the weather. All these factors have important implications for the kind of troops and equipment he can deploy, their rate of movement in advance or retreat, their ability to utilise concealment or their visibility, their ability to forage, the problems caused by civilians, the opportunities for resting and re-supply, and the maintenance of morale. It is easy, too, to get lost. The featureless steppe had the Germans and their allies struggling to pinpoint their location during the Second World War (**69**).

History is full of commanders who got these calculations right – and at least an equal number who got them wrong. Although the equation should be evenly balanced between winners and losers, it is the case that there are many instances where both sides have blundered to such an extent that victory was either extremely hollow or the result of blind luck. The Battle of Adrianople in AD 378, for example, was won by a timely but unplanned arrival of a large Gothic cavalry force which had been out foraging. The unit crashed into the Roman Emperor's left flank and won the day. Emperor Valens died of his wounds shortly after the battle.

Even those commanders who made the study of the military art their prime business got it wrong at times – after all, Napoleon Bonaparte stressed the importance of not overextending lines of communication and supply in his *Maxims*, but he still marched to Moscow.

69 *Soldiers marching astride the road in the featureless steppe. Dating from around 1942, this photograph shows German Allies, probably Hungarians.* Photograph: Julie Wileman's collection

The siting of defences obviously also depends largely on natural elements as well as demographic and political patterns. In simple terms, defences rely on features such as rivers and marshes, or cliffs and hills to augment and strengthen their man-made elements, and so the choice of site can be determined by geology, topography and drainage in a region. But of course, defences are there to defend other things beyond themselves: towns and villages, farmland and industries, mineral and other natural resources, and routes of trade, control and administration. And all these owe their location to natural forces. Designers of fortifications therefore sometimes have to compromise between ideal sites and practical effectiveness, and it is in this sphere that some of the greatest feats of ingenuity have been realised. This may seem like stating the obvious, but it has been the case on many occasions that military planners have failed to properly assess the balance between the demands of military science and those of practicability and usefulness. The abandonment of Fort Phil Kearny in the American West, outlined in chapter 2, was an example of a base too far into enemy territory. A castle on a high peak may be in a mightily strong defensive location, but if it is so remote that it cannot offer the possibility of counter-attack against an invader, it can simply be bypassed and immediately rendered redundant.

To be truly effective, a strong defensive point really needs to be part of an integrated system, as we discussed in chapter 3. It requires a system of communications, backup and mutual potential for attack as well as defence. An effective defence not only keeps the enemy out in a passive manner, it lets defenders out to undertake aggressive active manoeuvres.

The concepts of strategy and tactics are variously implicated in an investigation of the effects of landscape on warfare. Strategy can be defined, as Liddel-Hart stated, as 'distributing and applying military means to fulfil policy'. In the modern world, these sorts of decisions are undertaken at Chief-of-Staff level.[1] Tactics, on the other hand, are thought to operate on two levels: Grand Tactics and Minor Tactics. The former involves the selection of intermediate objectives and the allocation of forces required to achieve it, while the latter is focused upon the methods of fighting and manoeuvre.[2]

Essential to the prosecution of a successful campaign is the acquisition of a good map of the territory. On 19 December 1809 an angry Napoleon wrote to General Clarke ordering that the map of Germany which he had received be sent back, because it was so bad that he could not use it. The map's mixture of good and bad representations was perceived by Napoleon as being worse than if they were all bad, and consequently very dangerous. He was not understating the case. Several campaigns have demonstrated the appalling losses that can be caused when forces lose their way in alien territory. Full and proper information about terrain can enable a good general to snatch victory against overwhelming odds, as further examples illustrate.

Among the most important features that can affect campaigns are those that affect movement: slopes, broken ground, the softness or hardness of the soil to support the movement of guns, wagons and tanks, crossing points of rivers or passes through mountains, and obstacles such as built-up areas, forests and marshes. The problems of supply are also paramount – will the country sustain the troops as they pass through it or must supplies be brought in, and if so from where and by which route? In farmland or densely populated areas, troops can be billetted with the local population and derive much of their sustenance by the 'liberation' or 'capture' of local provisions, unless the defenders employ a scorched earth policy. This is a relatively rare occurrence; populations rarely have the opportunity to move wholesale out of the way of a military campaign, and are reluctant to risk their own supplies and survival by destroying them. In unpopulated, undeveloped landscapes, the available food and fodder can be very hard to come by. A large proportion of an army on the move must be constantly employed in either hunting and foraging, or guarding supply trains. Supply and logistics in modern armies is just as vital as ever. One soldier in the modern British army will require at least 18 other people acting in a support role to keep him or her in the field.[3] The more sophisticated an army is, the longer its tail becomes.

Methods of fighting are also dictated by the landscape; tactics in broken, mountainous or forested country must of necessity be very different from those adopted in open terrain. Historically, large unwieldy armies in the pre-industrial era, whose main strength was in close formation infantry fighting, fared particularly badly in difficult or rough terrain. There are a few successes, however, but they are the exceptions which prove the point. For example, for his Welsh campaigns of 1062, Harold Godwinson, then Earl of Wessex, ordered his housecarles (heavy infantrymen) to remove their chainmail in favour of lighter boiled leather armour, thus giving them a greater mobility and flexibility in the landscape (**colour plate 23**). The opportunities for guerrilla warfare are clearly much higher in such landscapes; concealment and ambush are the strategies of choice for defence in the wilderness or jungle. Before the era of satellite communications, the passing of orders and the receiving of reconnaissance reports were severely compromised in difficult terrain.

70 *A group of refugees head toward a burning barn in a familiar snowbound scene from the Russian front during the Second World War.* Photograph: Julie Wileman's collection

No army can be in constant motion; men and beasts need rest, re-supply, and often in difficult country, periods of consolidation and reorganisation. Therefore, strong points, at least temporary ones, must be created in defensible places where there is water, fuel and shelter. The sick and wounded must be tended somewhere or shipped back; there has to be somewhere to hold and process prisoners of war, to set up distribution points and to allow scouts or spies to rendezvous with their leaders. The Roman army had this down to a fine art, with their ability to create marching camps each night as they moved through hostile lands. Other armies have been less successful. Cold, tired, hungry troops are unreliable; the level of desertion rises and the effectiveness of the forces as fighting units is severely compromised.

Local knowledge of terrain can be a powerful ally. Some of the most heroic campaigns and actions in history have been carried out by small bands of often poorly equipped partisan fighters against vastly greater numbers of well-supplied invaders, and their successes, even if sometimes eventually futile, have relied on their superior use of the landscapes of their home territories. From the ranks of such troops, legends are born – Robin Hood in Sherwood, or Hereward the Wake, for example. But many factual examples can also be cited – the Breton resistance fighters in the Second World War, Geronimo and the other Apache leaders, and the Vietcong among many others. Canny generals have learned to use local scouts and tribes, exploiting rivalries and greed, to overcome this disadvantage. The French armies fighting the British in Canada employed the Huron Indians as spies and as shock troops; Wellington made good use of Spanish irregular bands in the Peninsula War. The British army today continues this tradition with the recruitment of Gurkha troops from Nepal, their role often being specifically related to fighting in specialised terrain.

The role of climate and weather should also not be underestimated, both for campaigns and as important factors in individual battles. The Russians famously relied for defence on 'General Winter', an important ally against Napoleon and possibly a vital component in their resistance to Hitler's forces in 1941 (**70**). In earlier wars, fairly strict 'campaign seasons' had to be observed in order for warfare to progress at all; once winter set in, tacit truces had to be observed. Rainstorms and blizzards have proved to be decisive factors in a number of important actions. One last example comes from the summer and not the winter, showing that good weather could have an adverse effect on a defending force. In the ninth century AD, the Vikings in Ireland had set themselves up an island camp at Dunrally at the confluence of the river Barrow and Glasham (its tributary), south of Dublin. The camp was comparable with those which the Vikings built in England at Benfleet, Shoebury, Mersea Island, Colchester and Reading. Ordinarily, it would have been almost impossible to storm this fortification with the resources available to local Irish leaders at the time, but in the long hot summer of 862 the waters and marshes around the island dried up so that by early September the kings of Ossory and Laois were able to attack overland and defeat the defenders.

The landscape of man

The placement of settlements in the landscape, the varying patterns of rural and urban economies, and the reaction of populations to warfare can be vital to the geography of war in many ways. Non-combatants are as much a factor as armies, formal or informal. The places where they live and the produce of their labour require protection, for wholly pragmatic reasons as well as any higher ethical considerations. Civilian populations represent the source of wealth, by their labour and skills, that sustain a community and by extension that community's ability to mobilise and support an army to defend it. The ability to protect civilians underlies the strength and legitimacy of rulers. Civilian populations also represent the source of manpower for future armies and for reconstruction after hostilities have ceased. The protection of their lives, homes and occupations must be accompanied, too, by the support of their morale and loyalty, to avoid their disaffection or the chance that they might succour the enemy's forces.

For an assailant, civilian populations represent a source of plunder; this may take the form of their lands, their portable wealth or even their life values as slaves. In the Anglo-Scottish border wars of the later medieval period, the Scottish soldiers received no pay – they were expected to reward themselves by raiding the houses and farms of the English along the border. It was during this period that many English resorted to the building of stone tower-houses and bastles for protection.

As early as AD 857, Charles the Bold tried to put into place rules for the protection of church property and members of religious orders, widows, orphans, and the poor during time of war. In subsequent centuries the Pax Dei (Peace of God) and Treuga Dei (Truce of God) movements continued attempts to impose rules for the conduct of hostilities to protect non-combatants. Ideas about formal declaration of wars, illegitimacy of private feuds and the distinction between 'spoils of war' and indiscriminate plunder were introduced and discussed. Several factors lay behind these debates. Depredations against Church property created a particular incentive for the Christian theorists, but less cynically there was a real concern for the plight of peasants, facing the brutality of the soldiery, destruction of their homes and crops, and then frequent devastating famines as a further result.

Despite this, civilian populations have continued to be targetted during war. From the medieval period,

> . . . as wars were gradually transformed into conflicts between whole and increasingly self-conscious communities, so it became increasingly difficult to argue that even the seemingly innocent farmer who tilled the land to grow cereal products, or bred cattle or sheep, should be immune from war. Some of his produce could be used to feed armies . . . other parts of the same produce [were] a possible source of taxation . . . out of which armies could be paid.[4]

In other words, his very productivity made the peasant culpable and therefore a legitimate target.

Shepherds with their flocks, herdsmen with their cattle – these were easy targets for raiders. Small villages could do little to prevent the destruction of their homes and harvests. Allmand notes that 'many recent studies have shown how large estates in normally rich agricultural areas contracted in time of war, the uncertainty regarding the future deferring work on outlying land which, before long, became unproductive wasteland'.[5] These effects could spread well beyond the immediate village or estate attacked, the local disruption eventually affecting the economies of much larger territories through fear, interruption of trade and markets, and famines.

In the 1300s, England was deliberately launching raids against the French. Armies, some as large as 10,000 men, rampaged across northern France. They often avoided defended centres – not only were these harder to attack, but attempts to do so would slow down movement, increasing the likelihood of coming into contact with the French troops. The English raids concentrated on seizing all the plunder they could carry away and destroying all that they could not.

These raids undermined the morale of the French populations, created insecurity and widespread fear, destroyed the regional agricultural economy (and by extension other forms of production) and severely damaged the credibility of the French crown. They also paid for themselves in booty.

A reaction was to concentrate, in the mid-fourteenth century, on the fortification of towns as refuges for peasants from the surrounding 'plat pays' into which they could bring not only themselves but as much of their produce as possible when danger threatened. Ironically, by the fifteenth century the English strategy had changed. Raiding was replaced by a policy of straightforward conquest which necessitated the subjugation of fortified centres, so the refuges of the previous century now became the foci of a new type of warfare, this time involving gunpowder artillery and sieges. At the siege of Rouen, between July 1418 and January 1419, thousands of fleeing peasants were trapped within the strong fortifications of the city by an English army. By midwinter, the old and the sick were expelled from the city to die in its surrounding ditches in a desperate attempt to conserve rations to maintain the garrison and the rest of the populace.

Sir John Fastolf regarded sieges as too expensive of men, time and money. In 1435, his advice to the king was to return to the policy of raids, '. . . brenning and distruynge alle the lande as thei pas, bothe hous, corne, veignes, and alle bestaile that may not be dryven, to be distroiede.' Fastolf claimed legitimacy for this policy on the grounds that French commoners had been given a chance to stay out of the fighting (i.e. by ceding their cities and leaving the war to the royal armies) and had failed to take this opportunity. Therefore, they forfeited any right to neutrality. Despite the many calls for clemency, citing the lack of effective control and brute savagery of the soldiers, and their motives of selfish greed rather than any moral act on behalf of king, church or country, civilians had become increasingly targetted as part of deliberate strategy.

The density of population also has a bearing on the development of warfare against civilians. In regions where wealth is concentrated in urbanised societies, the form of warfare most likely to develop is that of blockades and sieges – a relatively static, even rather formalised mode of conflict. By contrast, in more rural societies which lack many defended urban centres and whose valuables are distributed more widely in the landscape, warfare tends to be more fluid, raiding is more common (and indeed may be essential to the circulation of wealth) and battles are more frequently risked. This distinction is marked in the early medieval period in Europe between, on the whole, northern warriors such as the Vikings, and southern, Mediterranean campaigns.

The longer-term aims of aggressors have important connotations for the fates of civilians and their centres of settlement and production. For an invader determined not only to assault a territory but also to hold it, destruction of the population and means of production could be ill-advised. There might be far more value in maintaining agriculture and industry and utilising a cowed or enslaved population who could continue to work for the benefit of their conquerors. Both the Romans and the Normans knew this, and in theory at least embraced legal or moral codes that were designed to protect non-combatants once victory had been achieved.

If the aim of aggression is to gain plunder as part of what has been called 'pillage economies', then it also makes sense not to destroy everything or to so terrify civilians that they pack up and move out. If that happens, they cannot be raided again – the sources of plunder disappear. Better by far to intimidate, take what is offered or unguarded, and leave the infrastructure in place. This approach was typical of the Apaches, who would raid line cabins or outlying corrals, or attack isolated travellers and herdsmen, avoiding the larger villages and haciendas. Over several hundred years, the Spanish and Mexican ranch owners learned that by leaving a few unguarded horses or supplies in a distant location from time to time, they protected themselves against much more destructive raids.

If, however, the aggressor intends total subjugation of a territory, for political or religious reasons, then destruction of the means of support of the civilian population in a war of terror makes good sense (pragmatically – we are not discussing the moral or ethical parameters of war here). The English raids against the French in the fourteenth century had the political aim of bringing down the French state. 'Ethnic cleansing' is the terrible euphemism for wars of absolute destruction of a group of people for political and/or religious reasons – the Hutus against the Tutsis, the Whites against the Indian tribes of the Americas, the Serbs against the Moslems of Bosnia and Kosovo. It is clear that these types of campaigns also have an economic base, despite the avowed motivations of politicians. Economic greed and jealousy underlie many such atrocities. The aggressors can afford to destroy the means of production or subsistence either because the land holds something else that interests them (gold in the Sioux lands of the Black Hills of Dakota, for instance), or because they intend to repopulate the area with their own citizens, using wealth seized as plunder to rebuild the infrastructure to their own requirements.

So far, we have looked at some of the ways in which settlements and populations may influence the conduct of war on a grand scale, at the level of larger strategy. The effect on tactics and the methodology of warfare is no less significant. Man-made obstacles in the countryside may have great bearing on the conduct of hostilities – isolated buildings quickly become foci for major parts of the action (such as the struggle for possession of Hougoumont farm during the battle of Waterloo). Sunken tracks, field walls and hedgerows offer cover and opportunities for ambush in otherwise open-field engagements – perhaps one of the most famous examples of this being during the battle of Waterloo when Maitland's Guards Division lay unseen in a field of standing wheat until Napoleon committed his final reserve, the columns of the Imperial Guard, into the fray. The hidden troops were kept concealed until the columns were no more than 40 yards away when at the order they rose and poured point-blank fire into the heads of the columns, halting not only the march, but Napoleon's career and ambitions.

The modern military mind thinks of war in terms not of open fields or vast territories but of individual targets – specific places in or features of the landscape that must be controlled, or to which the enemy must be denied access. Some of these features are common to older conflicts (crossing points have been vital from Lars Porsenna to Montgomery at Arnhem) as have passes and communication routes; centres of population and production not only have tactical importance, they also have propaganda uses, particularly in the modern era. It was for the propaganda and political advantages that de Gaulle insisted on the early liberation of Paris. Tactically it was a less than persuasive primary target, and in fact the delay and re-disposition of troops to allow him to achieve his aim is considered by some commentators to have been very costly in both military and civilian lives in other parts of the European theatre of war, at the time and later.

Urban societies tend to concentrate on urban targets. In wars in areas of dispersed or small-scale settlement, even modern armies frequently find themselves at a disadvantage, and even superpowers can lose such wars – the lesson of Vietnam is obvious.

Specialised forces are required to cope with such wars: local armed scouts, Gurkhas, Chindits. Wellington made excellent use of Portuguese and Spanish irregulars and partisans during the Peninsula War, especially in the mountains, for purposes such as intelligence gathering, sabotage and raids to reduce the morale of the French. It was these partisans who helped carry out the 'scorched earth' actions that denied sustenance to Massena's troops even as the British were retreating towards the prepared lines of Torres Vedras in 1810–11. A German officer, August Schaumann, left vivid descriptions of this retreat, among other actions. The Portuguese peasants elected to join the retreat rather than face the French among their devastated fields, creating major problems for the movement of troops. Routes became blocked with livestock and vehicles. There was utter confusion as monks and nuns fleeing their convents, prisoners released from gaols, peasants and animals, mule rains and gun carriages and all manner of carts and wagons streamed down the same constricted roads littered with broken furniture, dead horses and abandoned goods.

> At one moment, an old grandmother, riding a donkey, supported by two old women, could be seen passing through the throng, and a little later she was knocked down by a mule bearing a load of camp kettles, and, amid piteous cries, trampled under foot. Ladies, who, according to the custom of the country, had perhaps never left their homes except to go to Mass, could be seen walking along, hand in hand, three in a row, wearing silk shoes.[6]

The streets of Leira became almost impassable with the detritus of the refugees – spilt coffee, sugar, chocolate, corn and flour, rags and broken crockery – and among all this British troops joined local criminals in looting the abandoned houses. The panicked movement of refugees caused similar problems of blocked roads for the retreating British troops in 1940 as fleeing Belgian civilians obstructed the routes towards the coast and Dunkirk. Schaumann also gives us a vivid picture of the Portuguese countryside once the people had fled.

> Everything was converted into a wilderness, in which soldiers, vultures, swarms of birds and pigeons grown wild, dogs without masters, wolves and foxes, lived their lives undisturbed. 50,000 of the inhabitants had fled.[7]

The scorched earth policy did indeed lead the French to suffer horribly, but so did the peasants who had remained. These people, already desperately poor, had not been able to bring themselves to destroy everything – they hid supplies in walls and roofs, in caves and cellars. The French resorted to torture and murder to find these caches. The town of Pyrnes, entered by the British on 7 March 1811, was described by a infantry soldier.

> Young women were lying in their houses brutally violated, the streets were strewed with broken furniture, intermixed with putrid carcasses of murdered peasants, mules and donkeys, and every description of filth, that

> filled the air with pestilential nausea. The few starved men inhabitants who were stalking amid the wreck of their friends and property, looked like so many skeletons who had been permitted to leave their graves for the purpose of taking vengeance.[8]

The cruelty of the French backfired, as it stiffened the resolve of the Portuguese and Spanish guerrilla bands and gave the British invaluable advantages during much of the rest of the campaign. A similar error was made by the Germans in 1914.

> Not surprisingly, after the main Belgian military resistance had crumbled, there were still some people who weren't aware that it had crumbled, who carried on fighting, and there were also misunderstandings, confusion and a sense of paranoia on the part of the German troops which led them to clearly enormous overreaction when they encountered problems. We know that in those days in August and into September 1914, when the Germans were moving most rapidly through Belgium, thousands of Belgian civilians were shot in response often to imaginary attacks on German troops. This notion that there was a kind of sinister guerrilla army which you had to root out before you lost men to sniper fire was deeply embedded in the historical memory of the German Army, and this must explain why so many casualties are inflicted on the civilian population . . . However it happened these thousands of civilian deaths had massive political consequences for the war as a whole. Nothing did more to mobilise British and later American opinion against the Germans.[9]

Despite the atrocities against the Portuguese, by February 1811 the French were dying at the rate of 500 a week and on 4 March Massena was forced to begin his retreat. Atrocities against civilians were not, however, confined to the French during the Peninsula campaign. During the 7-9 April 1812, after the city of Badajoz had fallen to Wellington, the British troops ran amok.

> The infuriated soldiery resembled rather a pack of hell-hounds vomited up from the infernal regions for the extirpation of mankind than what they were twelve short hours previously – a well-organised, brave, disciplined and obedient British army, and burning only with impatience for what is called glory[10]

reported a captain at the time. The two-day orgy of drunkenness, riot, arson, looting, rapine and murder was only brought under control after the men had raved themselves into exhaustion. The violence was excused by some participants on the grounds that the inhabitants of the city were all French sympathisers. Despite feeling sickened by what had taken place, some officers felt that the sacking was in part a necessary catharsis for the soldiers, and noted that once sated they were much more biddable. The civilians had provided a mechanism for the release of the excess

71a-e *(continued overleaf) Photographs taken by a Luftwaffe Officer who seems to have travelled widely on many fronts including Greece, France and Russia. These show warfare in the urban environment. It is easy to see how tank crews were nervous with their limited fields of vision in surroundings where snipers could conceal themselves. The surviving chimney stacks give a forest-like appearance.* Photographs: Julie Wileman's collection

aggression of the troops, allowing their commanders to regain control of the beast they had unleashed in the attack.

Fighting inside cities is generally reckoned to be particularly difficult and hazardous. Modern wars had needed to devise increasingly sophisticated strategies for dealing with conflict in the urban landscape. Visibility is restricted by buildings, routes are often narrow and easily blocked, every window can conceal a sniper and booby traps are easily put in place (**71a-e**). Where defended by partisans who know every alley, cellar and rooftop, infiltration by enemy troops is a lengthy and expensive process.

In some ways, the kind of tactics required for urban warfare are similar to those demanded in jungle or deep forest landscapes, but are further complicated by the presence of non-combatants. Targets must be chosen with extra care; they have to be specific and justified. The modern commander is always aware of the presence of the mass media and the consequences of the use of their material for propaganda both by his enemies and by his own political masters and their opponents at home. For him, war can be a far more complex jungle than for his predecessors. The accidental American bombing of the Chinese embassy in Belgrade on 8 May 1999 became an international scandal of possibly even greater proportions than the atrocities of the Serbs. The Duke of Wellington's chances of remaining in command at Badajoz would probably have been slight had the war been covered by modern media techniques.

Campaigns in the landscape

There can hardly have been a land campaign in all of human history where the nature of terrain was not an important factor in the minds of those organising the opposing forces. Selected below are some accounts of those campaigns and battles in which landscape features and the way in which they were used or neglected by commanders proved to be a decisive factor in the outcome of the campaign. The importance of intelligence, deployment, visibility, rough and difficult ground, weather and the use of ambush is mainly what concerns us here. Whilst some of these encounters are well known others are less so, yet all have been placed here to bring one or more aspects of the usage of the landscape to the fore.

Local terrain intelligence – the Apache Wars

A fierce and independent people, the Apaches moved into territories in the south-west United States at some time between AD 1000 and 1400. They are first recorded by Spanish settlers as early as 1540, and over the following centuries established a reputation as fearless raiders. The word 'apache' means 'enemy' in the Zuni language, and 'fighting men' in Yuma – the Apaches adopted the name with pride. In fact, they were made up of a number of different sub-tribes: the Kiowa, Lipan, Jicarilla, Mescalero, Western Apache (Coyotero) and Chiricahua, each divided into several bands. Their range extended from Texas to south-eastern Arizona and deep into the Mexican states of Chihuahua and Sonora – the land known as Apacheria.

Long a thorn in the side of the Spanish and Mexicans, during the nineteenth century the Apaches began to clash with the settlers and miners opening up the western United States. It was clashes with miners in 1861 that precipitated the Apache wars; a group of prospectors was asked by a great leader, Mangas Colorado, to leave his lands. They refused, tied him up and whipped the 70-year-old chief. From that time Mangas and his son-in-law, Cochise, began a campaign to drive the whites from their territory. Mangas and Cochise were Chiricahuas, among the most implacable fighters of their nation. On 15 July 1862 they deployed 500 warriors along the rocky heights above the pass and spring at Apache Pass to intercept a column of volunteer soldiers under Colonel James Carleton (the California Volunteers) who had been ordered into the area to protect the overland stage route. The Apaches had designed a superb ambush, but had reckoned without the superior technology of their enemies. Their attack broke up when the Americans brought up two wagon-mounted howitzers and opened fire. The Apaches withdrew, losing 63 warriors.

The Americans now began a programme of genocide aimed at the Apaches, but the tribesmen had learned a valuable lesson. Never again did they attempt a full-scale confrontation. Instead, they relied on their knowledge of their harsh and mountainous home and their own extraordinary endurance and fighting skills to carry on a guerrilla war that was to continue until 1886.

> We were essentially a mountain people, moving from one chain to another, following the ridges as best we could. If there were no mountains we took cover in arroyos, but survival on the desert and plains was much more difficult. I think we may have invented trench warfare, and we infinitely preferred a mountain at our backs. I doubt that any people ever excelled us as mountain climbers. Scaling walls was taken for granted. When closely pursued we killed our horses and scaled cliffs no enemy could climb. Men tied ropes to women and children and lifted them from ledge to ledge until they could take cover or escape. If the women and children could go ahead the warriors picked off the scouts, who always preceded the cavalry. We moved at night only when forced to do so and never fought in the darkness unless attacked. There was a belief that he who kills at night must walk in darkness through the Place of the Dead. I cannot say that all Apaches believed this, but many did.[11]

Cochise died in 1874, but other Apache leaders continued the war in defence of their land and freedom. Appalling atrocities were committed by all sides (American, Mexican and Apache). Eventually various bands of Mescaleros, Chiricahua and other groups began to be brought into reservations. However, a combination of mismanagement, graft and racial hatred led to a number of incidents resulting in Apaches breaking out and returning to their mountains. The reservations were badly sited and malarial; food supplies were stolen by venal agents; there were insufficient blankets or fuel to keep the people warm; warring tribes were forced on to the same reservations; smallpox and TB began to ravage the previously unexposed tribespeople.

The last great leader of the Chiricahua and Ojo Calientes people was called Goyathlay by his own people, Geronimo by the Mexicans and Americans. A Chiricahua, he was not one of the great chiefs, but to him goes the honour of the final great resistance of his people.

In May 1885 Geronimo and Naiche, son of Cochise, fled from the Turkey Creek reservation into the Sierra Madre. His band consisted of about 35-7 warriors and 80 women and children. The United States and Mexican armies both went after him. General Crook committed 80 companies of infantry and cavalry into the pursuit – some 3000 men. Early in 1886 Crook's scouts caught up with Geronimo and persuaded him to go back to the reservation. However, on the way back, Geronimo and part of his band broke out again. General Crook found himself in bad odour with his commander, General Philip Sheridan, and he resigned his post. Sheridan appointed General Nelson Miles in his place.

Miles set up 30 heliograph stations in south-eastern Arizona, and put some 5000 troops into the field. He offered a bounty of $70,000 to the scouts for the capture of

72 *Cañon de los Embudos, March 1886. Geronimo and General Cook meet for a peace conference*

Geronimo and Captain Henry Lawson was sent into Sonora in advance of prepared lines on the American side of the border. His job was to flush Geronimo out, but despite travelling up to 2000 miles through the unforgiving Sonoran mountains, losing most of his horses in the first week of campaign, and 40lb of his own weight, Lawson only managed to catch up with Geronimo's band once, on 14 July – the Apaches escaped unscathed.

Opposed to these troops and thousands of Mexican soldiers was Geronimo's band of around 18 women and children and 18 or 19 warriors, of whom at least two (Kanseah and Chapo) were little more than children, and one (Lozen) was a woman.

In March 1886 two scouts reached Geronimo at a stronghold on a flat-topped mountain in a bend of the Bavispe River accessible only by a gruelling half-day climb up a zigzag trail. He told them, 'This is my home. Here I stay. Kill me if you wish, for every living thing has to die sometime. How can a man meet death better than in fighting for his own?'

It was not until 3 or 4 September that Geronimo finally brought his band into voluntary surrender at Skeleton Canyon, Arizona. The great warrior was then about 57 years old, and his band consisted at the end of about 37 people, including 14 women and children. His surrender was forced by the concern of his warriors for the families they had left behind on the reservations. To 'teach them all a lesson' the Chiricahua, whether they had stayed peacefully on the reservation or not, and even including the scouts who had worked for the US Army, were shipped to imprisonment in Florida. A little later, 112 children were forcibly removed to a school in Pennsylvania where they were to be 'civilised'. Within 3 years, 30 of the children had died, and a further 12 were sent back to their families severely ill. One of these was the young warrior Chapo, who had fought to the end with Geronimo and was now to die of TB in Florida.

Geronimo died in captivity in 1909, a tired and broken old man. But for 6 months he and 20 or so warriors, encumbered with women and children, had held one third of America's standing army at bay and were not beaten.

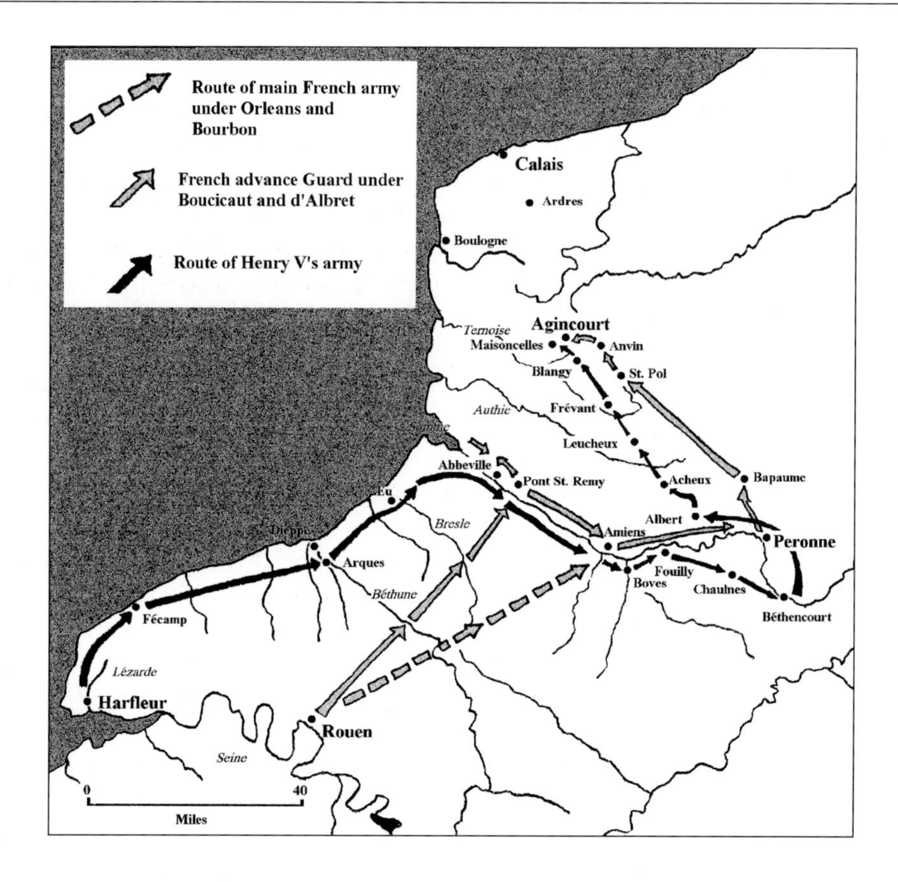

73 Map of Henry V's 1415 campaign in France showing the English march and its attendant French Shadowing operation

Terrain and deployment – the Agincourt Campaign, 1415

The Agincourt campaign provides a clear example of the dangers of campaigning in a hostile landscape with a small force. What happened to Henry V in 1415 clearly taught him a lesson. He was later able to employ tactics developed from the siege of Harfleur and learn from his long and dangerous march to Calais. He subsequently changed his strategy in northern France in 1417 to one of besieging and taking strongholds and dominating territory from them, the taking of Rouen in 1419 perhaps being the crowning example.

The battle itself, fought on 25 October, marked the turning point of English fortune in a wretched campaign. The original campaign plan had been to march to Paris after securing a coastal port and then to link up with English held territory in Bordeaux. By the day of embarkment 1500 vessels had been assembled in the Solent. It is estimated that because of the importance in medieval warfare of the horse as both a beast of burden and a fighting animal, and the fact that a knight was unlikely to go on such a campaign with less than his allotted six horses, the number of horses transported across the channel for Henry's expedition was around 25,000.[12]

The invasion force landed off the coast of Harfleur. If taken, it would serve to keep lines of supply and communication open with the Cinque ports of England and it was also within campaigning distance from Paris. Two and a half miles of walls surrounded the town, punctuated by 26 towers, and there were three gates (Leure, Montvilliers and Rouen) each with a drawbridge across the moat and barbicans, earthworks and counter approaches. As well as these human-built defences, the town was naturally protected by the rivers Seine, Lézarde and some marshes to the south. There was also a large and deliberately flooded area to the north.

Early in the morning of 14 August the English launched their invasion in a fleet of small craft, landing at a shingle beach where the port of Le Havre now stands. Henry pitched his camp to the north-west of the town on high ground and began besieging Harfleur in earnest on 18 August. The Duke of Clarence was sent to blockade the eastern side of the town, a task made difficult by the dammed streams and flooded roads. His roundabout journey took him into the path of a supply train from Rouen on its way to Harfleur. Clarence captured the supply wagons and enriched the English army with their plentiful contents of arms. He took up a position to the east of the town, but the Sire de Gaucourt had slipped into Harfleur with a further 300 men-at-arms on the orders of the French King Charles VI, assuming control from the Sire d'Estouteville. With the English king and the Earl of Suffolk surrounding the west side of the town, and a flooded valley to the north over which small boats communicated to the Duke of Clarence on the east, the scene was set for a protracted siege which was to cost the English heavily in time and in men.

Henry attempted to undermine the walls of the town by digging mines towards and beneath them. This was effectively nullified by accurate French counter-mining operations. Henry chose instead to deploy his heavy guns and other artillery equipment, risking the attention of the garrison's missile troops. The French proved very active enemies and frequently sallied from the gates capturing men or destroying equipment. Henry's guns, one as long as 12ft with a 2ft calibre capable of firing a 500lb stone, were set-up with accompanying field defences of timber screens. A week of bombardment followed, with the guns proving more effective than the traditional mangonels and trebuchets.

Henry's army was tiring of its work. The walls were being repaired at a notable rate and only in places, mainly at the south-west gate, were they seriously in danger of being breached. Disease too, in the form of dysentery, began now to take its toll, accounting for as many as one in five men in the English army. The French sallies became increasingly desperate, particularly out of the south-west Leure gate, whose outer barbican was all but smashed to pieces. The last French sortie occurred on 17 September and resulted in the loss of the Leure gate barbican. This meant that the English could draw their siege equipment up to a devastatingly close range. The town was about to fall. The bombardment continued again after Gaucourt's initial refusal to surrender. This time it was irresistible. Some protracted negotiation followed, with the French requiring that the terms for a surrender should be that they could at least send a detachment to Vernon to inform the Dauphin of the town's demise. The town would surrender on Sunday 22 September, sparing itself a sacking. Disease and the attrition of siege warfare had cost the English up to 2000 casualties they could ill afford. Among those who had to return home to Southampton was the Duke of Clarence.

During the last weeks of the siege at Harfleur, Charles VI had raised the Oriflamme banner at St Denis in early September signalling an intent to meet the English in the cause of national defence. Charles d'Albret, the Constable of France, was at Rouen trying to raise a force and Jean Boucicaut, the Marshal of France, was putting together a force at Honfleur on the other side of the Seine estuary from Harfleur. Henry's original campaign plan of pushing on to Rouen and then Paris and finally linking up with English Bordeaux now had to be re-thought. His force, cut to a mere 7000 troops, none of whom were in the peak of health, was not prepared for an extended march. Besides, Harfleur would need a sizeable garrison of 1000-1500 troops if it were to be held for any length of time.

Henry gambled on a quick march to link up with English Calais (**73**). The nearest French troops under d'Albret at Rouen would surely not catch him in time. Boucicaut at Honfleur and the Dauphin at Vernon could also be outpaced and would surely not fight until all parts of the force were combined against the English in the field. The problem for Henry was that the terrain over which he must march was traversed by no less than 10 rivers. The most formidable obstacle was the river Somme which Henry wished to cross at the ford at Blanche-Taque five miles downstream from Abbeville, where Edward III had crossed in the early years of the Hundred Years War. The garrison commander at Calais, Sir William Bardolf, had been ordered to send a force south to divert any French forces in the district. He headed towards the Somme with 300 men. Henry set out for Calais from Harfleur around 7 October. He started by taking a coastal route through the town of Fécamp and then on to Arques, where he arrived on 11 October. Some opposition was encountered there during the crossing operation at the bridge over the Béthune, and the Castellan at Arques even fired a shot at the English force. After the threat of a wholesale sacking, the Castellan turned into a provider, giving the English bread and wine. The next river crossing also proved difficult. The English arrived at the river Bresle, just south of Eu, to be met with gunfire and a determined mounted sortie from the town, which it had to fight off with losses. Consequently, the town was threatened in the same way that Arques had been and the result was the same – more supplies.

Just a few miles from the Somme, however, the capture of a French prisoner brought unexpected news. The ford had been prepared by the French with stakes and beyond it was waiting a force under Boucicaut of 6000 men. Henry decided to turn east along the banks of the Somme until a crossing point could be found. He had been outguessed and outpaced by Boucicaut. Meanwhile the size of the main French force was becoming larger by the minute. As well as up to 15,000 men-at-arms under the Dukes of Orléans, Alençon, Bar and Brittany, there were up to 20,000 lesser armed peasants and crossbowmen. Henry would be outnumbered if these armies met, and that is what the French Council of War, against d'Albret's wishes, decided they should do. The French plan was that Boucicaut and d'Albret's advance guard should deny the English their preferred crossing place at the ford near Abbeville, forcing them to travel upstream looking for another one. The English would be driven straight to the main body of the French forces with which Boucicaut and d'Albret would meet at the gathering point at Péronne. The operation seemed to work well. The English tried, but were denied suitable crossing places at towns along the way upstream and were consequently forced deeper into enemy territory. The French had also denied the English an opportunity for foraging by abandoning farmsteads in Picardy and removing from them all stock and food produce.

When the English reached Corbie, a group of straggling archers were set-upon by a small detachment of French knights who had crossed the bridge, resulting in some English casualties, but most importantly one or two French prisoners were taken. These prisoners had told Henry of the contempt in which his archers were held by the French knighthood. In fact, they scarcely spoke to their own cross-bowmen. The knights intended to ride down every English archer before they had even got their arrows in their bows.

Henry made preparations. Each archer must cut himself a stake sharpened at both ends to be placed into the ground at an angle in front of their ranks when battle came. This would form an anti-cavalry obstacle behind which the archers could shoot. The archers did this, but were well aware that the stakes which they now had to carry had become an additional burden. A change in course of the English army can be traced from the Corbie incident. Henry, probably acting on information from his captives, did not follow the twists of the Somme as he had done before, but headed out to the south-east and the towns of Chaulnes and Nesle, creating a bulge of land between himself and the French on the other side of the river. The enemy would have to thin itself to cover the north bank of the Somme now that the English seemed to be out of sight. By 19 October Henry had reached Nesle and had received information about crossing places at Béthencourt and Voyennes, just a few miles away. That morning the army split into two and attempted to travel down the Béthencourt and Voyennes roads across a marsh on small causeways, only to find that they had been broken up near to the river. The English, by nightfall, would be over the marsh and through the ford, having used all manner of timber and thatch to fill the holes of the causeways leading up to the villages. This giant obstacle had at last been overcome, yet Henry's men were a hundred miles away from Calais, not a great deal closer than when they had started in Harfleur. Worse still, the French army had just entered Péronne to the north and would now surely block the route to Calais.

The French squabbled about who was to lead the army. In the end it was neither the king nor his son, but Charles d'Albret, who was still rather defensive minded and favoured shadowing the English until they had tired themselves out. Orléans and Bourbon had other ideas and sent heralds to the English king asking him to choose a place of battle. Henry refused to name a place, but warned the French not to impede him on the road to Calais. On 21 October the army moved past Péronne and on to Albert with no serious impediments. They did, however, cross behind the path of the French army on its way to Bapaume, its footprints in the trackway telling of a huge host. Henry posted a flank guard on his east side and kept marching nervously through Forceville, Leucheux and Frévent. On 24 October his scouts reported that the French force, which had kept its distance marching alongside the

English, was drawing near and that it was huge. Crossing the Ternoise to the south-east of Maisoncelles, news was brought to him that the French had crossed the river at Anvin and were pouring into the valley to the north of his own army. They were deploying for battle and had again succeeded in outpacing him and now blocked the road north to Calais. Henry moved his men down into the village of Maisoncelles half a mile to the south-west of Agincourt. Here they spent a rain-soaked night quietly waiting for the battle which would follow the next day.

During the night Henry sent scouts around the area, and on learning that the French had curiously hemmed themselves between the Tramecourt and Agincourt woods, he began the next morning to prepare the ground in front of his archers against a frontal assault using the stakes they had been carrying since Corbie. The news that so large a force had deployed in a manner where only a proportion of them could meet the enemy line at any one time gave the king some hope.

The English probably numbered between 5500 and 5900 men opposing a French force of somewhere between 20,000 and 30,000, not all of whom were to fight. At dawn on the morning of 25 October, the armies adopted their positions. The English drew up at the southernmost end of the channel created by the two flanking woods of Agincourt and Tramecourt, pinning their flanks on these woods and preventing the enemy taking the vulnerable archers in flank, while the French remained in position blocking the road at the northern end of the channel (**74**). The vast majority of Henry's archers were on his flanks in two large units. It was they who were to provide the overwhelming firepower in the fight. From west to east there were three central units drawn up under the leadership of Lord Camoys, the king, and the Duke of York respectively, each unit comprising dismounted armoured men-at-arms at least four ranks deep. The French had drawn up in three main divisions with several flanking cavalry units. At the front was a line of dismounted men-at-arms containing, from west to east, the leaders Bourbon, d'Albret (the supposed commander-in-chief), Boucicaut, Orléans and Eu. This preponderance of leaders in the front rank, with Bourdon and Vendôme providing flanking cavalry units, reflected an eagerness on the part of the French which was to be their downfall. The Dukes of Bar and Alençon headed a less congested second line of dismounted men-at-arms which had at its front a long unit of crossbowmen and, beside them, more flanking units of mounted men-at-arms. The third line, set back from the funnel-mouth, consisted of at least six units of mounted men-at-arms flanked by other similar units and gunnery units whose field of fire was already blocked by their own army.

The English archers drove their stakes into the ground and waited. The French remained still. Henry had hoped that they would attack down the channel, but they did not. By 11 o'clock, Henry determined that he would have to take the battle to the French and he gave the order to up-sticks and advance towards the enemy line. At about 250-300 yards from the French line (within bow range) they halted and drove their stakes into the ground once more. The first volley of arrows aimed at the line of infantry and flanking cavalry units sparked the French into action. The cavalry charged at the bowmen as Henry had been told they would. None of them made it to the English line as the archers' black rain fell upon them with increasing effect.

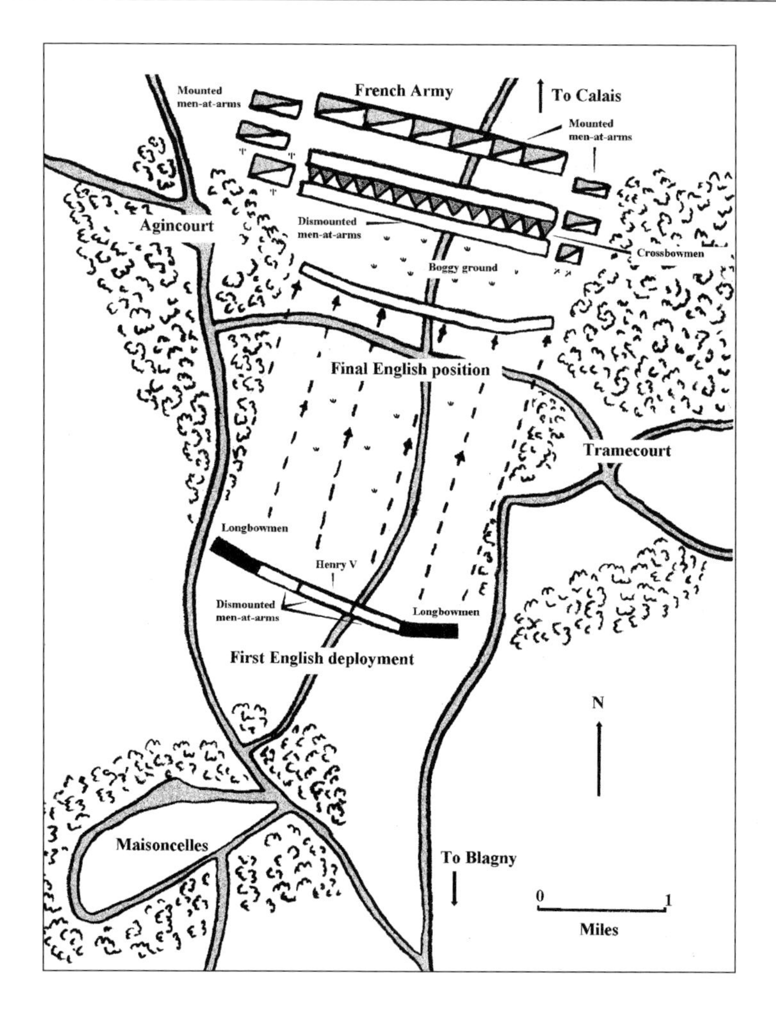

74 *View of the Battlefield at Agincourt, France, 1415. Henry V's route to Calais was blocked by a massive French force. His deployment was to his advantage. The French had positioned themselves at the mouth of a funnel-neck and could not bring their numbers to bear. Wet conditions made fighting in the mud a near impossibility. Powerful English longbows secured an overwhelming victory*

Moreover, those mounts which were not killed outright recoiled into the flanks of the congested infantry line under d'Albret which was lumbering towards the enemy. The ground was sodden and heavy. Despite the attempts of d'Albret to form parts of the line into a column, the arrow storm kept up its deadly work. The French men-at-arms, it seemed, wanted to head for their worthy feudal opponents – their English cousins at the centre of the line. In doing so, they channelled themselves into a position where the English archers could pour fire into their flanks. When the French finally contacted the English infantry line it reeled temporarily with the shock of the weight of impact; the archers in the small flanking units dropped their weapons, picked up their clubs and set about the knights who were now fighting in thick mud at the end of a disorganised charge and with enemy to their front and sides.

Only half an hour had passed and already the Duke of Gloucester was wounded and countless Frenchmen were dead, including the Duke of Alençon who had come up with part of the second line, trampling crossbowmen on the way. Even the king was not untouched by the fighting, having his helmet and crown damaged. D'Albret was dead and Boucicaut, Orléans and Bourbon captured. Some time then appears to have passed with the French threatening to regroup themselves before a small detachment of knights and peasants made for the English baggage, looting Henry's crown and precious sword. There then followed the infamous killing of the French prisoners which was carried out lest they rise in support of the attack on the baggage train.

The battle lasted in total for only about three hours. By the middle of the afternoon, the French third division had wheeled away from the fray and split up, not wishing to suffer the fate of its comrades. The casualties were horrendous. As many as 10,000 French lay dead and as few as 200-300 English, although among them lay the Duke of York. The victory had been emphatic due to the constriction of the battlefield brought about by Henry's tactical position and the presence of flanking woods at the archers' sides. This enabled the archers to concentrate their firepower in time and space to deadly effect, firing at up to ten arrows per minute towards a forward killing-zone into which the impetuous French seemed only too willing to throw themselves. It was a battle probably just as much lost by the French as won by the English.

Despite the differences in approach between the French leaders (with d'Albret and Boucicaut preferring a campaign of attrition and Orléans and others preferring a direct assault on the English), their forces had frequently out-paced Henry's. His way was blocked from the moment of his first arrival at the banks of the Somme and when he finally crossed it, the French still held the initiative. The French mistake was to fight when and where they did and in a hopelessly uncoordinated manner. This is not to belittle the campaign efforts of d'Albret or Boucicaut, however, whose policy of wearing down the enemy seemed to have paid dividends until they lost the argument.

Henry made it back to Calais and returned to England in triumph. His future campaigns in Normandy were to be different from the Agincourt campaign. He preferred to use the landscape in a different way and not to be a slave to its features and the machinations of a clever enemy. He would learn from Harfleur. The taking of strongholds was to be the key to holding territory and protecting troops. He would now have to prosecute his claim to the French throne with better strategic planning and considerably less luck.

The importance of high ground – the Battle for Mont Pinçon 5-7 August 1944

> We took-off into the blue, driving into the dark, told to prepare for anything. It was close wooded country and we saw and heard little. Normally, we felt comparatively safe, compared to infantry, but not in this position. In general, we couldn't hear much, all speech done on intercom and a 400hp engine belting away. A bloke would get out of a slit trench to yell at you there was an mg over there. But you couldn't hear. We were frightened of the ditches

> along the roads and bazooka teams in them. If attacking along a road, the infantry would stay parallel with the tank, and protect us from bazookas, while we fired with both mgs at the trees and everything else in sight, to protect the infantry who were protecting us. We felt reasonably safe, if we had infantry beside us; if not, then just naked.
> Raymond Arthur Frank Hill, a Sherman gunner of the 13/18th Royal Hussars (QMO)[13]

The battles in Normandy which followed the historic landings on the 6 June 1944 were fought in what Field Marshall Montgomery later called ideal defensive country. What he meant by this was that the German forces could use the natural features of the landscape to great effect, and being experienced and well-trained soldiers, were able to make life extremely difficult for the British forces which were slowly advancing against them. It was noted by some of the men who fought the battle at Mont Pinçon that whenever the British took a position and were able to interrogate the enemy, they found that the unit they had been facing was commanded by a Warrant Officer and not the usual Commanding Officer. It was discovered that the Officer would invariably have made his way back to reconnoitre a new defensive position. Such was the tactical flexibility in the German command structure. Montgomery was concerned that during this campaign the British Infantry divisions were losing three men to the Germans' one. Much has been written about the difficulties of fighting in the Bocage in 1944, with its high hedges and hilly landscape (**75**). It certainly was not the right country for open tank warfare, but tanks were of course employed nevertheless.

The Battle for Mont Pinçon highlights the importance of a natural terrain feature in modern warfare. It has been said that the whole battle for Normandy was the story of an advance from one set of commanding heights to another.[14] Of all the heights in Normandy, Mont Pinçon was the highest. It is easy to see why German resistance was strong. The hill at its apex was 365m high and it commanded a considerable view over the landscape for miles around. The weather, for the most part, was very clear and visibility was good. Above all, armoured movement was easy to spot because of the dust that the tracks threw up. This gave the hill a vital significance for both the Germans and the British in that it could be used for observation – the 'eyes' of Normandy, so to speak. The Germans would fight hard to keep their position here.

Following the successful American breakout on 26 July, Montgomery ordered General Dempsey, commander of the British 2nd Army to launch Operation Blue Coat, an advance to the south and south-east of Caumont. The task was given to the 43rd Wessex Infantry Division, consisting of 129, 130 and 214 brigades, supported by Divisional Artillery (94th Field Regiment) and tanks from the 8th Armoured Brigade under the overall command of Brigadier Errol Prior-Palmer comprising the 13/18th Royal Hussars (QMO), 4/7th Dragoon Guards, and Sherwood Rangers. Also with 8th Armoured Brigade were the Essex Yeomanry and 12 Battalion KRRC mechanised Infantry. The job of taking Mont Pinçon itself was given to an Assault Brigade comprising of 129 brigade, supported by tanks from the 13/18th Hussars.

In the early morning of 5 August the attack began. The original plan had been that the 5th Wiltshires with A Squadron of the 13/18th Hussars would advance towards

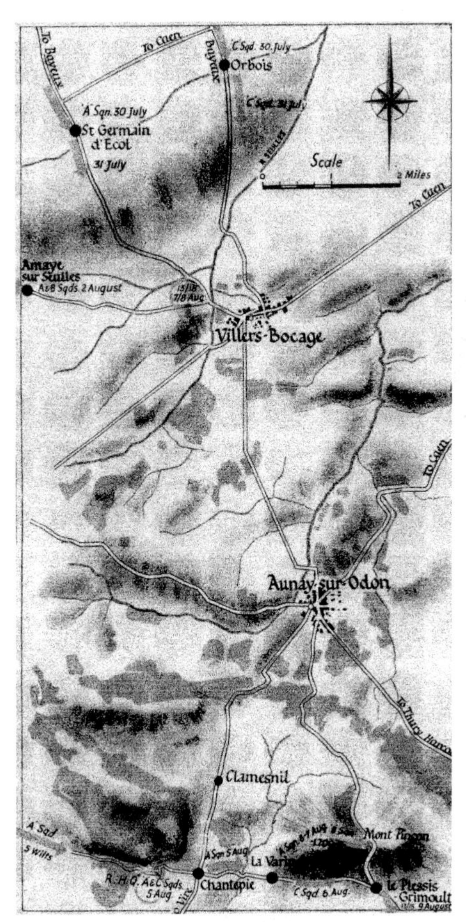

75 *Map of the battle for Mont Pinçon from the History of the 13th/18th Royal Hussars (Queen Mary's Own) 1922-47.*
Courtesy of the Light Dragoons

Mont Pinçon via La Varinière. The 4th Wiltshires with B Squadron of 13/18th Hussars would advance and take the village of St Jean le Blanc to the south of the hill. Around the west flank of the hill between the British and their objectives ran a small river, large enough, as it turned out, to prove a difficult obstacle. The 4th Wiltshires came under fire almost as soon as they advanced and the fighting was said to be almost hand to hand. Casualties soon mounted.

By 16:00, pioneers had managed to get a bridge across the river and a troop of tanks from the 13/18th Hussars were across and heading towards the bottom slopes of the hill. It took a further two hours for this local action to be concluded in favour of the British, and it was noted that Germans were not keen on surrendering. They had either retreated or lay dead. The action was not over by 18:00 however, since the Germans had reformed for a counter-attack but were heavily bombarded and subsequently withdrew.

The fight for St Jean le Blanc which followed cost the lives of one Officer and 21 Other Ranks, with 37 Other Ranks wounded. Given that the Companies involved in the action were already under-strength, these casualties were severe indeed. At 21:00 the Brigade commander ordered a withdrawal from St Jean le Blanc, preferring to concentrate some force upon the main objective, Mont Pinçon. Meanwhile, in the north, 5th Wiltshires with A Squadron of the 13/18th Hussars were moving to secure the bridge west of La Varinière. The crossing was chaotic. 18 Platoon of D Company led the way and the rear Battalion HQ received a direct hit accounting for the Battalion padre and cook. As dusk fell only one Company could say that it was across the river. D company, however, had got itself surrounded, and it knew it. The attempted withdrawal which followed all but decimated the unit.

The 4th Wiltshires had moved on to Danvou, a position selected for them by the Brigade HQ. Danvou, regrettably, had enemy within it in the form of artillery observers and the 4th Wiltshires received a sustained mortar and artillery wake-up call the next morning. After this pasting, the unit was given orders to form up behind the 4th Somerset Light Infantry who were some miles away.

76 *Elements of the 13th/18th Royal Hussars (QMO) operating in the Normandy countryside shortly before the action at Mont Pinçon.* Photograph courtesy of the Light Dragoons

On 6 August there was a change in strategy. 7th Hampshires would now lead a diversionary attack in the north and 129 brigade (5th Wiltshires and 4th Somerset Light Infantry) would attack Mont Pinçon. The 4th Somersets were carried into battle on the back of the tanks of B Squadron 13/18th Hussars, which according to some eyewitnesses threw up an alarming amount of dust. Keeping to the north of La Toque and La Roguerie, the 4th Somersets were ordered to advance in the direction of point 365, on high ground on the eastern side of the hill. At 15:00 the barrage began, followed by an infantry advance which came under heavy machine-gun fire resulting in the halting of the advance for several hours as the infantry hit the ground for cover. The lessons of Hill 112, fought earlier in the campaign had not been heeded. The British were still attacking in a frontal assault up a hill in open ground in broad daylight against an enemy with superior firepower.

Meanwhile, the 5th Wiltshires were ordered to resume their attack on the bridge which they had failed to take the previous day, with the support of the 13/18th Hussars. Their attack began at 14:00 with an artillery barrage, but still little headway was made on the advance towards the hill. The leading company suffered greatly, whilst a troop of tanks managed to get beyond the bridge. The taking of La Varinière was not quite so hard as the getting there. At 16:30 the final assault went in and the village fell just 20 minutes later. Morale was very high at this point and it was resolved to push on to Mont Pinçon. With orders to get to the top, the British tanks were still struggling at 18:00. Two tank troops from A Squadron were ordered to follow a tank commander who had found a trackway leading up the side of the hill. They raced up the track which had a bank on the right and a steep drop to the left, encountering no opposition. One troop sergeant's tank slipped into a quarry and another, the Squadron leader's tank, hit a mine. The other seven tanks reached three quarters of the way up the hill and went into a holding position. The success of the rush up the hill had been its element of surprise coupled with the effects of a very good smokescreen which covered the advance. During the wait for reinforcements, the mist descended and there followed an eerie period of some hours when the British could hear German voices just yards away. In due course, the rest of A Squadron and the depleted infantry joined with the two advanced troops of tanks. Some German counter-attacks were launched but lost their way in the mist.

Meanwhile, at the base of the hill, B Squadron was given orders to advance from the south. The 4th Wiltshires were ordered up the hill whilst the 5th Wiltshires would stay and defend the crossroads at La Varinière, an action which was to cost 52 killed and 158 wounded. Some success transpired with the capture of German machine-gun nests, although later that night, German scouts captured some English signallers in a daring patrol.

In the cold mist and in the middle of the night, led by major R. Neave on foot holding a compass, the British moved in single file between the Germans up the hill, hearing voices to both left and right. Also that night, due to some intense homework by the new battalion commander Col. Bill Roberts from the 4th Somersets along with a senior artillery officer, there was a heavy and accurate bombardment of German positions.

The terrain had caused the British some immense difficulties, and at times their strategy was found wanting. It was not until Le Plessis Grimoult was taken the following day that the British could claim victory at Mont Pinçon. But it had been a pivotal battle. The Germans were to throw more troops in from vital sectors to try to take the hill back, but it would be in vain. When Lieutenant-General Horrocks (commander of 30th Corps) came to Mont Pinçon on 8 August (a bold and morale-boosting visit which surprised some officers due to its forward position), he told the 13/18th Hussars that the next time they moved, they would be doing 60 miles a day. They chose not to believe him, but within two weeks they were in Belgium.

Wooded terrain – the Battles of the Wilderness and Spotsylvania Courthouse, 1864

The American Civil War marks a transitional period in human aggression. Industrialisation had led to weapons of greater killing power than ever before and some harsh lessons were to be learned about their effects. Infantry weapons now had an increased range, but artillery was still lagging behind. Certain aspects of command, control and communication were carried out in the old-fashioned way, however. Also, the period marks the beginning of an attritional style of warfare with vast systems of entrenchments and breastworks which have led some to draw parallels with those of the First World War. The battles of the Wilderness and Spotsylvania Courthouse in the spring of 1864 are good examples of these factors, although they have been chosen here because the ways in which the two armies were brought together and fought each other were dictated by the constraints of a heavily wooded Virginian countryside. Every aspect of these two encounters shows the difficulties presented to the commanders by such a landscape. The loss of life was appalling.

At dawn on 4 May 1864, the army of the Potomac under General Ulysses S. Grant and Maj. Gen. George Meade arrived at Germanna ford just 18 miles west of Fredericksburg and, it seemed, were intent on a move towards Richmond. Grant and Meade's army was organised into three corps under Maj. Gen. Gouverneur K. Warren, Maj. Gen. John Sedgewick and Maj. Gen. Winfield S. Hancock, with Ambrose Burnside's Independent 9th Corps swelling the numbers to around 120,000 troops. Watching the Union moves from his signal stations was General Robert E. Lee, commander of the Confederate forces, who had recently reorganised his own forces promoting A.P. Hill and S. Ewell to corps command following the death of 'Stonewall' Jackson. The forces at Lee's disposal amounted to around half those of the Union.

Lee knew that if the Federal forces reached Richmond then it was all over. He ordered his forces to push out into the wilderness where the quality of the terrain might even things up a little and where he stood a good chance of stopping the Union march on the capital. Ewell took the Orange turnpike and Hill the parallel Orange plank road to the south. Both were ordered not to engage the enemy until Longstreet, an experienced Confederate commander, had turned up with his corps. Meanwhile Grant, not wishing to fight in the woods, ordered his forces to press to the south-east where there were some clearings. Grant and Meade could only guess what was in front of them, as intelligence reports were thin on the ground and very vague. Reports suggested a body of Rebels were headed towards Warren's corps, so Warren detached a division to investigate. About noon on 5 May, Warren's men entered a clearing known as Saunders Field and discovered Ewell's entire corps lying in wait for them. Warren's men were fired upon the very moment they entered the clearing. Despite the clearing, much of the fighting was in woodland. Both of Warren's flanks were stuck in the woods and here they fought an action which ended in a costly stalemate by nightfall. The Battles of the Wilderness had begun.

While the two sides had been wearing each other down at Saunders Field, three miles further south two of A.P. Hill's divisions had been pushing east along the Plank road towards the Brock road with the objective of taking and holding the crossroads there to isolate Hancock's corps. Grant saw the importance of the crossroads and pushed one of Sedgwick's divisions there. Sedgwick won the race and was soon backed up by Hancock. Between them, they pushed Hill back into the woods with substantial loss on the Confederate side. Nightfall saw a cessation of fighting and Hill's troops had taken a mauling. He was expecting Longstreet to relieve him and failed even to properly deploy for action in the morning of the 6 May. Hancock was at him again bright and early at 5:00am and it seemed Hill was doomed. Then, Longstreet finally arrived out of the jungle with a Texan contingent which he threw almost off the line of march straight into battle, taking huge casualties, but also inflicting some loss on Hancock, giving him something else to think about. Longstreet's master stroke was to push four brigades up an unfinished railroad to get behind Hancock. They were successful and rolled up Hancock's line 'like a wet blanket'. Here, Longstreet could have won the wilderness for the Confederates, but as he pushed east along the Plank road, he was shot and badly wounded. Although Lee took charge of the drive, the impetus had gone. Hancock hung on. Failure to

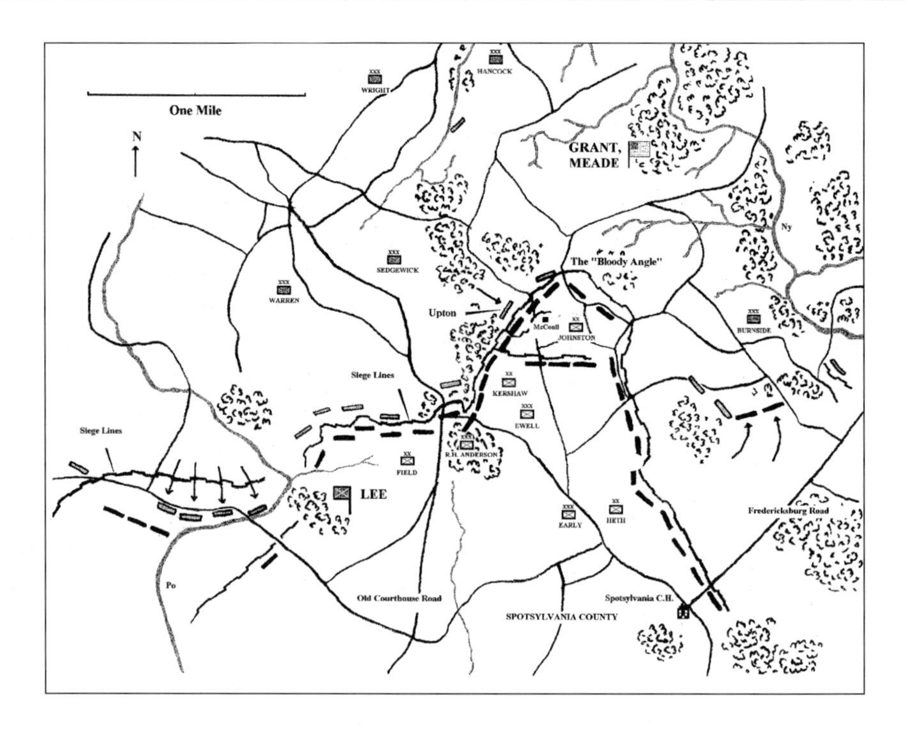

77 *The Battle of Spotsylvania Courthouse 8-21 May 1864. In their attempts to break the bulge in the Confederate line, Union troops could not follow up their successes. The heavily wooded Virginian countryside meant that visibility was so poor that commanders could not see where successes had taken place. A bloody stalemate resulted*

exploit success was a notable feature of the Wilderness and Spotsylvania Courthouse battles. Again, late in the day on 6 May, Georgian brigadier John B. Gordon assaulted Grant's right flank, routing it and capturing two generals. But it was too late for any one to do anything about it. Grant reformed his troops. The stalemate had resulted in the loss of 18,000 Union soldiers and 8000 Confederate. Worse was to follow.

Some expected Grant to call it all off. He indicated on 7 May that his army would press towards Richmond along the road which led past Spotsylvania Courthouse. The cheers with which this decision was greeted must soon have turned to groans, as the night march of 7-8 May saw Union troops subjected to not only sleeplessness, but small-scale ambushes, obstacles and entrapments. Meanwhile, Longstreet's replacement, Maj. Gen. Richard Anderson was leading a confederate column on a parallel course to the west, headed for Spotsylvania courthouse. Whoever held it would have access to Richmond.

Warren continued his advance and came across a clear area (later known as Laurel Hill). It seemed that only a few cavalry were defending the ridge in the clearing, but when Warren deployed for attack, he was met with a barrage from Anderson's artillery. The confederates had won the race through the jungle. The Battle of Spotsylvania Courthouse had begun. It grew from this initial encounter. Ewell's corps filed-in on Anderson's right and began entrenching in the dark. Daylight revealed that their position had brought about a huge bulge in the confederate line, a salient known as the 'Mule Shoe' (**77**). 9-10 May saw further probing on both sides, followed by an attempt on the salient by Colonel Emory Upton who with 12 regiments attacked its west face using the element of surprise and managed to force a deep penetration through the defending Georgians in that part of the Mule Shoe. However, due to the lack of adequate support for this action, put down simply to the fact that Meade could not see where breakthroughs had occurred, a confederate counter-attack saw the situation restored to its earlier state. The attack had given Grant the idea, however, that more force was required to destroy the salient.

Thursday 12 May was the bloodiest day of this series of battles. Having withdrawn their artillery from the Mule shoe, believing that Grant had withdrawn, the confederates found themselves assaulted by Hancock's corps that had come through the woods. This giant effort succeeded in taking most of the salient, but delays in the aftermath of the action involving the rounding-up of prisoners gave Lee a chance to direct a successful counter-attack from the region of the McCoull house. Positions were restored again and it was only mid-morning. More bitter fighting followed when the Union VI corps went into action against the Mule Shoe. The apex of the salient had a slight bend in it. Here the fighting was bloodiest and this place became known as 'The Bloody Angle'.

The Union attacks against the salient were thwarted by a number of factors: poor visibility and communication made local successes difficult to follow up so that counter-attacks would restore confederate positions. Heavily wooded land made the deployment of tactical reserves for this purpose a virtual impossibility. The defenders' breastworks, which were constructed of log barricades 6ft high with traverse walls at 20ft intervals (resembling a roofless log cabin) were built well enough to withstand artillery bombardment. At one point in the battle the Union artillery was brought into almost point-blank range, but failed to establish a breach.

The battle turned into a slogging match which went on through the night. Orders were eventually given on 13 May for the Confederate troops to withdraw to the base of the salient. In the morning, when the Union troops reached The Bloody Angle, the only people they found were the dead and dying. Grant probed for weaknesses in the confederate line for a few days, but with the Mule Shoe flattened out, Lee's lines were less vulnerable than they had been. By 20 May, the confrontation at Spotsylvania had become meaningless. Grant moved off southwards and Lee again put himself between Grant and Richmond. A further 18,000 Union and 10,000 Confederate dead added to the numbers lost in the Wilderness. Although the Union dead amounted to a greater total, the Confederates with each battle found it harder to replace their men.

The mountain pass – Thermopylae 480 BC

The events at Thermopylae in 480 BC have passed into military legend (**colour plates 24 & 25**). It is a story of how a small force of Spartan hoplites and their allies, under their leader Leonidas, held at bay the mighty Persian army before being treacherously outdone by a local Greek, who gave his knowledge of the terrain to the enemy. The Persians wished to gain access to central Greece. Despite the fact that the pass at Thermopylae was not the only way to do this, it was the most obvious way. The importance of the mountain pass at Thermopylae, situated on the east coast of central Greece between the Kallídhromon massif and the Maliakōs Gulf, cannot be underestimated. It has been a strategically important place on many occasions after the battle for which it is principally famous. In 279 BC the Greeks fought the Gauls there and in 191 BC, the Romans under M. Acilius Glabrio in conjunction with Philip V won a victory against Antiochus of Syria. More recently, in 1941, the New Zealanders fought a rearguard action against the Germans at the same place. It should perhaps be remembered that each of these actions ultimately led to the defeat of the defender, but these encounters should be set against the successful obstruction of the pass in 352 BC when the Athenians denied Phillip II, and again in 323 BC when Athenian troops were once more stationed there as a deterrent.

There has been much argument as to the exact nature of the terrain at the time of the battle. Herodotus stated that the pass had cliffs on one side and the sea on the other. Today, the tourist is presented with a site that hardly looks like a traditional pass at all (**78**). Subsequent geological activity has led to a retreat of the coastline by several miles. Some have found reason to state that the pass may have been as narrow as 20m in places in 480 BC, although even these new revised estimates are disputed.[15] The road through the pass had three gates along it: west, east and middle. The latter was marked by a partially ruined wall showing for how long this pass had been considered important. In fact, the very word Thermopylae means 'Hot Gates' and comes from the hot natural springs nearby.

The Persian army was reputedly huge. There are extravagant claims from Herodotus that it was 2.5 million men strong. Whilst this is surely an exaggeration, one would only have to reduce the amount by a factor of ten to get a still sizeable and more realistic force of about 200,000 plus. What the Spartan leader Leonidas was counting upon was the fact that no matter how large the Persian force, his own men stationed at the gates of the pass would match the Persians one for one in such a constricted area. And if this was so, his optimism was justified, for the feared Spartan hoplite with his solid shield, body armour and long thrusting spear was probably a better warrior man-for-man than his Persian adversary.

The battle took place late in the summer of 480 BC. Xerxes, the leader of the Persian Imperial Army, had camped near Trachis to the west of the pass and waited there for a full five days, presumably for the remnants of a weather-torn Persian fleet to catch up with him. During this time, he decided to send out some spies who brought back reports that they had seen the Spartans preparing for battle by stripping down and fixing each other's hair. Later, Xerxes sent a herald to the Greeks offering them safety if they surrendered. This may have been a way of trying to split the Greek allies within Leonidas's command, but either way, Leonidas would have none of it.

Xerxes decided to assault the Greek position. The Greek defence was strong and the Persian archers' weapons were ineffective against Greek shields and armour. For days these assaults went on. Meanwhile Xerxes sent 10,000 of his famous 'Immortals' on a Flank March to try to take the Greek middle gate position from the rear. The Persians learned about a route through the mountains from a local

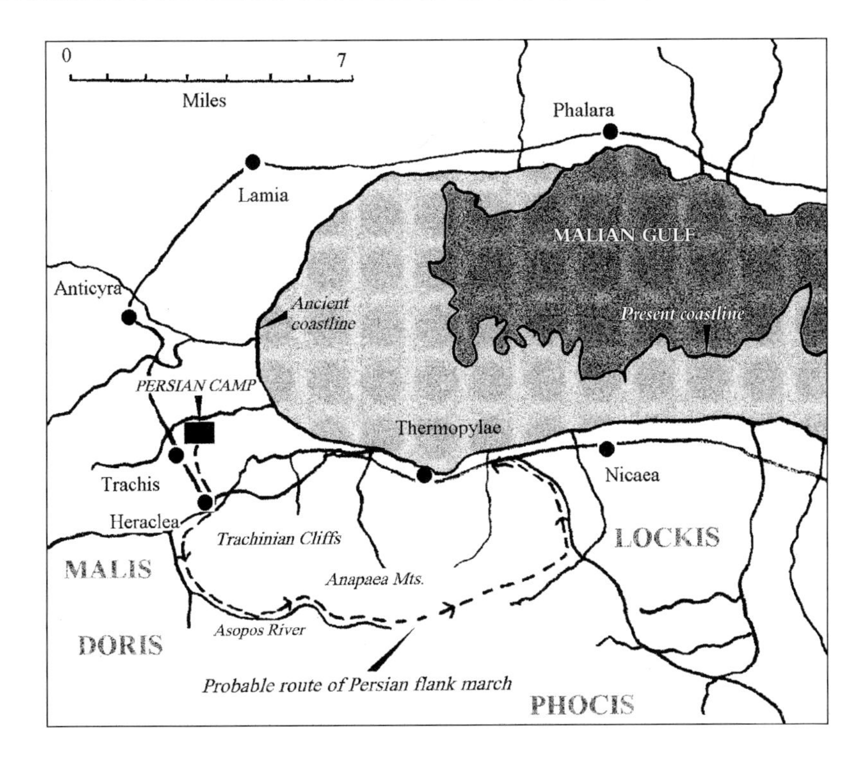

78 Map showing the location of Thermopylae. The topography has changed over the centuries since 480 BC due to the erosion of the coastline

Greek man named Ephialtes. There is some dispute as to the route that the Immortals took. It may have been along the gorge cut by the Asopos river which passes through the Anopaea Mountains two miles to the south of Leonidas's position in the pass, although in places this gorge is simply too rocky to be traversed at all. Whatever the route, Leonidas was ready for this strategic move. He had placed a detachment of troops from Phocis in the path of the intended march, who would at least be familiar with the terrain. But something unusual happened. Whether the Phocians were bribed, defeated or simply taken by surprise, the Immortals got past them. The tide had turned against Leonidas.

Leonidas, on hearing that he had been outdone, dismissed many of his allied troops. Curiously, he decided to stay on with his Spartans, ordering the Thespians and Boeotians to remain too. With only around 1400 men left, Leonidas would lose the battle of attrition which followed, but it was not without its minor successes. The Persians still had difficulty bringing their numbers to bear, but the Greeks were running out of men. Leonidas was killed during a Greek pursuit of the main Persian contingent towards the west gate. After this, the final act at Thermopylae was a retreat to a hillock in the pass where heroically, the Spartans resisted the inevitable until not one of them was left alive. The stone lion erected to commemorate the dead has never been found. Nor indeed have the bones of the Spartan hoplites who died on the hillock.

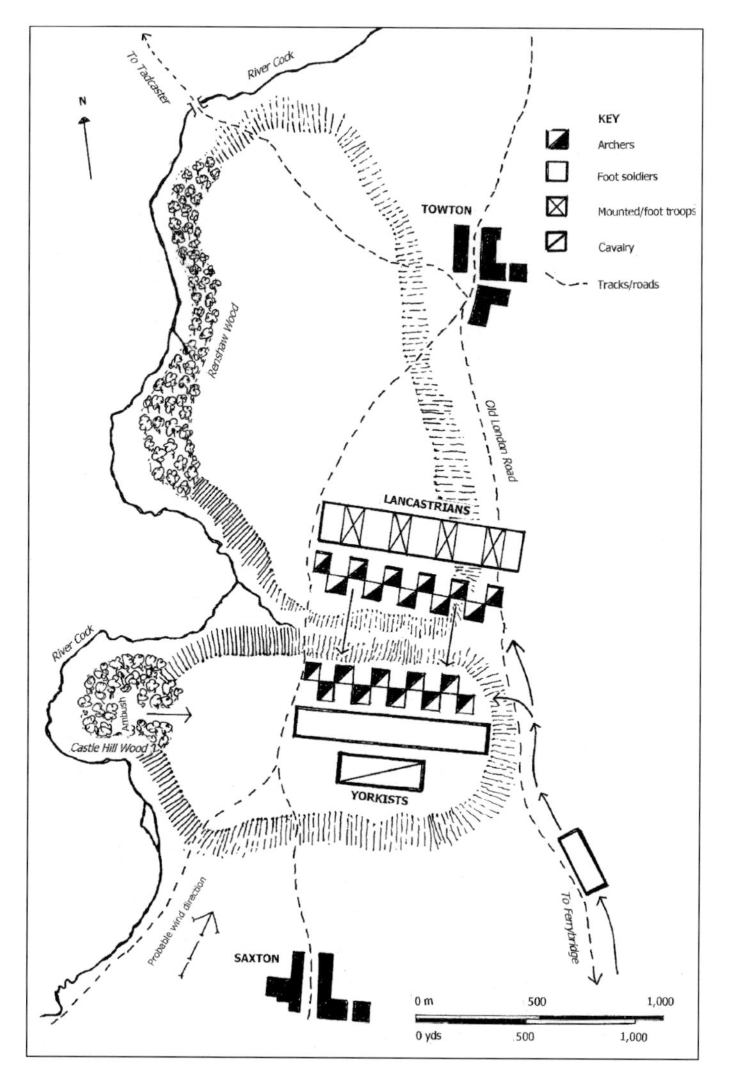

79 *Map of the Battle of Towton, 1461. The apparently open nature of the country-side was on the day rendered insignificant by the weather*

Weather – the Battle of Towton. Sunday, 29 March 1461

> . . . there was a great conflict, which began with the rising of the sun, and lasted until the tenth hour of the night, so great was the boldness of the men, who never heeded the possibility of a miserable death.

So George Neville wrote to the Papal Legate on 7 April 1461, a chilling description of this battle, brought back into the public eye recently with the discovery of a mass grave of soldiers apparently massacred as they fled. It was one of a series of bloody conflicts that made up what is called the Wars of the Roses.

The conflict had been precipitated by baronial opposition to Henry VI and his unpopular queen, Margaret of Anjou. Henry, who had suffered periods of lunacy, was the descendant of Henry IV, who had usurped the throne from Richard II. A rival candidate for the throne, Richard, Duke of York, had been supported by Richard Neville (known as Warwick the Kingmaker), and a deal had been struck whereby Henry recognised Richard as his legitimate heir. This agreement in effect disinherited Henry's own son Edward; Margaret violently opposed the deal and took up arms. Richard of York died in a battle on 30 December 1460 with Margaret's Lancastrian forces at Sandal Castle in Yorkshire. His claim was passed on to his son Edward, who was 18 years old. On 4 March 1461 Edward was 'elected' king by the citizens of London, becoming Edward IV.

Immediately, Edward sent his supporters the Duke of Norfolk and the Earl of Warwick to raise troops, and just over a week after his election marched in pursuit of Margaret's forces. The Lancastrians had enjoyed some success in the war so far, being victorious at a battle at St Albans on 17 February. However, Margaret had not felt sufficiently confident to continue an advance on London and had withdrawn northwards. Reaching Nottingham by 22 March, Edward advanced to Ferrybridge and after a fierce fight crossed the River Aire on 28 March.

A few miles north of the bridge, the Lancastrians deployed to meet the Yorkist forces. Some 25,000 men led by the Duke of Somerset had cut the bridge over the River Cock, their main line of retreat, and formed up on a plateau of land between the hamlets of Saxton and Towton.

This plateau is raised some 30m above the plain around it. Its slopes are fairly gentle except on its west side, where it drops sharply to the River Cock. The plateau is divided into two by a depression running east-west, again steepest at its west end. At the west side of the plateau are woods – Renshaw Wood along the edge of the northern section, and Castle Hill Wood on a spur on the west side of the southern part (**79**). The River Cock winds its course all along the west side of the plateau.

With the Lancastrians ensconced on the northern ridge of the east-west depression (known as Towton Dale), the 20,000 or so Yorkists spent a miserable night in the open along the southern ridge. Accounts mention the damp, freezing conditions that cause both men and horses to suffer. Both forces were probably drawn up in two main divisions, archers in front, possibly in a chequerboard formation to allow freedom of movement for each bowman. Behind them were the bulk of the armies, the foot soldiers. The Lancastrians may have interspersed their infantry with cavalry troops; a light cavalry detachment probably formed up at the rear of the Yorkist lines, perhaps with reserve infantry. Arriving at the battlefield first, the Lancastrians had also concealed an ambush party in Castle Hill Wood, on the Yorkist flank. The length of the southern ridge is some 1300m, of which 900m faces on to the northern ridge; this, according to Andrew Boardman, an expert on the battle,[16] must have represented the core of the battle's most bitter action. The woods and steep drop on the west, and the slopes to the east, would have served to anchor the flanks of each army, and the gently rolling depression of the strip-field farmland between them became the killing ground.

As day broke, the two armies faced each other across the depression. They were told to give no quarter – this was to be a no-holds-barred encounter as the young king Edward sought revenge for the death of his father. It was then that another factor entered the equation – it began to snow.

80 *Archers. Late fifteenth century. After* Chroniques d'Angleterre. *The Longbow, the most successful defensive weapon of its era, got the better of the offensive armoured knight at Crécy, Poitiers and Agincourt*

This rapidly turned into a blizzard, gusting and squalling into the faces of the Lancastrians. A great shout is recorded by witnesses as the armies prepared to engage. Lord Fauconberg, in charge of the archers in the Yorkist front line, ordered his men to fire their arrows at their Lancastrian counterparts and then to retire a little distance. This volley, aided by the following wind, reached its target. Immediately the Lancastrians retaliated, firing volley after volley into the blinding squall of snow.

> The northern men, feeling the shoot, but by reason of the snow, not perfectly viewing the distance between them and their enemies like hardy men shot their sheaf arrows as fast as they might, but all their shot was lost and their labour in vain for they came not near the southern men by 40 tailors yards. When their shot was almost spent the Lord Fauconberg marched forward with his archers, who not only shot their own sheaves, but also gathered the arrows of their enemies and let a great part of them fly against their own masters, and another part they let stand on the ground which sore annoyed the legs of the owners when battle was joined.[17]

The English longbow (**80**) of the period probably had a pull weight of between 90-120lb, and the length of the heavy iron-tipped arrows, based on estimates of the average height of the unlucky victims found in the mass grave (166.5-183.5cm or 5ft 6in-6ft) would have been between 64-72cm (27-30in). John Waller, an experienced archer, comments:

> Personal experience of having shot in a snowstorm, with white fletched arrows launched at 45 degrees for maximum range, demonstrated that they

> were soon lost from sight as they disappeared among the snow flakes. Having walked forward to the target we found, as the Lancastrian archers did at Towton, that most of the arrows had fallen short. Personal experience has also shown that it is not unusual for there to be a difference of at least 20 to 30 yards when shooting with or into the wind at long distance, even without a snowstorm.[18]

It was usual for archers to carry two sheafs of arrows each – 48 in total. If the reused Lancastrian arrows are brought into the equation, Boardman calculates '. . . then you've got about a million arrows – and that's about forty tonnes. So it was probably the biggest exchange of arrows in British history.'[19] The rate of fire was probably somewhere in the region of 10–15 arrows a minute.[20] Archers could reckon on consistently hitting a human target at 90m, and a group target at 230m. But the confusion of the snow made all the difference in the early part of the battle. As the Lancastrians closed to hand-to-hand combat, they were impeded by the piles of their own dead archers.

The snow continued to fall as the northern army rushed on to the slope where the Yorkist archers stood. Despite their earlier advantage, the Yorkists were being pushed back by sheer weight of numbers; the slowness of Northumberland's troops in backing up the Lancastrian attack, however, allowed Edward to bring up his reserves to plug the gaps in the line; for some hours, the main movement in the battle was simply that of fresh troops being brought forward to replace those killed, hurt or exhausted.[21]

> So followed a day of much slaying between the two sides, and for a long time no one knew to which side to give the victory so furious was the battle and so great the killing: father did not spare son nor son his father. Jean de Waurin, contemporary chronicler.

The lines eventually began to pivot as the Yorkists were slowly pushed back towards Saxton – the Bishop of Salisbury recorded that they were at the point of collapse, but in the afternoon, reinforcements led by the Duke of Norfolk reached the battle and joined on the right flank of the Yorkist line. This was not, immediately, decisive. The slaughter went on for some hours, until eventually the Lancastrians began to break. A trickle turned into a flood as demoralised and exhausted men turned to flee, most along the road to Tadcaster northwards.

This crossed the River Cock by a ford and the bridge earlier destroyed; the mass of men trying to cross it created a bottleneck. Edward Hall recorded that the Lancastrians,

> . . . like men amazed, fled towards Tadcaster bridge to save themselves, but in the mean way there was a little brook called Cock, not very broad but of great deepness, in this which, what for haste of escaping, and what for fear of followers, a great number were drent and drowned, in so much that the common people there affirm that man alive passed the river upon the dead carcasses, and that the great river of Wharfe, which is the great sewer of the brook, and all of the water coming from Towton, was coloured with blood.[22]

81 Roman Cavalry Officer's ceremonial facemask discovered under a collapsed part of the wall constructed by the Germans to ambush Varus's legions

Casualty estimates made by the heralds at the time, and confirmed by other reports, were in the region of 28,000 dead, 20,000 of whom were Lancastrians cut down by Yorkist cavalry which pursued them all the way to Tadcaster. It is thought probable that the 37 men aged between 16-50 years old and found in 1996, were among those massacred in the rout.

This battle clearly demonstrates the vital role weather can play in this type of engagement. If the Yorkists had not used the snowstorm to their advantage early in the battle, drawing the sting of the Lancastrian archery, it is doubtful that they could have held long enough to benefit from Norfolk's arrival. They were less in number, cold and miserable before the combat began; they had already fought several actions and been marched hard. Fauconberg demonstrated a touch of genius in his exploitation of the conditions, winning the day for York. Not until 1485 was the war finally won – by Henry Tudor, a Lancastrian.

The use of ambush – the Lost Legions of the Teutoberg Forest

In AD 9 the seemingly unstoppable expansion of the Roman Empire under Augustus came to a violent and shocking halt in the dark misty forests of Germany. A train of civilians, servants and auxiliary troops followed three Legions, led by Publius Quintilius Varus, to annihilation by a confederacy of German tribes under a 25-year-old German called Arminius. Arminius was the son of a tribal noble; he had been educated in Rome, fought with the Roman army in the Balkans, and been made a citizen with the rank of Roman Knight. He was thus completely familiar with the Romans' fighting abilities and strategies, and had been appointed to lead a troop of German auxiliaries as part of Varus' bodyguard. Arminius, however, had not bought in to *Romanitas* – he still dreamed of a free Germany.

For some 20 years, Roman expeditions had been crossing the Rhine in an attempt to bring Germany into the sphere of influence of the Empire. Varus had been appointed governor of the region and his brief was to encourage the tribes to sign treaties and enter into peaceful commerce with the Empire; he seems to have approached this task via a programme of bribery and corruption of the local German war chiefs, and by AD 9 it was going well. The area was peaceful, large towns were growing up on the west bank of the Rhine, and new foundations were beginning to be created in barbarian territory. Recent excavations at Waldgirmes, some considerable distance across the Rhine east of Mainz, have revealed the presence of a Roman-style town, with stone-built houses and typical Roman artefacts. By the time of Varus' ill-fated expedition, this town had been growing for some 10 years. The trip, begun in the spring of the year, had taken Varus and his train along the course of the River Lippe and then across to the River Weser, making contact with local tribes as they went. As the weather turned at the end of the summer, they began to turn back to make the long and difficult trip back to their winter quarters on the Rhine.

Varus was completely unaware of the fact that Arminius had been busy bringing together the local tribes and preparing an ambush. He therefore accepted without question a report that was brought to him of an uprising to the north, and turned with his entire entourage away from their known path, striking out into the 'fearful forest and stinking bog' described by Tacitus. The message was a ruse; skilfully timed, it set Varus on a path that would take him to certain death. Some 20,000 people, with pack animals and carts, struggled through pathless dense pinewoods and bogs and over crags. The column became dangerously strung out, with the rear perhaps a full half-day behind the leaders. From the deep cover, the Germans began to harry the rear, picking off groups as they became isolated from the main march, and as they tried to find rest. For at least two days and nights, those at the back came under constant hit and run attack, while the leading party forged ever onwards, unaware of what was happening behind them. By the time Varus and his officers realised the situation, there were miles of corpses along the trail. Then the head of the column was attacked; in violent thunderstorms and mist, the Romans were slaughtered, Varus and several officers committing suicide rather than face capture. No one survived.

When Augustus learned of the disaster he was overcome with grief and even panic, for no army now stood between Rome and the Germans. Conquering Rome, however, was not part of Arminius' plan – he just wanted to keep the Romans out of Germany. In AD 16, Germanicus took troops back into the region and, it is reported, found the bodies. Some had been mutilated, and skulls had been fixed to tree trunks, but all had been reduced to skeletons, human and animal alike. Carefully, and with great anger and sadness, his men dug mass graves and placed into them all the bones they could find, hiding forever the traces of Rome's greatest defeat. Augustus decreed that there was to be no more expansion across the Rhine and set the frontier at the river forever. The numbers of the three legions, the XVII, XVIII and XIX, were never used again.

In the late 1990s, a British tank commander, Major Tony Clough, stationed with NATO at Osnabruck, was exploring an area of farmland near Kalkreise with a metal detector. He found a number of coins of the Augustan period, and then discovered some lead slingshots. Considering it possible that these might represent evidence of the massacre, excavations of the site began in 1999. In addition to large amounts of military and civilian equipment, including a magnificent Roman cavalry officer's face mask (**81**), in 1994 the archaeologists found carefully dug and arranged mass graves, evidence of Germanicus' reburial of the dead. Analysis of the material in the graves showed that the bodies of people and animals had spent some years in the open between the time of death and the time of burial, adding weight to the contention that these remains were those of Varus' people.

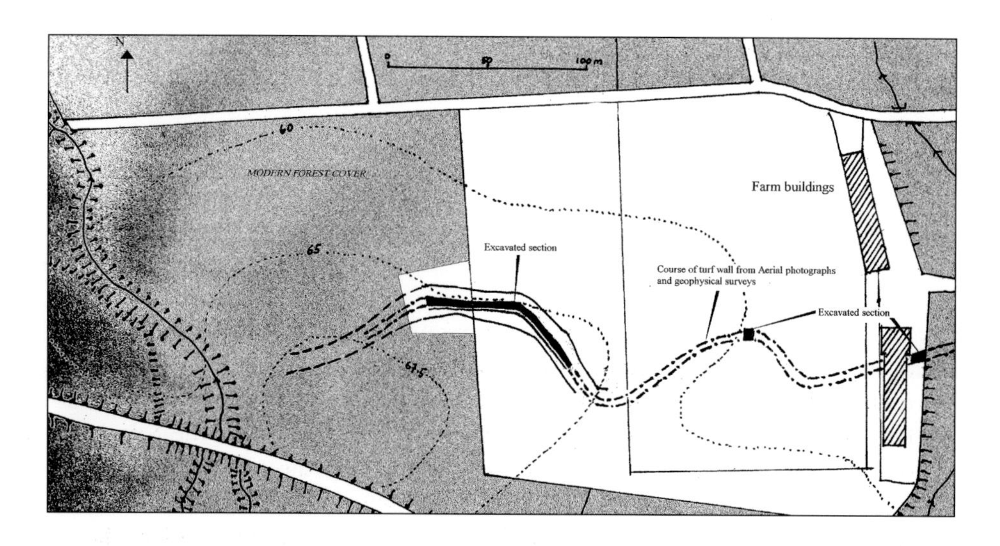

82 Traces of the wall built by Arminius's tribal allies to entrap Varus and his legions have been surveyed through a combination of excavation, geophysics and aerial photography. This plan shows an interpretation of this material

Even more surprising, however, was the discovery of traces of a turf wall surmounted by a hurdle palisade (**82**). This structure, some 4-5m across and 1.5m high, meandered more or less east to west down a slope towards a place where steep forests on the south angled down towards a deep bog to the north.[23] The wall had been built over a period of a few weeks, proof of Arminius' planning. As the head of the Roman column struggled through the trees in the rain and mist, they would have found themselves forced into a narrow neck, with the Germans waiting behind their wall on the south and nowhere to escape on any side. There was less than about 80m between the wall and the edge of the bog – a prepared killing ground. It has been suggested that Arminius learned how to construct such a wall from the Romans themselves; there is no evidence elsewhere of any such construction and use of this type of tactical fortification by the German tribes.

Arminius showed consummate military skill in the timing of his false message and the building of the wall that was the final trap; he was aided considerably by the nature of and his ability to utilise the terrain – the deep trackless forests and the bogs – and by the weather, for not only did the rain and mist confuse the Romans and make their efforts to travel and fight even more difficult and miserable, but the thunder also struck fear into them because they would have regarded it as a portent of doom.

The town at Waldgirmes was burned down and never reoccupied around AD 9 or 10, the fate of its inhabitants unknown. Arminius himself was assassinated by his own countrymen at a tribal meeting in AD 19. But the Romans never conquered Germany; some commentators have suggested that it was the Varus disaster that set the pattern for the division of Europe ever since.

5 Cycles of war

> . . . the Norsemen, were under the hurdles piercing the walls. What the Saxons and the Irishmen who were among them did was to throw large rocks so that they destroyed the hurdles over them. What they did in the face of this was to place large posts under the hurdles. What the Saxons did was to put all the ale and water of the town in the cauldrons of the town, to boil them and pour them over those who were under the hurdles so that the skins were stripped from them. The answer which the Norsemen gave to this was to spread hides on the hurdles. What the Saxons did was to let loose on the attacking force all the beehives of the town, so that they could not move their legs or hands from the great number of bees stinging them. Afterwards, they left the city and abandoned it.
>
> Third Fragment, *Annals of Ireland*, tenth century, recounting the Norse attack on the Mercian City of Chester[1]

The pattern of war has been one of invention and counter-invention, development and response. Each new weapon is met by a new form of defence and a new, even more effective, piece of armament, and these in turn are met by further innovations in armour, fortifications, munitions and strategy. The use of weapons against people led to the development of body protection – shields, corselets, helmets and the like, and the building of fortified settlements, as we have seen. Some of these relate to close fighting and, others, increasingly during history, to long-range projectile weapons.

Through the ages, a number of important stages can be identified in the process of the sophistication of aggression. These include developments in the management of troops: professionalisation, training, generalship and organisation; the direction and form of aggression and defence; battle formations, siege tactics, mining and trench war; and in the improvement of mobility in warfare – the use of horses, the development of the stirrup, mechanised transport and the tank, development of chemical and biological weapons; and finally long-range capability via airborne and satellite armament. Defensive progression has involved increasingly complex architectural design, early warning systems, intelligence procedures, the use of traps, sabotage and decoys, and political and social manipulation. Accompanying all these have been the almost constant arms races that have typified the best financed and supported scientific efforts of mankind – it might almost be claimed that the technological progress of the world has been only a side effect of the battle to invent ever more effective and destructive weapons. Certainly the impetus that helped to develop such inventions as accurate time-keeping, manned flight, penicillin, communications systems and many others was directly related to warfare.

In the following sections, we shall look at a few examples of these aspects of war and its cycles of developmental spiral. In chapter 1, the causes of human aggression were discussed; we looked at emotional, ritual and competitive stimuli touching upon the problem of defining the point at which aggression becomes actual warfare. We must look more closely at what might be termed larger-scale aggression, and consider its causes and the means by which it may be perpetuated and escalated. The role of technology in these processes also needs to be studied, with a consideration of examples that illustrate human ingenuity and reactions towards military imperatives.

How should we define war? Is it dependent upon the involvement of a specific number of participants or communities? Does the use of the term 'warfare' imply specific patterns of events, or particular degrees of intensity, duration or geographic location of conflict? There has been little agreement about the answers to such questions. Clausewitz defines warfare in terms of a duel regardless of its level. It is, he says, a mechanism which compels the enemy to do our will. 'Force, to counter opposing force, equips itself with the inventions of art and science.'[2]

What have been called wars have lasted for as few as six days, or as long as a hundred years. Warfare involving great nations has been confined to a few small islands or has spread itself across several continents. Wars have occurred intensively, sporadically, or even, in the case of the Cold War, with hardly any combat activity at all.

Common to most wars seems to be the need for an initiating factor, although this may not necessarily be in direct relation to the true underlying causes, and there do seem to be some patterns that emerge in the way wars are prepared for and then develop, although it must be clearly recognised that any such patterns are by no means universal or necessary to an absolute definition of warfare.

In the first instance, wars imply the mobilisation for conflict, or for the support of conflict, of large proportions of the participating populations. By mobilisation is meant the directed or mutual consensus that not only will men (and more rarely women) prepare themselves to fight, but that the community as a whole is also prepared to devote a proportion of its economic and social effort to the prosecution of that fight, and perhaps to allow its normal social, productive and even ritual life to be disrupted or altered to that end. The term 'warfare' seems to imply an acceptance and commitment on the part of all or most of a society towards the justice and desirability of conflict. This, in turn, implies a degree of directed or consensual organisation for its support.

In lesser, smaller forms of aggression (however deadly or frequent) the majority of people, or at least large sections of the group, may have little or no involvement, even as spectators. Such conflicts may be held at the personal level or within the province of specific groups only – such as warrior societies, official champions or groups of young males – and everyone else can simply get on with normal life. The number of actual combatants in a population at war seems to be very variable, where figures are available.

Group	Male population	% males mobilised
Rome (AD 100-200)	25,000,000	2
US Second World War	66,000,000	17
USSR Second World War	91,000,000	22
Germany Second World War	34,250,000	32
Zulu State (1879)	125,000	40
France First World War	19,500,000	43[3]

The above data suggests no clear correlation between size of population, size of territory and degree of mobilisation. The data set is too small to draw any sensible conclusions but we can perhaps note that those populations facing invasion (the Zulus, or the French in the First World War) may mobilise higher proportions than the more predatory nations, or those whose own territorial sovereignty is not threatened, perhaps unsurprisingly. Unfortunately, for most ancient or historical conflicts we have generally insufficient information to be able to ascertain overall patterns, but it would seem likely that the greatest response often occurs in the face of the greatest threat where there is a sufficient degree of leadership to co-ordinate it. What these figures do not tell us is the degree of involvement of the rest of the population – the women doing war work in the fields and factories, the elderly or infirm driving lorries or manning fire engines, and the specialist engineers and theoreticians working at improved weaponry or the development of strategic planning. Nor do these statistics really show how many of those mobilised were actually involved in battle. In more recent years, the greater part of the manpower commitment has been in the form of support personnel – stores and munitions workers, technicians and mechanical service engineers, communications and technological surveillance operatives and a thousand other vital but non-combat roles.

It is thus very difficult to quantify the percentage of populations actually involved in warfare. That there is a high degree of organisation, however, seems to be beyond question. However many men are under arms, the management of material, supply and communications in warfare must be well directed if the combatants are to be effectual. Nevertheless, the level at which such management operates can be very variable. In guerrilla groups, tribal warfare or mercenary units the practical direction is often in the hands of a single war leader or chief, perhaps supported by a few trusted deputies and only loosely controlled by the body politic. In more formal units, direction emanates from appointed bodies – the chiefs of staff, often under very direct political control. This has, of course, been a source of great frustration to a large number of generals in the past.

The introduction of the idea of political control in warfare begs the question of whether warfare is, therefore, a phenomenon of states rather than of smaller social entities. It has been argued that only at the level of a state can the necessary political will and social control be manifested in order to pursue true warfare. It is said that true warfare exists only between politically complex organisations and only between larger polities; this is rather a naive position. Most of us are only too aware that even very low-level social organisations can be politically complex. If relations between members of the golf club or vestry committees can approach open warfare, it is easy to understand how the political preconditions of war can be met by those running the affairs of clans, villages, tribes and chiefdoms that otherwise lack the trappings of statehood.

Warfare, it is sometimes claimed, differs from other forms of aggression through its method of prosecution – the employment of both strategic and tactical science, the sustaining of its intensity and the duration of actions. These assertions seem to contain a good deal of truth. While individuals involved in smaller scale raids and fights often employ great tactical skill, the formation and carrying out of strategic planning appears to be confined, on the whole, to much more general and sustained campaigns of aggression or attrition where motivations are claimed to be on a grander scale than those of personal revenge, animosity or short-term acquisition. Political motivation and organised direction together combine to allow the prosecution of aggression for longer term ends, ends that are not necessarily those of the actual combatants. It is suggested that soldiers who fight for pay, or under the coercion of a powerful politically dominant leader are more inclined to maintain their assaults and to continue their advances than warriors fighting for personal and emotional causes. This, it is suggested, was the reason for the overwhelming success of the professional Roman army over the tribesmen of Gaul and Britain. That is not to suggest that formal large-scale warfare is any more deadly than lesser forms of conflict. On the contrary, mortality rates for so-called 'primitive' war tend to be much higher. But it is the tendency for formal war to be more sustained for longer periods of time that breaks down opposition more completely – the effort of maintaining resistance destroys not only the fighting units but the productive and emotional capacities of the defenders. In any case, in 'civilised' war, a high death rate among a conquered people may actually be counter-productive for the victors, who may desire to control a large population of potential slaves, tribute or tax payers, or otherwise economically useful workers.

Analysis of a number of wars by several writers suggests some patterns in their development and the ways in which they escalate. Conflicts involving large proportions of populations, whether in active or supportive roles, seem to have several overt and covert causes. In many cases, one or two events serve as sparks to light the powder – the assassination of an arch-duke or an incursion of a rival's forces into your own or someone else's territory, for example. But the spark could not ignite the powder if the powder had not already been laid. Other less plainly stated, even less obvious or more fundamental issues generally underlie the start of wars. Still other reasons may subsequently be offered as excuses or rationales for the outbreak of hostilities. Many honestly held or downright cynical justifications can be offered for wars: upholding religious or political principles, defending various underdogs, preventing atrocities, protecting specific ethical standpoints or customary usages, for example. It is possible, however, that the true and underlying cause of just about every conflict is, in essence, economic: wars are to do with resources, their ownership, availability and distribution.

Inevitably, therefore, landscapes contain the causes of war as well as its stage. In 1870/80s America, ranchers fought range wars over water sources for their cattle. In

EARLY WEAPONS DEVELOPMENT IN HUNTING AND FIGHTING
▼
DEVELOPMENT OF PERSONAL ARMOUR and DEVELOPMENT OF SMALL SCALE DEFENCES
▼
INCREASED ORGANISATION – DEVELOPMENT OF THE FIRST ARMIES
▼
LARGER SCALE DEFENCES AND LOOK OUT TOWERS/POSITIONS
▼
SIEGE WARFARE
▼
INCREASED SOPHISTICATION IN DEFENSIVE ARCHITECTURE and POPULATION CONTROL METHODS FOR SUPPLY AND PROTECTION
▼
MORE DESTRUCTIVE LARGE SCALE WEAPONRY
▼
CREATION OF DEFENSIVE ARMIES
▼
INCREASED PROFESSIONALISATION AND ELITISM GIVING RISE TO MOBILITY
▼
EXPANSION OF KINGDOMS AND FORMALISATION OF WAR AND FRONTIERS
▼
PREPARATION AND MOBILISATION FOR WAR AT NATIONAL SCALES
▼
INDUSTRIALISATION OF WAR
▼
COMMERCIALISATION OF WAR AND COMMERCIAL WAR
▼
SABOTAGE, INFILTRATION AND BLOCKADING TO ALIENATE POPULATIONS
▼
COVERT, PARTISAN AND GUERRILLA WARFARE
▼
SOPHISTICATION OF SURVEILLANCE AND COMMUNICATIONS
▼
AERIAL AND SATELLITE TECHNOLOGIES
▼
REMOTE WARFARE
▼
CIVILIAN DEFENCE STRATEGIES AND COUNTER-TECHNOLOGIES
▼
WEAPONS OF MASS DESTRUCTION
▼
DETERRENCE CAPABILITIES AND STALEMATES
▼
ALTERNATIVE BIOLOGICAL AND CHEMICAL WEAPONS
▼
ANNIHILATION?

83 Theoretical diagram showing a possible cycle of warfare over the centuries. Accompanying this cycle is the constant struggle between aggressive and defensive postures and their associated arms and defence races

the same country, the wars against the Dacotah Sioux in the Black Hills were motivated by the desire to gain access to the gold deposits of the region. Norman and Breton younger sons joined William the Bastard in the Conquest of England in 1066 in order to gain land and to carve out their own dynastic territories. In 1991, the West could not abandon Kuwait's oil resources. Malthus, in his 1798 *Essay on the Principle of Population*, suggested that conflict becomes more frequent and intense as populations grow in size and density; this growth leads to an increase in pressure on and competition for subsistence and resources, which then becomes if not the stated aim, at least the expected and desired spoils of war. The four horsemen are Famine, Pestilence, War and Death – and they ride together.

Many historical examples appear to support Malthus's view; but, equally, there are many that do not. While pressure on resources due to population density may be an important factor, it is not an exclusive cause of war. Expectations, proximity to rivals, perceived grievances about exchange values, and political ambition must also be considered. Landscape factors have an important part to play in many of these scenarios. In addition to competition for particular resources, we must consider how rival communities are located in relation to communication and exchange networks and routes, how their utilisation of the land has shaped their social and political expectations and systems, and where and how the borders between groups are sited and controlled in relation to the opportunity for intrusion and conflict. The effects of climatic and biological change on subsistence and resource availability must also be considered. It has been suggested that those societies which have the greatest history of surviving natural disaster tend to be more prone to bellicosity than societies dwelling in more temperate regions, and that aggression rises in line with the severity of naturally-created stress. It was during a period of low rainfall in southern Africa in the early nineteenth century that there was an increase in the frequency of Bantu raids upon their neighbours, and that the Zulu state began to emerge as a considerable and forceful entity.[4]

The periodic effects of El Niño events may have had a strong influence on the rise and fall of various South and Central American states in the pre-Columban periods; drought and its effect on the Anasazi culture is an example of the importance of the climatic change as a causal factor for aggression.

The Anasazi of the American south-west

Over some 1000 or more years, a number of cultures developed in the region of the South Western states of Arizona, Utah, Colorado and New Mexico centuries before Columbus discovered America. Among these cultures were the Hohokam, the Mogollon and the Anasazi or Pueblo people. Between about AD 500 and 1000 the Anasazi group increased its population significantly, and increasingly relied on the growing of crops, particularly corn (maize) for subsistence. By about AD 700 several distinct groupings had emerged within the culture, including the Cibola group and the Mesa Verde group, each with slightly different assemblages of artefacts and styles, and possibly slightly different religious practices. The various sub-groups traded with each other, exchanging pottery, food and some exotic trade items such as turquoise and shells from the shores of the Pacific.

During the ninth century AD, villages became ever larger. Some became part of a very extensive road network; the settlements in Chaco Canyon were linked by over 400 miles (645km) of roads up to 12.2m wide and running in stretches 60 miles (96.5km) long,[5] bringing over 30 settlements into contact with trade routes that covered vast sections of what is now the western half of America and Mexico. There do seem to have been incidents of internal conflict between about AD 900 and 1100. The work of Professor Christy Turner and others has led to the strong suggestion that ritual cannibalism was being practised among the Anasazi, or upon them by intrusive people possibly originating among the Toltec peoples of central Mexico; the Toltecs were the precursors of the Aztecs, and it is from the Toltecs that the Aztecs inherited their most bloody ritual practices.[6] Further theories proposed to explain the evidence for violence include the possible arrival in the region of hostile Atapasca peoples, ancestors of the present day Navajos and Apaches. Alternatively, hostilities may have arisen within Anasazi communities as a result of rivalries between clans or secret ritual societies.

By about AD 1150 the Anasazi people had reached their greatest population density. The south-western region seems to have climatic cycles that recur every 300 years or so. From AD 1030 up to 1150, the predominant weather pattern had been one of winter rains, resulting in a build-up of soils and a maintenance of a relatively high water table. Then the pattern changed to one of summer rains – soils were quickly eroded and water became ever more scarce. Between AD 1272 and 1285 the Great Drought occurred and much arable land went out of cultivation. Efforts were made to conserve water and install irrigation systems, but these could not, in the long run, deal with the stress put upon the subsistence economy by the climate change, and by the changes that had occurred within Anasazi society during the eleventh and twelfth centuries.

In Chaco Canyon, at least 13 substantial villages demonstrate a general tendency for people to start to come together into larger communities during this time. Similar patterns can be seen at Mesa Verde where some 500 people from the Far View settlement in AD 1100 had relocated by 1200 to a much bigger community about 10 miles (16km) south. In Chaco Canyon, the settlement of Pueblo Bonita had some 800 'rooms' or family dwelling spaces, and 32 kivas, or subterranean ritual chambers. Unlike much building in the American south-west, these later Anasazi villages were built not of adobe but of carefully cut sandstone blocks, roofed with massive pine timbers brought from many miles away. These great 'pueblos' were much more defensively sited than the earlier smaller settlements, and where smaller settlements remained in use, they began to surround themselves with defensive palisades. Balcony House, a settlement in Mesa Verde, could only be reached by a guarded tunnel.

Dendrochronology suggests a building date of AD 1278 for this structure. Stepped terrace construction of the buildings, some four-storeys high, allowed defenders to fire missiles down on any attackers from unassailable platforms, and access within the buildings was often by trapdoors and ladders that could be drawn up in times of danger. Doorways at ground level were very rare.[7] Despite the massive building programmes, the skeletal evidence shows that this was a society in crisis – Harris lines on bones demonstrate periods of malnutrition, and there was a rise in the mortality of infants and children.[8]

84 Anasazi dwellings in New Mexico after a photograph taken in 1873. Late in the life of the Pueblo Cultures, stone houses were built on almost inaccessible ledges among the sandstone cliffs

By the thirteenth century there are clear signs of warfare across the whole region, with houses burned and villages destroyed; bodies are found that had been decapitated, and many show evidence of arrow wounds. It seems to be clear that people were clinging together for defence. In the first half of the century, few communities housed more than 25 families, outside the great pueblos; by the second half, nearly all the population was living in groups of between 75-400 'rooms'. At the end of this period, the heartland of the Anasazi culture appears to have been abandoned; occupation did continue in more peripheral zones and the climate began to improve. Signs of warfare begin to disappear. Nevertheless, the habit of defence was not given up; later villages still often have strong defences, and there is some continuing evidence in the skeletal material for isolated bouts of violence. Around this period a new people entered the region, the Navajo, who saw the spectacular remains of the great pueblos and named their builders the 'Ancient Ones' – Anasazi. This culture seems to have gradually been absorbed into the other groups that make up the tribes of the region today; the breakdown of their period of greatness is clearly attributable to climatic change, but it is worth noting that the period of warfare that may have contributed towards this breakdown is evidenced archaeologically in almost direct correlation with the palaeoenvironmental evidence for the period of severe drought and soil erosion.

Several writers have pointed to the fact that once a society has turned to war it retains an acceptance of aggression as a problem-solving strategy even after the original cause and outbreak of war is over. A readiness for war remains part of the behaviour of societies which before the first conflict appear to have been peaceful.

In other words, once learned, warfare cannot be unlearned. Its form, scope and frequency may change over time, but it does not disappear entirely.

Military posture and technology

Sometimes in military history, technological breakthroughs can mark a change in the way warfare is approached. Improved performances in rifles or artillery may supply good reason to adopt different stances or postures on the battlefield. Other times, it is not so much the technological improvement as such which changes the way things are done, but the manner in which existing technologies are combined to produce a weapon of hitherto unheard of capabilities. This is especially true of the post-industrial era. The development of the tank, outlined below, is a classic example of this. The tank's transformation into its Second World War role reflects a change in posture from the entrenched defensive lines of the First World War to the Blitzkrieg-style mobile offensive warfare of the latter war.

In the nineteenth century, industrialisation made a number of things possible that were not before. Weapons technology was of course an immediate beneficiary of the process, allowing theoretical designs to see fruition. The Minié bullet, for example, the base of which expanded after firing so that it gripped the rifling of the barrel, virtually doubled the range and accuracy of the weapon. The British soon employed the principle in the 1850s with the result that ranges increased from 300 to 600 yards. Just 150 soldiers armed with the Minié would equal 525 armed with a musket.[9] Strategic capabilities were also improved with the coming of the railways and the use of the telegraph. In fact, the railways became such a mainstay of troop transportation, munitions and supplies movement, that they have been important ever since. All of this made it possible to increase the size of the armies who were fighting. Forces at war in the years before and during the Industrial Revolution were becoming national in scale. It is the factor of size which put paid to the usefulness of the fortification systems of the era of Vauban as outlined in chapter 3. As early as 1672, the French army was increased from 30,000 to 120,000 men to fight the Dutch war, and later to 360,000 men. Fortress strongholds simply could not hold out against an aggressor. Instead, a new posture was adopted: that of positional warfare.[10] The trench systems of the American Civil War and the First World War were to become the new static posture. The chilling thing about both these wars is that the posture adopted by the opposing forces made armies vulnerable to the devastating killing power of the new modern weapons. This was attritional warfare at its most deadly. Whoever ran out of men first would lose the war.

Technological change also has a causal effect in warfare, as well as being stimulated and advanced by military demand in preparation for and during conflicts. Those societies which have developed and practise settled agriculture find themselves in conflict with hunter-gatherer or nomadic and pastoral groups – in competition for land and water, in arguments about access and boundaries, and in disputes over ownership and rights to food. Improvements in transport have led to expansion, incursion, imperialism and colonialism as well as providing opportunities for increased ranges for raids and other conflicts. Improved subsistence methods and resource utilisation also, of course, tend to lead to animal and human population expansion and thence competition for resources.

Technology is also a factor in the escalation in warfare, as each side strives to produce more decisive weaponry and more effective defences against the improvements made by enemy science. It is a case of measure versus counter-measure. Eventually, technological spirals can even lead to stalemates and the preconditions for negotiating truces and even peace terms. Other causes of escalation can include the drawing-in of other communities because of accidental or deliberate actions (bombing errors, or the need to gain extra resources to continue the struggle, for example); the perception of an increasing scale of atrocity perpetrated by the enemy, often the reporting of specific events against civilian victims but equally often, historically, based on little real fact; and by the increase in personal power and the opportunity to exert political and physical force to achieve dominance gained by military leaders during the course of a struggle. These stages seem to occur in a pattern of steps and plateaux in the chronology of a war. The Roman success against the Carthaginians allowed them to gain their first overseas colony in Spain. Their desire for a land route to this new bonanza led to their involvement in Graeco-Gaulish southern France. Their involvement in southern France eventually provided the platform for Julius Caesar's campaigns which were motivated as much by personal ambition as by any other cause.

The case of the tank outlined below demonstrates a good example of the problems encountered by those who had the vision to see that a combination of technologies could change the face of battle in the twentieth century.

Armoured warfare – the tank

There is no doubt that the tracked armoured fighting vehicle has revolutionised warfare. At the heart of the beginning of the story was the desire to see mobility introduced to the battlefield, to find a way of assisting the infantry in smashing through enemy machine-gun and other fixed positions. Eventually the weapon became incorporated into giant mobile armies capable of long-distance strikes whose vehicles included a balance of mobility, firepower and protection. The tank became, and still is today, a decisive land weapon.

An officer of the Royal Engineers, Major E.D. Swinton (as he then was), was the first exponent of mobility. Parallel with his ideas of developing the Holt caterpillar tractor as a mechanism for carrying forward a gun were the ideas of Winston Churchill, then First Lord of the Admiralty, who also wanted to introduce a mobile aspect to the capabilities of the Royal Naval Division and Royal Naval Air Service. Swinton's observations were very clear. The problem in the early days of the First World War was that the enemy had ample heavy artillery and plenty of time to fortify his defences and dig-in. In other words, the defensive aspects of warfare (on both sides) had got the better of the offensive. Swinton saw the caterpillar tracked machine-gun destroyer as the way to break the cycle. It would flatten barbed wire entanglements, provide some support for infantry, be bullet-proof and have enough firepower capability to knock out fixed positions. Swinton argued that up to 12 miles could be covered a day by the tanks and also went as far as suggesting that artillery and aircraft should support the vehicle, a controversial idea for the time.

Early in 1916, trials of prototype vehicles named 'tanks' for purposes of deception were undertaken in England. Despite impressing many, it was not until June 1917 that tanks were organised into Tank Corps.

On the 1 July 1916 the Battle of the Somme began; by this time the British forces had taken delivery of 40 tanks. Towards the end of the battle, tanks were deployed in small detachments in very difficult muddy ground. Also, they had not been employed in numbers sufficient enough to exploit the element of surprise which Swinton had recommended. The tanks were not successful and GHQ wobbled.

With the passing of the beacon of mobility to Maj. Gen. J.F.C. Fuller, who knew nothing of Swinton's writings, came the continuing pressure for tanks to be used en masse. On 20 November 1917, a mass tank attack involving 378 tanks with 6 infantry divisions, supported by a cavalry reserve, took place at Cambrai. The ground was dry and firm, and there was no preliminary bombardment to tip off the enemy. Although the surprise element was achieved, 179 tanks had been taken out of action on the first day, 71 from mechanical troubles, 43 from ditching and only 65 from direct hits. The Germans, through counter-attacks, re-established their positions in a short time as the British attack had advanced so far that the cavalry could not exploit its success. In a way though, Cambrai was a success for the tank, in that it showed what it could do if used in numbers to break the stalemate of trench warfare.

German tank-building was not initiated until late in the War, and the main vehicle, the A7V, was not a great success. The French developed heavy tanks, but were particularly fond of a small two-man tank, the Renault FT (**colour plate 26**).

Until the period between the wars, few people had considered the employment of tanks as part of a long-distance strike-force in a combined arms fully motorised unit. This was to become the great passion of General Heinz Guderian when he was in charge of motorised troops. Drawing upon the work of an Englishman, Captain B.H. Liddel Hart, Guderian frequently pushed for what he saw as a new form of decisive mobile warfare, turning his own mobile supply troops into combat troops. He met with many obstacles on the way, not the least of which were the attitudes of his superiors during his early career. The commander of the German Inspectorate of Motorised Troops, General Otto von Stüpnagel, told him in 1931, 'You're too impetuous! Believe me, neither of us will ever see German tanks in operation in our lifetime.'[11] There was a reason for this. The German mentality since the punitive Treaty of Versailles had become somewhat defensive. What Guderian was proposing was an armoured strike force of such magnitude and concentration that it in itself could take and hold ground on an Operational level (a level somewhere between the tactical and strategic). Improved wireless and communication facilities would ensure that command could be maintained despite the speed of an advance. Even as late as 1933, when two Panzer Divisions had already been reluctantly accepted, General Beck, the Chief of the General Staff at the Inspectorate, disliked the philosophy of the tank unit commanders being as far forward as possible. He was very much of the old school and believed in delaying defence down to the last rifle section.

The German tank exercises of the late 1920s and early 1930s were carried out with canvas dummies pushed about on foot at first. Then came motorised dummies with mild steel plates, and things began to improve for Guderian and his colleagues when General Lutz took over at the Inspectorate and Guderian got the Chief-of-Staff job. Guderian envisaged a panzer division with two types of tank: a light tank with armour-piercing gun and two machine guns (hull and turret mounted), and a medium tank with a larger calibre gun and two machine guns. While he waited for the endless arguments to resolve themselves about methods and materials of manufacture, Guderian needed a training tank. The training tank was based on the Carden-Loyd chassis, an English design originally intended for a 20mm anti-aircraft gun. This meant that the training tank could mount nothing larger than machine guns, but it could at least be made ready for service by 1934. This tank became the Panzer I (**colour plate 26**).

In 1933, Hitler came to see Guderian's exercises at Kummersdorf and proclaimed 'That's what I need! That is what I want to have!' With this kind of support, although there were some reversions to using the tank as infantry support (particularly in the case of the 4th Panzer division), Guderian's dreams would become a reality. On 15 October 1935, three Panzer Divisions were created: 1st Panzer under General Freiherr von Weichs (Weimar); 2nd Panzer under Colonel Guderian (Würzburg) and 3rd Panzer under General Fessmann (Berlin).

In an article of the 15 October 1937 entitled 'Tank Attack by Fire and Movement', published in the Journal of the National Union of German officers, Guderian set out the principal philosophy of armoured warfare in the new age. The tank was to be a harmonious balance between armoured protection, firepower and manoeuvrability. Upon movement he had this to say:

> Everything is therefore dependent on this: to be able to move faster than has hitherto been done: to keep moving despite the enemy's defensive fire and thus to make it harder for him to build up fresh defensive positions: and finally to carry the attack deep into the enemy's defences.

The tank could bring its firepower to bear whilst actually advancing, so Guderian argued. It was true. Although it is harder to register a target on the move, it was not impossible. Within a few years Panzer Divisions would be employed exactly as Guderian had envisaged as part of Manstein's clever reversal of the Schlieffen Plan, in a drive to the English Channel, with fatal consequences for French and English Forces.

Captain B.H. Liddel Hart remarked upon reading Guderian's own account of his drive to the channel as being 'like the repetition of a dream, as it was just the way that in pre-war years, I had pictured such a force being handled . . . only to be told, then, that the picture was unrealistic.'[12]

In 1940 the Blitzkrieg tactic gained Germany's rapid early successes in Holland and Belgium, and allowed them to punch through the Ardennes, covering 240 miles in 11 days and cutting the Allied defensive lines in half. Tank production in Germany was well organised, but by no means as rapid and successful as that of the Russians. The Russian T-34 (**86a & b**) was greatly superior to the Panzer III and IV series,

85 *A knocked-out French Somua S35 tank. Embodying the right balance of firepower, armour and mobility, this tank could have been one of the best of the Second World War, but it was hampered by the fact that the man in the turret had to perform several jobs at once.* Photograph: Julie Wileman's collection

despite having a cramped interior. It had armour 45mm thick compared to a German maximum of 30mm, guns capable of taking out most tanks, and a top speed of about 32mph. These factors represented an agreeable mixture of protection, firepower and speed, which combined with its low silhouette made it one of the best tanks of the war. The T34 was not the only tank which had the right mixture. The French Somua S35 (**85**) was another candidate for the accolade, but suffered by having only a one-man turret, which meant that the jobs of loading, firing and commanding the vehicle were given to just one crew member.

During the bitter struggles of the Second World War in Russia, it was the Russians' ability to churn out highly effective tanks at an amazing rate, coupled with the combined advantages created by the sheer distances involved and the severity of the winters, which eventually overcame German military efficiency and courage. The Russians, however, did not readily accept the proposals of the proponents of mobility at the beginning of 1941, preferring to use tanks more in an infantry support role.

The entry of the Americans into the war brought the Sherman, among other vehicles, into the action. Many different versions of the Sherman were developed,

86a/b Two knocked-out T34 tanks being examined by German soldiers. The top picture probably shows an earlier model. Photographs: Julie Wileman's collection

notably the amphibious type used in the D-Day landings. Shermans were regarded as simple to maintain; they were fast and manoeuvrable, and the Americans could match the Russian rate of production. They did however have an alarming tendency to catch fire when hit. Among the other versions produced were a mine-clearing flail tank, a flamethrowing type, a bridge-building tank, and a bulldozer.

Despite a long period of peace in Europe since 1945, tanks have continued to demonstrate their importance on the battlefield, not least in the Arab-Israeli wars of 1956 and 1973. It is not yet the case that anti-tank capabilities, or the accuracy of aerial smart bombs, have signalled the end for the tank. It is still the best way to move and fight on the modern battlefield.

Irregular and special troops

Before the formalisation of armies and war, all fighters might be termed 'irregular'. The concept of 'primitive war' discussed by Keeley and others is one that is also familiar in respect of guerrilla, partisan or insurgent warfare, characterised by a lack of recognition of the so-called rules of war, and by special levels of ferocity and high numbers of casualties. Operations tend to be carried out by small, more or less autonomous bands, often out of uniform and with a variety of weaponry, sometimes old or home-made. These types of forces are experts in the utilisation of specific landscapes – the *maquis* fighters of southern France during the Second World War, for example, or Vietcong guerrillas in the jungles of South-east Asia, or the urban tactics employed in Bosnia or Chechnya.

The above list demonstrates the resurgence of this type of warfare in modern times. When war is no longer confined to mutually agreed battlefields but spills over into areas previously considered too difficult for formal operations, or when aggression is covert, carried out against occupying powers or by disaffected groups against their own governments, irregular troops are typically those which are called for.

The British began to recognise the usefulness of irregular troops alongside regular armies in the campaigns in North America at the end of the eighteenth century, as did the French, both sides making particular use of Indian fighters for their scouting abilities in the dense and unknown forests, and the fear their fabled ferocity struck in the hearts of the enemy, and also using units of Rangers for intelligence and sabotage missions. Wellington's war in the Peninsula was greatly assisted by the actions of Spanish irregulars, and it was this war that coined the word 'guerrilla'. The partisans' ability to move quickly through the desperately difficult landscapes of central Spain and the Pyrenees and to disappear as quickly as they came contributed vastly to what Napoleon came to regard as the 'Spanish ulcer'. Whilst not contributing greatly to major actions, the constant harrying of troops and supplies by these bands tied up a great many French troops. Occasionally, however, they achieved major successes: a young farmer, Francisco Espos y Mina, led a raid in spring 1812 on a huge French supply train at the Salinas pass, freeing nearly 500 Spanish prisoners and accounting for the best part of 5000 French casualties killed or injured. The Peninsular campaign also offers examples of other facets of irregular war; the French refused to recognise the Spanish irregulars as anything other than bandits and would shoot them out of hand if they were captured. The guerrilleros responded with equal brutality against French soldiers, who then took vicious reprisals against civilians suspected of aiding the partisans. This had the effect of driving the peasants into offering even greater support to the guerrilleros. This pattern can be observed in numerous subsequent campaigns all over the world.

By the twentieth century, the regular armies of many nations began to recognise that the best way to combat guerrilla troops was to create specialist units of their own, trained in guerrilla and covert tactics. Britain created Commando units, the Special Air Service and the Special Boat Service; the USA formed the Green Berets; and the French have formed several special operations units, within which roles the Foreign Legion now features strongly.

The SAS was born in the desert war of 1941-3 in North Africa; Lt David Stirling, confined to a hospital bed in Cairo, designed a force that would be made up of small highly-trained autonomous units capable of creating havoc behind enemy lines and somehow managed to sell the idea to his senior officers and gain promotion to captain at the same time. Deep penetration, parachute drops, survival training and specialist technical skills have all become the hallmarks of the SAS. Despite some early setbacks, this unit, originally comprising just 66 Commandos, has come to be recognised as one of the most efficient covert forces in the world.

The other side of the coin has been the rise of the various terrorist 'armies' during the last century – groups like the IRA, PLF, the Al Qaida network or Japanese Red Army. Rather than direct their efforts solely against military targets, these forces often use paramilitary tactics against civilians. Civilian targets are easier to hit, gain more publicity and create conditions of low morale and distrust more easily. For these groups, it is the modern technical urban landscape that is their hunting and killing ground, and they have learned to camouflage their activities as effectively against this background as Norwegian partisans did in the Arctic during the Second World War.

The archaeology of irregular troop actions is even more difficult to recognise than conventional warfare, usually lacking permanent bases or fortifications, uniforms or regular munitions. In some cases, traces may be left of their actions – the famous Vietcong tunnels, for example – but, for the most part, the traces left for posterity are likely to be as insubstantial as the evidence of their actions was likely to be spotted at the time. It may be that the most visible aspects of covert war result from the over-reaction of regular forces in response to such attack. The destruction of villages and crops by the French in reprisal for guerrilla actions in the Peninsula may be traceable; the village of Vassieux was systematically razed by the Germans as reprisal for Resistance activity, burning many of the people alive inside their homes.

On the whole, however, there is likely to be little that the future can recognise. Irregular forces trade off their invisibility, leaving scant archaeological trace. They have the advantage in many cases of being able to live off the land. Moving in small groups and often with minimal technology, they can survive in terrain which is impossible for larger armies because of the necessities of providing sufficient fuel, equipment and food to the forces.

Logistics and supply

No single aspect of warfare is more immediately influential on the life of the countryside than the supply of food, fodder and raw materials for weapons, vehicles, uniforms and equipment for the forces. These activities can have lasting effects on the landscape. In the case of south-east England, for example, we can still see the results of Neolithic flint mining, Roman and later iron quarrying, the water management, earthworks and buildings associated with the gunpowder industry from the sixteenth to the early twentieth centuries, shipbuilding yards, and the building of canals and turnpikes to bring products and supplies to embarkation points, depots and training grounds for most of recorded history. Perhaps the most far-reaching aspect of military supply in the region has been deforestation – for fuel to run the case mills, iron foundries and gunpowder works, for building timber especially for ships, and many other purposes. Local legend has it that Walnut Tree Clump, at Norbury Park, Surrey, once boasted 22,000 walnut trees all cut down by one Andrew Chapman in the late eighteenth century as part of his war profiteering; he is said to have sold the wood to make musket stocks for use against the American colonists in the War of Independence. Certainly, not a single walnut tree survives there today.

For most of history, armies carried minimal supplies with them – it was generally expected that they would, once campaigning began, 'live off the land'. It was a mark of the rise of professional armies that they needed to think more seriously about provisioning. Supplying an army, particularly a mobile force, is a complex feat. The raw materials must be acquired, packed and placed on to carriers; suitable routes must be found and supply caches and depots set up. Storage facilities must be built and equipment for utilising the provision (mobile kitchens, forges etc.) must be designed and provided.

The Roman army was notable for its organisation of supply, although it was by no means the first to think of logistics in a holistic way: the Assyrian king Sennacherib (704-681 BC) had grain and hay sent ahead of his army prior to his devastating assault on the kingdom of Elam in 694 BC. The Romans, however, designed basic rations (corn baked into hard biscuits called *buccellati*, somewhat similar to later ship's biscuits), basic kit including tents, stakes, shovels, mobile workshops, and storage depots. A familiar aspect of Roman fortresses is the rows of raised granaries always provided, theoretically capable of holding up to two years' supply. Each legionary carried a heavy basic pack, and other items were transported on the backs of mules for speed. Byzantine armies similarly marched with supply carts loaded with a basic set of equipment designed for the use of each group of 16 infantry soldiers.

Keegan notes a particular feature of the need to supply early professional armies:

> Wheeled vehicles needed roads. It is significant that two of the greatest empires of the ancient world, the Persian and the Roman, left as enduring monuments the roads they made. The Persian Royal Road connected Susa, near the head of the Gulf, with Sardis, close to the Mediterranean coast of Asia Minor, sweeping across 1500 miles of wild country. The

> Romans constructed a network of roads right across their Empire to ease the passage of marching troops, their wagons and pack-animals.[13]

Hitler's Germany prepared for war in part by the building of autobahns in the 1930s.

The difficulty of passage on poor roads is a major reason for the short campaigning season of most medieval armies. In many cases the depredations of foraging troops were far more feared than actual warfare, and did far more damage to populations. In later centuries, armies moved with vast baggage-trains – 'The armies of seventeenth-century Europe resembled nothing so much as huge maggots gnawing their way across the face of the land, leaving a trail of famine and destruction behind them.'[14]

By the nineteenth century, technology provided a new form of transport for the military – the railway. France in 1859 moved hundreds of thousands of men and horses by rail during the war with Austria, and the notable superiority in miles of track and numbers of locomotives was an important advantage to the Union army during the American Civil War.

The trenches of World War I also relied to a large extent on rail transport for supply, although the invention of motorised road transport was also important, especially for the increasing demands on ammunition supply created by the adoption of rapid-fire weaponry. In 1914 the British forces possessed 827 cars and 15 motorcycles; by 1918 they had 56,000 lorries and 34,000 motorcycles. The mid- and later twentieth century saw the almost universal adoption of air transport, which in the case of bulk carriage by aircraft necessitates the building of landing strips.

The horse or mule has not completely been superseded by modern technology, however. Even with the rapid rise in the amount of supplies carried by motorised or rail transport during the First World War, four-legged assistance was vital. As well as the 25,000 horses owned by the British Army in 1914 and the 400,000-500,000 supplied from home to 1918 (165,000 of which were impressed into service during the first 12 days of the war), a further 700,000-800,000 were purchased in North America, and others were bought from South America, Australia and New Zealand, India, Spain, Portugal and South Africa, along with thousands of camels, oxen and donkeys.

The attrition rate on these animals was awful, despite rapid advances in care and veterinary attention.

> First, [during the hard winter on 1916-1917] there were weeks on end of rain, then weeks of rigorous cold and icy winds, and then rain again with the thaw. The greatest care could not overcome the evils that followed on those dreadful conditions. Flanders and the Somme country are appalling areas in such circumstances. The mud was awful and literally engulfed horses. There were parts where wheeled traffic could not go, and yet supplies had to be got to their objectives and the guns moved as directed. So loads had to be carried as packs, and, in this way weighed down, our war-horses and mules were pulled to pieces.[15]

87 Mule supplying ammunition to the front line during the First World War

A major side-effect of the demand for horses during 1914-18 was the increase in speed of the adoption of motorised transport for commercial and agricultural purposes at home, leading to road building programmes, traffic signals, garage and service stations, scrap heaps and all the other effects so visible in the modern landscape. Horses and mules continue to be used in war in those places where roads do not exist and conditions are not suitable for air transport – in recent years they have been employed in the mountains of the former Yugoslavia and in Afghanistan.

It was the Duke of Wellington who laid the foundations for modern logistics and supply corps during the Peninsular War. Most armies, from the Romans onwards, with an organised supply service, rely on contracting materials from civilian sources; this has always provided great opportunities for graft and fraud, or worse. Civilian muleteers were said to sell 'pork' to soldiers in Portugal that they had carved from the bodies of dead Frenchmen. The new commissariat issued tickets in exchange for requisitioned supplies, cutting down to some extent on the desertions, fights and other problems caused by allowing troops to forage for themselves. The problem was one that the French army was plagued with to a much greater extent. The system was not perfect, and rations were often short or rotten, but it did allow a much greater degree of discipline to be maintained among the British troops.

Nineteenth-century armies were vast compared to their predecessors, and the demands made on the countryside were proportionately huge. A division of 7000 men in Wellington's army would require 10,500lb of bread, 7000lb of meat, and 7000 pints of wine each day. To this could be added (in ideal conditions) a quarter of a pint of peas, 1oz of butter and 1oz of rice per man, and 14lb of hay, 10lb of oats and 4lb of straw each day for each horse (the army in early 1813 had over 20,000 horses).[16] It is almost impossible to appreciate the sheer acreage of agricultural production this represents, and the figures for the World Wars are almost unbelievable. Apart from the vast overseas purchases necessary, the Second World War saw the 'Dig For Victory' campaign, which brought many areas into cultivation that had never before been utilised. The problems in supplying forage for animals in particular have had major effects on the speed and success of military actions:

> an early thirteenth-century Caliph of Baghdad sent his troops to plough up the land ahead of an invading army since destroying the grass was a more effective method of driving off the enemy than meeting them in battle with inferior forces. Similarly the Mongol army which invaded Syria in 1260 had to withdraw, not because it was beaten in battle but because all the grass was used up.[17]

A further technological advance of the nineteenth century was the introduction of preserved foods; Napoleon's troops were provided with boiled beef in glass jars. The French term 'bouilli' (boiled) is the origin for the 'bully beef' that by the American Civil War was being issued in cans, along with vegetables and other foods.

By the end of the last century, major campaigns were supported by incredibly sophisticated commissariats – in Vietnam basic supplies for US personnel included hot dogs, ice cream and Coca Cola, a far cry from the rations of the soldiers of previous centuries. Small supply towns appear for even relatively transient military or police actions; similar towns, or *vici*, grew up outside more permanent Roman fortresses throughout their empire, some of which have survived as settlements to the present day.

In many societies and over many periods, there have been trends towards urbanisation, central places for settlement surrounded by the agricultural lands necessary to support them, and linked together by networks of roads and other lines of communication for trade and control of surrounding territory. Wealth becomes centralised in towns, as does power, and they therefore become targets for aggressive action within the landscape. The response to this has been a long series of defensive designs and the use of sophisticated technologies designed to protect the inhabitants, their property, and their symbols of power, such as religious, judicial and administrative centres, elite residences and public buildings. Equally intense attention has been paid to ways to attack and capture urban centres. In a more purely military arena, castles, strongholds and forts, often in themselves symbols of power, have been developed with siege warfare in mind, even where the primary aim in their construction has been more generally aggressive – to control conquered or restless populations, or to threaten neighbours, for example. It is in the ebbs and flows of siege warfare that we can see some of the most innovative military thinking at work over the ages. In many ways, it is in siege warfare that we find the most important applications of science and technology for war developing over the centuries, and from earliest times the complex stratagems of this form of battle have taxed the ingenuity of armies and their leaders.

Siege warfare

Why doesn't the enemy simply go round a city, cutting it off from its territory and supplies? There are several reasons for engaging in a siege; in the first place, it would be unwise to leave an undefeated centre in the rear of an advance – attacks could easily be mounted on the rear of the army unless troops are stationed to pin the defenders inside, and that means tying up a goodly part of the force every time a town is encountered. Additionally, the town's defeat will provide prestige, booty, further supplies, and the demoralisation of its territory and of other towns. It may also be the case that capture of the town may result in the capture or death of the leaders of the defenders, destroying the political infrastructure of the area, perhaps of the nation. There have, of course, been situations where the besieging of a city has been the wrong move, as was the case at Stalingrad in the Second World War. Military hubris has always played a part in siege warfare too.

The main weapons of a besieger have always been starvation and disease, but these are double-edged. The besieging army also has to be fed and kept healthy, often a tall order in enemy territory and the factor behind some notable failures in history. If the surrounding farms have been destroyed by their owners before they flee behind the protecting walls of a city, the besieger has to expend much effort and many troops to forage over long distances to maintain his effectiveness. Sieges can be lengthy affairs – not all as long as Troy, by any means, but long enough for both sides to suffer badly without sufficient logistical support. At the siege of Harfleur in 1415, despite numerous attempts to take the town, which included diverting a river to flood it and contaminate its water supply, resistance continued so strongly that by the time it capitulated, the English had lost one third of their army through desertion and dysentry. They fared better at Rouen, however, where it was the townspeople who suffered worst. The town had been militarily well prepared, with a numerous garrison, freshly dug ditches and pits, strong walls, towers and gates well supplied with guns and catapults, and retaining dumps of earth banked against the walls to resist bombardment and mining. The English strategy was to build campaign forts in front of each of the town gates, connected to each other by palisaded trenches, and to block the river access to the town. The battle became one of the most vicious of its period, with increasing levels of atrocity carried out by both sides. About 12,000 non-combatants were sent out of the town to preserve supplies for those who could fight, but they were not permitted to pass through the English lines. They remained trapped between the walls and the besiegers, throughout the winter, in continuous rain without food or shelter except for a small dole given by the English at Christmas. Inside the town, there were tales of cannibalism and it was claimed that 5000 people starved to death before the defenders capitulated halfway through January.

Castles were more vulnerable to starvation and disease than towns in some instances, being smaller and more crowded, especially if they had opened their gates to fleeing peasants from the surrounding district. For this reason, a

> medieval campaign was best timed for the mid or late summer. The harvest would be in the fields, flocks would be grazing, and wooden defences would be dry enough to burn. A castle would have low stocks of food, a well affected by dry weather, and a moat diminished in size.[18]

Other siege weapons were designed either to be used against the defenders on the walls, or to attack the walls themselves, to remove the physical barrier by going over, under or through it. Castle and town walls, especially in the earlier medieval period, were designed to be tall and to have very few openings, thus putting the defenders out of range of the projectile weapons of the period. To counter this advantage, besiegers built towers to reach the top of the walls, dug tunnels to bring them down, or constructed machines capable of lobbing missiles over them. Siege towers went under a range of pseudonyms, including malvoisins and belfrariums. They were cumbersome timber structures, moved on wheels or sledges up to the walls; once in place, troops could scale ladders within the tower and over-reach the defensive wall. The main weapons against towers were the use of fire (countered by soaked timber shutters or hides draped over the structure) or traps dug and concealed near the foot of the walls designed to collapse under the weight of the tower as it approached, tipping it over. Among the machines designed for sieges were the mangonel, capable of throwing stones of up to five hundredweight, the heavier but more accurate trebuchet, and the ballista, a form of giant crossbow. Generally, the effect of the missiles launched from these machines seems to have been more psychological than actual; alternative recorded uses of mangonels included throwing the carcasses of diseased animals over the walls in the hope that they would infect the defenders, and on at least one occasion, using the machine as a way of returning a messenger whose terms of surrender were not satisfactory.

The aim of miners was to dig under the walls of the town or castle, and if the fortifications did not collapse by this method, to set a great fire beneath the structure that would weaken it sufficiently that collapse would soon follow. At the siege of Rochester (**colour plate 27**), King John's engineers famously used the carcasses of 40 fat pigs under the south-east corner of the keep; the resulting heat brought down not only the corner tower but a large section of wall. This apparently surprised the attackers so much that the defenders had time to withdraw behind the keep's crosswall and continue the siege for some time. When the corner of the keep was rebuilt, the new tower was constructed round, rather than square like the other three corners, as it was by then realised that the round shape was inherently stronger and more resistant to this form of attack. Mining was detected by means of bowls of water placed at strategic intervals – if the surface of the water quivered, it indicated activity below ground. The problem was that by the time the warning was given, the mine was far advanced, so the practice of counter-mining developed, driving tunnels aimed at breaking into the attacking galleries and halting their activities. It is said that during the siege of Melun in 1419, a second battlefield was created underground due to the number of mines and countermines, with fights arranged by mutual appointment and heralded by trumpeters.

Advances in technology began to change the face of siege warfare in the medieval period; from the fourteenth century, gunpowder artillery started to appear. Development was rapid and great interest was displayed by rulers in the new weaponry. The interest of James II of Scotland was too personal – his desire to watch from close quarters the performance of a giant bombard called the 'Lion' resulted, as it accidentally exploded, in his own death and the wounding of many of his courtiers. Another fan of artillery was Henry VIII, who invested heavily and took great interest in experiments in the design of new forms of cannon. The use of cannon changed everything; within a short period the traditional castle had become redundant and a new form of stronghold was required – the artillery fort. The massively strong walls, curved low-profile design and utilitarian aspect of Henry's castle such as Deal (**64**) and Walmer (**65**) set the pattern for much defensive building right up to the present day.

Would-be besiegers also have to make sure that they themselves are not vulnerable to attack behind; a siege requires a very great many people tied up in a variety of tasks. Apart from the foragers and miners already mentioned, scouts would be needed to patrol the surrounding countryside to guard against this danger. Specialised personnel would also be needed to man artillery weapons, and messengers would have to be used to pass orders and information to and from all sides of the attack. Cavalry troops would make sorties against relief forces, bowmen or soldiers armed with handguns were used to pick off defenders on the walls, and of course the ordinary infantry soldier was needed to make the assault once a breach had been achieved. A common feature of siege warfare is the use of spies both inside and outside the walls, involving intelligence corps. Propaganda activities are also a recurring feature, attempting to demoralise one side or the other. All these various activities would require advanced logistics and a co-ordinating staff. It is therefore in siege warfare that we see the development of the combined force strategy in full effect. In modern wars, air support is also provided.

It is tempting to think of sieges as geographically confined warfare, but in fact their effects are often felt over much wider areas than the besieged city itself. The surrounding countryside becomes depopulated, agricultural activities come to a standstill, and communications, trade and commerce are affected, sometimes over long distances. Rivers may be redirected, massive earthworks undertaken, stands of timber cut down for fuel or for building engines, providing props for mining or for creating trackways. Bridges and roads are blocked or destroyed; those industries located outside the walls (usually those which present a risk or a nuisance inside a town, such as metalworking and pottery-making or tanning) are terminated. Mills are frequently also located outside towns and were vulnerable. Other settlements curtail much of their own activities too, and take on a more defensive posture, in case they are next to be assailed. Thus a single well-directed siege can bring the life of an entire territory to a standstill. Add to this the effects of conscripting and supplying relieving forces, and the logic of siege warfare becomes even more apparent.

A badly-directed siege, however, can prove catastrophic to an invading force; if the objective cannot be taken rapidly, or its assault proves overly costly in men and equipment, an invasion can grind to a halt within enemy territory. When that happens, the invaders are in great danger of being picked off piecemeal by their foes, and of becoming committed to a rate of expenditure that can cripple their entire campaign.

The three examples of historic sieges outlined below demonstrate the way sieges have been undertaken and the effects that they have had. The loss of Vercingetorix and his forces as a result of events at Alesia were so generally devastating to the Gauls that the Roman takeover could proceed if not without opposition, at least without co-ordinated resistance. Caesar's success in this siege gained Gaul for the empire. The cycle of defensive and aggressive measure and counter-measure is well demonstrated at the siege of Chateau Gaillard. Medieval military technology meant that stalemate was easily reached until the advent of gunpowder changed the nature of siege warfare. This siege also shows that however well-designed and complex the defences are, there is always an element of fortune involved in the outcome of an encounter. Stalingrad, the final example, is a siege gone wrong, where attackers find themselves surrounded and besieged by a giant relieving force.

Alesia

In 52 BC, the spirited Gaulish opposition to the Roman conquest came to an end at the siege of Alesia (**88**). The Gaulish leader, Vercingetorix, after a brilliant campaign which came within a whisker of destroying Julius Caesar's ambitions, was forced to retreat into the oppidum, or native town, with 80,000 of his followers. There is modern dissension over the site of this event. During the nineteenth century, several places claimed the honour, including Alaise in Franche-Comté, but excavations at Alise-Ste-Reine in 1861 seemed to identify the site, and it is now the traditionally accepted location. Napoleon III took great interest in the site, and it is said that the massive statue of Vercingetorix erected nearby has an uncanny likeness to him. More recently another site in the Jura has been suggested; it is claimed that Alise-Ste-Reine is simply too small, and does not have other features mentioned in Caesar's description.

Caesar says that the site was impregnable and could only be taken by siege. He describes a hilltop with steep sides, with rivers on two flanks and a large plain below; around the site were equally tall hills, with a larger mountain to the north. He built two lines of siegeworks around the oppidum, to enclose Vercingetorix and to keep any relieving force at a distance. A relieving force did indeed arrive; according to Caesar's account, it comprised some 200,000 infantry and 8000 cavalry and was composed of tribesmen from all parts of Gaul. There was certainly one Briton at least inside the besieged fortification – Commius of the Atrebates, who had accompanied Caesar back to Gaul after the second of the abortive Roman attempts to conquer Britain in 54 BC. Commius had changed sides, possibly as a result of first-hand experience of the devastating effects of the Roman war machine. The figures given for the participants in the siege must, of course, be taken with a certain amount of reservation. Caesar was

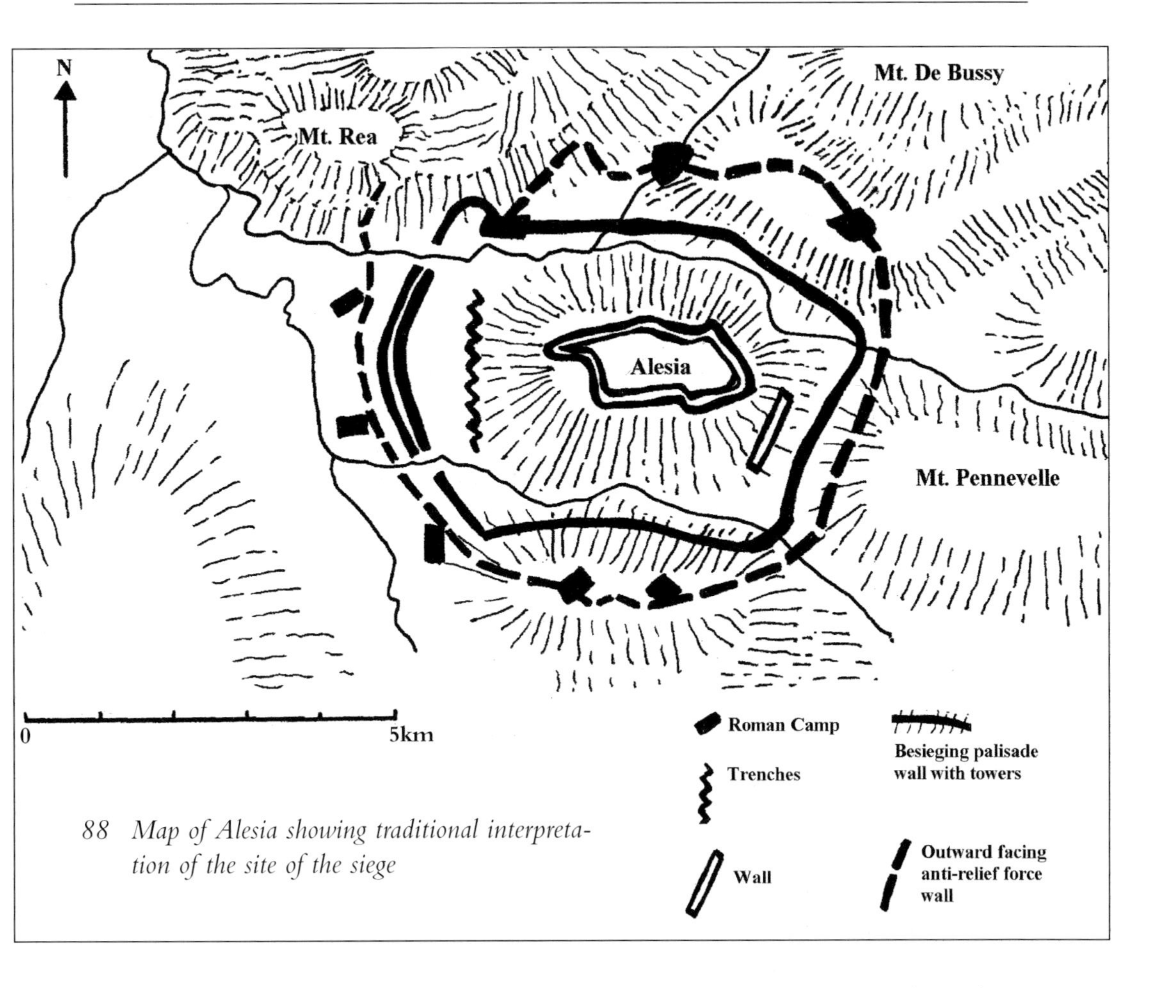

88 Map of Alesia showing traditional interpretation of the site of the siege

certainly not the sort of man to miss an opportunity for self-promotion and may have inflated the numbers of the enemy to enhance his own reputation.

Despite valiant efforts of the relief forces, led by Vercingetorix's cousin Vercassivellaunos, to break the siege, including night raids and desperate efforts from inside to break out, starvation finally drove the Gaulish leader to surrender, to spare his followers further suffering. Vercingetorix was taken to Rome, where he was held in solitary confinement for six years, until the day of Julius Caesar's triumphal procession, when he was executed. Commius managed to escape the siege and returned to Britain, perhaps to the Atrebates' oppidum at Chichester, where he continued to lead the tribe for many years.

The Siege of Chateau Gaillard

Richard the Lionheart's castle on a sharp bend of the River Seine was a state-of-the-art building in its day, but its day was surprisingly short (**89**). It remained 'impregnable' for only seven years. It sat on a 300m-high spur overlooking the river and the town of Andelys. Deep valleys and steep slopes meant that the only possible route for an attacker was from the east. The would-be assailant would first be faced with the defences of the

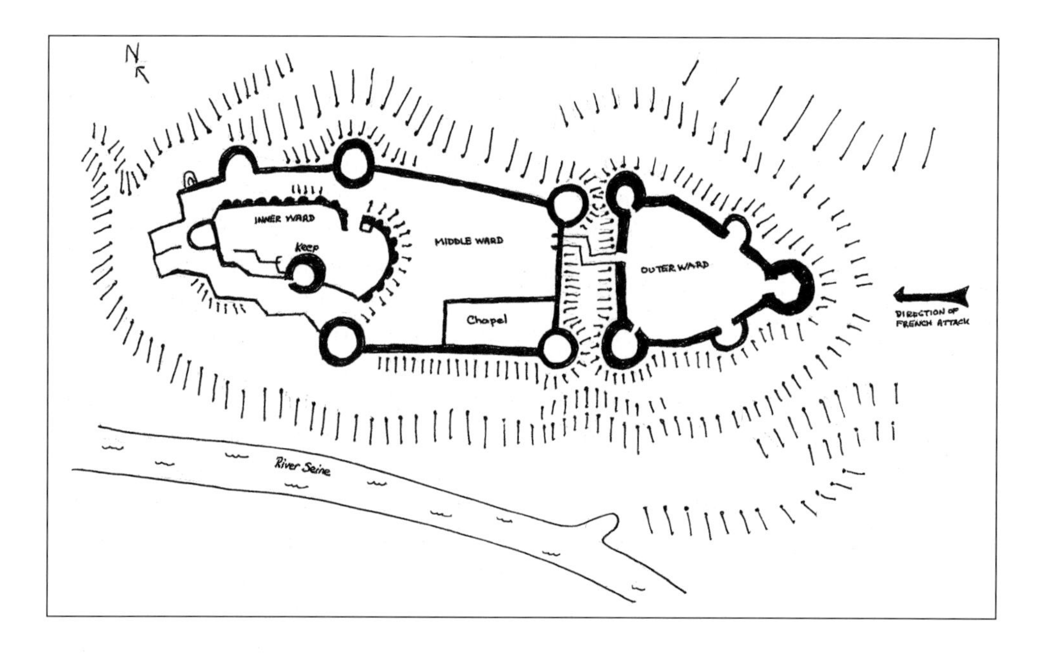

89 Plan of the surviving features at Chateau Gaillard

Outer Ward, protected by massive projecting forward towers. If he managed to fight his way into this ward, he would find access to the next obstacle, the Middle Ward, barred by a 30ft-wide and 20ft-deep ditch, traversed by a causeway that zigzagged across, making it impossible to bring siege engines or towers close to the wall. The eastern towers of the Middle Ward were built to run down flush into the rock of the hill, frustrating any attempt at mining beneath them. Even when this barrier had been overcome, there was still the Inner Ward to take, within the Middle Ward and protected by a 500ft-long curtain wall, its whole length comprising 17 convex buttresses which provided an extremely complex pattern for defensive fire. Much care and attention had been paid to almost every feature of the castle's design – even arrowloops were staggered so as not to weaken the strength of the masonry overall.

In 1203, Philip Augustus, king of France, laid siege to Chateau Gaillard. He began by making a careful reconnaissance, taking out the river defences below the castle first, and making camp at the base of the hill. An early relief attempt by the Earl of Pembroke involving co-ordinated land and boat actions failed, unable to bring the boats up in time. Philip Augustus then isolated the castle by means of trenches and the placement of timber towers; his main assault on the castle itself did not begin until six months after the initial reconnaissance. His engineers managed to mine the towers of the Outer Ward, but this success came to a halt when faced with the defences of the Middle Ward. Siege towers were built, but could not be brought near enough to the walls; engineers climbed the rock face by means of daggers thrust into the chalk face to form ladders, but could not find a way to undermine the towers. It was stalemate – until a French soldier noticed that a latrine shaft on the outer wall had an opening high up near to an unbarred chapel window. He and some fellows managed to clamber up the latrine shaft and pull themselves into the chapel crypt via the window. They started to make a great noise, hoping to frighten the defenders into believing that a large force had gained entry. The defenders' attempt to smoke the French out of the crypt backfired, literally, as the wind changed direction and blew the smoke towards themselves. This, coupled with a great noise being made by the French army at the main gate, was so demoralising that they abandoned the Middle Ward and fell back into the Inner Ward. The crypt party were able to open the gates for their comrades, but the siege was still far from over. The walls of the Inner Ward proved just as resistant to mines as had the outer walls and towers. Philip Augustus had to bring up a great catapult to hammer at the walls while the miners worked under cover of the bridge over the ditch to chip away beneath. Their efforts were eventually assisted by the countermine begun from the inside, intended to scare the French off. Unfortunately, the combined assaults on the structure weakened it sufficiently for a collapse to occur, and the French were finally able to take the keep. The small surviving remnant of the garrison surrendered, some seven months after the siege began. (The population of the village under the castle's walls fared particularly badly; having taken shelter within the castle at the start of the siege, 1000 were sent out as non-combatants and allowed to escape, but the 400 later expelled from the castle were not so lucky. Held between the lines, they eventually resorted to eating grass and, finally, each other. Very few were still alive by the end of the siege.)

Stalingrad

In 1942 the German forces were deeply committed in Russia. Several major objectives were being pursued. The oilfields of the Caucasus were to be seized, and the line of communication provided by the River Volga was to be cut. In the early stages of the push towards the Volga, things went almost too easily – huge distances were covered rapidly, with little opposition. By 23 August, units of the German 6th Army had reached the outer suburbs of the city of Stalingrad (**90**). It immediately became clear that it was here that the Russians were determined to make a stand. The battle to take the city became the most costly in human life of the whole of the Second World War, with total casualties approaching two million lives. In many ways, the battle was unnecessary – the German advance could have taken another approach, cutting the Volga elsewhere and taking the city at more leisure once its support had been severed. However, it was the very name of the city that led Hitler to take a personal interest in its capture and for Stalin to commit a vast amount of resources to its defence, driving his countrymen without mercy to achieve this. During the battle, some 13,500 men were executed for failure to fight well enough, and many others were sent to penal battalions where they were used as expendable gun fodder and even as human mine detectors.

The German advance did not have sufficient heavy armour simply to drive straight at the city. By this time, the Nazi lines of supply were very extended, the need for fuel being one of its greatest problems. They faced a battle of attrition in an urban centre

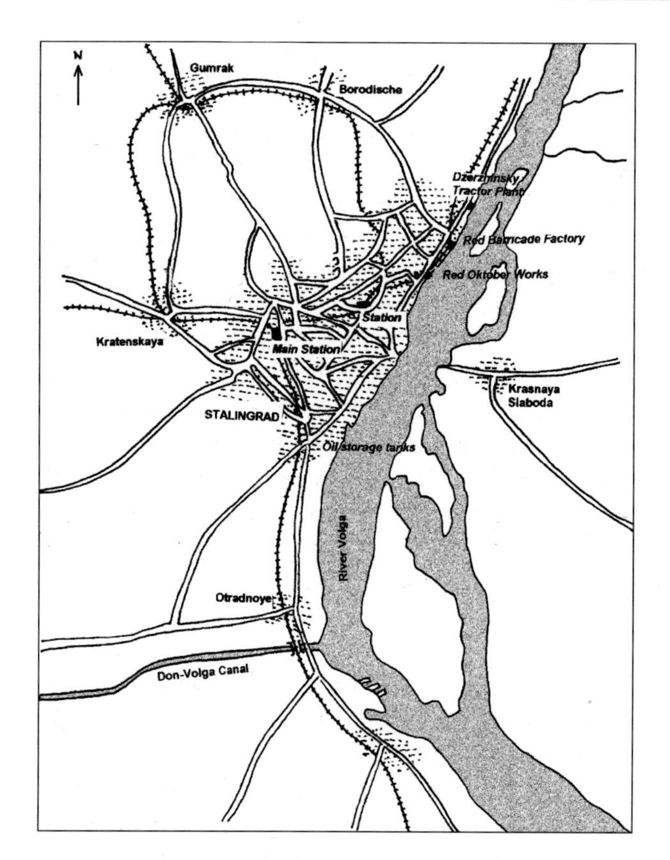

90 Map of Stalingrad in the 1940s

that stretched for over 20km along the west bank of the river; towards the middle of the city were three industrial sites that became the foci of resistance and attack. These were the Barrikody ordnance factory, the Red October steelworks and the tractor factory. On 13 September the Germans launched their attack against one of the Red Army's positions, and succeeded in taking the railway station and pushing far enough forward to come in range of the wharves. The Soviet commander, Chuikov, threw everything into the battle. He brought up his last 19 T-34 tanks and managed to establish a bridgehead at the river, from where he launched counter-attacks. Despite frequent Luftwaffe strikes, he managed to bring the German advance to a stop. The railway station was retaken within an hour, lost and then won back by the afternoon of 14 September. Fighting was hand-to-hand, and the Russian losses were staggering. Attempts to attack the German north flank failed, and for a month Chuikov's forces held doggedly on amongst the rubble and almost constant fire. The Germans found they could gain very little ground and some commanders felt that the attempt should be abandoned, but Hitler was adamant, and General Paulus was obliged to gather his men and supplies for a renewed and stronger push. On 14 October, a massive attack was launched against the ordnance and tractor factories, a battle that continued for a fortnight without an hour's respite. The ferocity of the fight was such that at the tractor factory, four whole German divisions, together with battalions of engineers, were engaged along a front of little over half a kilometre.

Little by little, Stalingrad fell into German hands, until by November they held the tractor factory and virtually all of the rest of the urban centre. The Russian forces had become divided, and it seemed to the Germans that one last great effort, aimed at the Red October steelworks, would finish the job. They seemed to have failed to recognise, or dismissed as unimportant, the meaning of reports of a huge army coming to face the poorly equipped Axis forces (mainly Romanian and Italian, with some Hungarian units) who were stationed on the outer flanks of the attack. They had also failed to react to reports that the Soviet industrial machine was churning out new T-34 tanks at an incredible rate, despite the knowledge that the T-34 was more than a match for their own Panzer tanks. The Soviet relieving force was over a million men strong, well supplied with tanks and heavy field artillery and with strong air support. They began their counter-attack on the day of the first winter snows, 19 November, and four days later had encircled the German forces, possibly nearly half a million troops, support personnel and conscripted Russian labour.

The Germans were ill prepared for such a move – they had not brought up enough food and supplies for any more than six or seven days, and they were still waiting for winter uniforms. The most pressing need was for ammunition and fuel. Nevertheless, Hitler demanded that rather than try to break out, they should hold what they had gained and wait for relief. Supply was organised by Goering personally – he had claimed to Hitler that there was no problem in making sufficient air drops. He reckoned without the distances involved, the accuracy of Russian fighter planes and anti-aircraft weapons, and that old Russian ally, 'General Winter'. Quite apart from dreadful weather conditions, the aircraft were not designed or prepared for use in the sub-zero temperatures that soon set in. A total of about 590 aircraft were lost during the operation. Conditions became too bad to try to land supplies, so they were dropped by parachute, but as the winter wore on, the besieged German forces lacked sufficient fuel to bring lorries to the dropping zones and '. . . supplies built up around Pitomnik while men starved to death only a few miles away'.[19]

A relieving force was being prepared under Field Marshal von Manstein, but his efforts were hampered by fast moving events in other theatres of war, denying him the troop numbers and equipment he needed. The Allies had made landings in North Africa, forcing the Germans to take over Vichy France in case of an invasion from the Mediterranean. In Russia too, large sectors of the German forces were pinned down or heavily engaged. The 57th Panzer Corps began to advance, taking 12 days to cover about 45km. The idea was to drive a passage through the encircling Russian armies, down which the beleaguered survivors of the Battle of Stalingrad could escape to the west. But the Soviet army had broken through to the north-west, destroying the Italian and Romanian resistance, and was heading for the German airfields and supply dumps behind the lines. The need to try (unsuccessfully) to protect these stretched the resources of von Manstein's command even further, until the relief vanguard consisted of just 35 tanks. The encircled 6th Army began to pull its meagre capacity back towards the point where the Panzers were expected to break through, and behind the Panzers, efforts were being made to bring up the necessary supplies to enable them to make a run for it out of the trap. But continued Soviet attacks and the chronic shortage of fuel brought the efforts to ruin. By New Year's Eve, the Panzer were back where they had started and the attempt abandoned. With the loss of the supplying airfields, the conditions of those trapped became utterly desperate; there was insufficient medical provision to deal with the wounded and starving, and dysentry and typhoid fever struck hard. Those still able to move fell back into the ruins of Stalingrad itself. 160,000 died during December and January, although the survivors continued to fight on, until 30 January, when their surrender finally came.

> A party from 11th Corps headquarters broke out of the city as it fell, as did elements of the 71st Infantry Division and an unknown number of little groups. A few were seen by German aircraft but all were swallowed up on the vast frozen steppe. No one escaped alive. German aircraft flying over the city on 2 February could see no sign of movement among the ruins.[20]

The whole German campaign in Russia achieved little more than had Napoleon's, 130 years earlier. It cost Germany terribly in men, industrial output, national investment and morale. The vast distances and above all the Russian winter combined to make Hitler's grandiose plans turn into nightmares, as they had done for others before him. The determination and acceptance of the cost of that defence in human lives and production effort by the Russians, with the tyrannical Stalinist whip to spur them to even greater sacrifice, cannot be discounted, but in the end, when the invasion of Russia is contemplated it always comes down to a question of geography.

The pathology of war

A final consideration must be that of the changing effects of warfare on the bodies of the participants. In earlier chapters we noted that the evidence in prehistory included examples of trauma inflicted by weapons on the bones of individuals. In recent years there has been a growing amount of work undertaken on the pathological study of signs of war trauma on physical human remains. The study of the bones of people involved in military activity can be very illuminating, not just in terms of the injuries caused by different kinds of weapons, but in the ways in which arms training affected the bodies of specialist fighters. A number of the skeletons found in the wreck of the *Mary Rose* had unusual shoulder developments – a condition called *os acromiale*, where part of the shoulder has failed to fuse at the joint. Because these skeletons were found alongside archery equipment, it has been suggested that the condition was caused by the commencement of archery training at a very young age. The constant stress of pulling a bow did not allow the bone to join and harden in childhood.[21] However, it is with weapons injuries that we can more clearly see the terrible effects of warfare. Much has been written about the theoretical effects of sword injuries, or the crushing effects of receiving a wound from a Dane-axe, for example, but only when we see the full effect of the injury on the surviving bone do we get a full picture of the power of ancient and medieval weaponry.

Two Anglo-Saxon examples might serve to illustrate the point. Recently, the York Archaeological Trust excavated some bodies from a churchyard which were thought to be victims of the first English encounter with the mighty Harald Hardrada at Fulford Gate in 1066. The skeletal evidence showed multiple cut marks to the long bones of the legs, and one decapitation. At Eccles, in Kent, six skeletons showed signs of fatal edged-weapon injuries, with each having damage to the cranium, two having suffered repeated blows. The deductions made from the Eccles material were that the injuries were caused by sword blows, cutting the bone rather than leaving the depressed marks that would have indicated axe blows, and that the blows were aimed downwards on to the head, shoulders and arms. The majority of the injuries were on the front and left sides of the victims, indicating right-handed opponents. Multiple blows are probably the result of 'finishing-off' a victim once the first blow has brought him to the ground. These types of injuries can be seen on the backs of victims who have fallen forward, but the most common injuries occur on those parts of the body that would have had least protection – the heads, the right arms, and the legs below the shield or chainmail.[22]

Healed wounds can show that an individual may have been a professional soldier; the report on the skeletal material from a mass grave associated with the Battle of Towton revealed that 32 per cent of the bodies had suffered previous wounds to their heads that had healed over before their fateful arrival at their final battlefield.[23] This type of evidence also tells us something of the effectiveness of battlefield medical practice of the time. Remarkably enough, none of the healed injuries at Towton showed any signs of infection. Analysis of the trauma at Towton has also demonstrated the range of weaponry available – swords, daggers, maces, poleaxes, and a variety of arrowhead types.

In general, it is hard to establish that weapons trauma on a single skeleton is the result of warfare – the unfortunate victim may have been murdered, or died in a brawl. It is, however, with the rare survival of mass graves such as Towton that the effects of war can be most devastatingly obvious.

With changes in types of warfare come changes in types of injury. In chapter 1 we listed some examples of skeletal trauma suffered in prehistory – spearheads and arrowpoints still embedded in bone, for example. We have noted the results of close-combat injuries such as those at Towton; one of the most famous examples of a possible sword injury comes from the study of a cremated skull tentatively identified as that of Philip II of Macedon (**91**), father of Alexander the Great. Tradition says that Philip had suffered and recovered from an arrow injury; the slash across his face, however, which almost certainly blinded his right eye, cut so deep into the bone that it has been surmised that it was caused by a heavier slashing blow.

These types of injuries would have been sustained by warriors in many combats throughout the centuries, as well as some whose evidence is less likely to be clear in archaeological evidence. The injuries sustained at the Battle of Agincourt, for example, although we have no remains from that encounter, may have included:

91 The reconstructed head of Philip of Macedon, showing damage done to the face by either a sword or an arrow

> those which had pierced the intestines, emptying its contents into the abdomen [which] were fatal: peritonitis was inevitable. Penetrations of the chest cavity, which had probably carried in fragments of dirty clothing, were almost as certain to lead to sepsis . . . Many of the French, of course, had not been collected from the battlefield and, if they did not bleed to death, would have succumbed to the combined effects of exposure and shock during the night, when temperatures might have descended into the middle-30s Fahrenheit.[24]

The effects of gunpowder weapons were, if anything, even more terrible. Close proximity to an explosion can result in the fragmentation of the bodies of men and animals in a way unknown to the ancients. Injuries and causes of death recorded after Waterloo in 1815 included decapitation or the removal of limbs by cannonball, the effects of major trauma suffered from the lightweight but deadly musketballs, and the injuries caused by grapeshot. Musketballs could penetrate the body and cause lethal trauma without knocking the victim over; a few lucky individuals suffered musketball injury even in the head and survived to tell the tale. Much of the lightweight grape and musket ammunition was received at low velocities, causing bruising or sometimes fractures of bones rather than severe penetrating injury, but even these could be fatal if the head was hit or if the effect was to cause a rider to fall or an infantryman to stumble at the wrong moment. Some injuries were caused by flying pieces of other victims, blown apart by shells, which hit and penetrated their comrades.

Some evidence of battle trauma demonstrates very clearly how terrible were an individual's final moments. Some of the skeletons of a trooper of Custer's Seventh Cavalry recovered from the Battle of the Little Big Horn in 1876 have been analysed forensically to demonstrate the sequence of death. One individual had suffered a fractured skull and a blow to the face which knocked out his teeth. Shot twice in the chest, he had then suffered cuts to his wrist and slashes, made by an axe, across his thighs; despite these terrible injuries, the evidence suggested that he had taken a long time to die. Another skull had an unusually rectangular-shaped bullet entry, suggesting that the projectile had hit the trooper as the result of a ricochet. Like the archers of the *Mary Rose* and the battle of Towton, Custer's men showed pathological clues to their occupation, including deformation of the hip bones caused by constant horseback riding.[25] Comparisons of the size and age of the remains with the rosters of the troops known to have been involved has led to the tentative identification of some with known individuals; of particular interest is the case of Corporal George Lell, possibly identified by his dental work, one of the earliest such occurrences. Facial reconstructions have also been attempted, comparing the results with another new feature of the nineteenth century – the photograph.

Battlefield trauma in industrial war, since the American Civil War, brings new forms of injury, both that which is recoverable archaeologically and that which is invisible even in life. Casualties during the Battle of the Somme in 1916 suffered relatively few slashing injuries; more bullet wounds were inflicted than in earlier campaigns because of the use of machine guns. Shell and bomb wounds were much more terrible. A shell could completely destroy a man's body – there are records of comrades only being able to retrieve the boots of a victim. Even those not actually hit by a projectile could suffer terrible and fatal injury because of blast effects:

> Shell blast could create over-pressures or vacuums in the body's organs, rupturing the lungs and producing haemorrhages in the brain and spinal cord. It was effects of this sort that killed three Welch Fusiliers 'sitting in a shellhole . . . with no more visible mark on them than some singeing of their clothing'.[26]

Splinter damage was often severe, and new forms of high velocity bullets produced fatal wounds far more often than older ammunition. Another new and terrible aspect was the use of chemical weapons – the first discharge of chlorine gas by the Germans occurred at Ypres in 1915, later followed by mustard gas and phosgene gas, delivered in canisters or in shells. Ernest Shepherd serving with the Dorsetshire Regiment on Hill 60 recorded for the date Saturday, 1 May 1915:

> At 6pm started the most barbarous act known in modern warfare. We had just given orders guarding against the gases the Germans use. These orders had just reached one platoon (No. 7) when the enemy actually started pumping gas on to us. This gas we were under impression was to stupefy only. We soon found out at a terrible price that these gases were deadly

> poison . . . The scene that followed was heartbreaking. Men were caught by fumes and in dreadful agony, coughing and vomiting, rolling on ground in agony . . .[27]

The panic caused by this new weapon, specifically designed to be used in trench warfare, and the horror of it, are best described in the words of Wilfred Owen:

> Gas! GAS! Quick, boys! – An ecstasy of fumbling,
> Fitting the clumsy helmets just in time;
> But someone still was yelling out and stumbling
> And flound'ring like a man in fire or lime . . .
> Dim, through the misty panes and thick green light,
> As under a green sea, I saw him drowning.
> From 'Dulce et Decorum Est', August 1917[28]

A further form of casualty, if not new to war, certainly highlighted by the war in the trenches, was the psychologically damaged soldier – suffering from 'shell shock' (called 'battle fatigue syndrome' in the Vietnam and later conflicts). At first, soldiers whose wills and minds were destroyed by the conditions and constant danger of trench warfare were regarded as cowards; the concept of shellshock was in fact a kindly response to a recognition of human frailty. Other euphemisms have been employed, then and since – 'exhaustion', 'nervous', etc. Perhaps the only archaeological trace of these victims will be the excavation of the psychiatric hospitals built to house them after the war.

As weapons have become capable of greater destruction, the evidence for human suffering has changed. More and more weapons are capable of totally destroying bodies – like the effects of the bombs at Hiroshima and Nagasaki – or of killing later by means of accidentally or intentionally introduced pathogens. These include bioweapons such as anthrax, and carcinogens resulting from nuclear explosion and the use of chemical weapons.

The desire to recover the bodies of the fallen and to identify them is a relatively modern phenomenon. Dog-tags and other such insignia are now normally issued and worn by all soldiers; mass battlefield graves are less common as nations, particularly the Americans, undertake massive efforts to retrieve the bodies of their fallen, even at the risk of the lives of the recovery details. It is sometimes the case, sadly, that there is little to recover; few of the bodies of those who died on 11 September 2001 in New York can ever be retrieved. Mass burials relating to recent conflicts have tended to be those of civilian victims, and here archaeology has been of great service, identifying the dead and building up evidence for the prosecution of individuals accused of war crimes.

We end the material in this volume with an account of the revelations of a discovery which shed dramatic new light on the nature of medieval weapons and their effectiveness whilst also providing unique examples of body armour from a period that was in transition between chainmail and full plate armour.

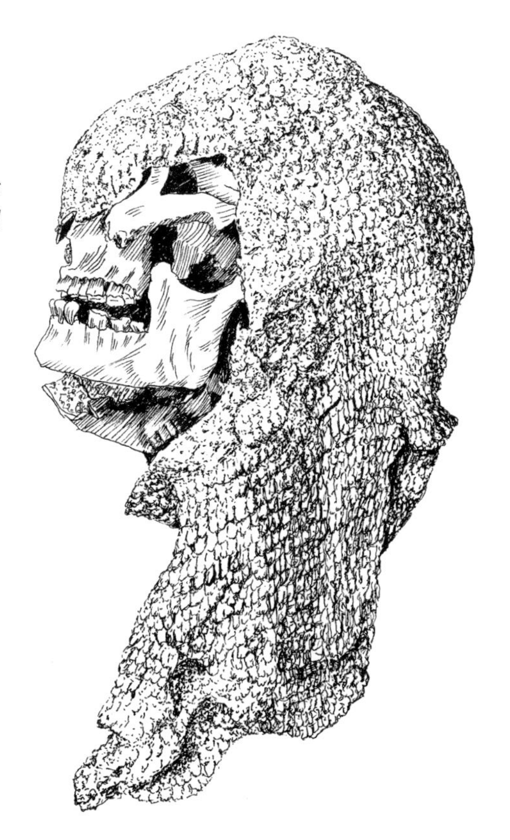

92 After the battle of Visby, in Gotland in 1361, the bodies of the dead were not quickly buried. Instead, sometime after they had rotted into their armour, they were thrown into a huge pit. The results were revealing for there were pathological signs of weapons injuries on all the bodies as well as some unique examples of armour from the period

The Battle of Visby 1361

Excavations in Gotland outside the city of Visby between 1928-31 revealed mass graves of the victims of a battle which took place on 27 July 1361. King Waldemar Atterdag of Denmark invaded Gotland in that year and after defeating several bands of militia was confronted at the gates of Visby by another poorly trained body of warriors. The battle which followed was a resounding victory for the feudal army of the Danish king, who with a combined arms force of infantry, cavalry and archers, defeated a collection of infantrymen. Visby fell to Waldemar after the battle. Around 1800 Gotlanders had paid with their lives for trying to defend the city, a figure which was recorded in historical texts and which can be reasonably accurately supported by archaeology. The extraordinary aspect of this battle was not that it was so one-sided (for there are countless examples of such confrontations), but that we have any evidence of it at all in the archaeological record. The dead from the battle – nearly all Gotlanders with one or two Danes – were buried in a collection of giant and rather hurriedly dug mass grave pits. It may well have been some time before this burial took place, since not all the bodies had been stripped of their armour indicating that they may have rotted into their suits and coifs during the hot summer days while they were lying around.

Among the types of armour discovered on the bodies in the graves were 185 chain mail coifs (**92**), a form of head protection worn in conjunction with a padded arming cap beneath a helmet, and 24 coats of plates. The coats of plates from Visby represent an antiquated form of body armour for the time. The militia probably bought their armour themselves, or had it passed down to them and it is not unlikely that these suits were first made sometime in the preceding century at least.

Excavators were able to determine three types of weapon injury on the hapless victims of Waldemar. Cutting weapons (swords and axes) accounted for 456 wounds, while 126 were the result of piercing weapons (arrows, spears and the grisly 'morning star', a spiked iron ball on a chain attached to a handle). Crushing blows accounted for an innumerable amount of injuries and were probably caused by blunt weapons such as maces and the like. The amount of soft body tissue damage caused can only be imagined. Flesh wounds must have been very numerous indeed. The bodies varied in age from boys to old men, emphasising the makeshift nature of the force. Sword blows which actually cut through bone only amounted to 29, indicating that these were well chosen and decisive blows. One man had both his legs cut off in one go. Cranial injuries were not unusual either, with one old man having his jaw cut away and another victim with most of the left side of his face cut off. 15 per cent of all injuries were sustained to the arms, mainly the humerus. Tibia injuries amounted to 56.4 per cent of the total, with fibulas at 16.46 per cent and femurs at 12.2 per cent. A great majority of the injuries were to the left side of the body, indicating right-handed opponents. The angle of entry of some of the piercing wounds – almost certainly arrows – shows that they entered at a steep incline. The only sensible way to interpret this is to view the body as already prone when an archery attack came in. This would mean that arrows falling out of the sky onto a body that was lying down would seem from the wound which they left, to have been travelling upwards.

What picture are we to draw from the extraordinary evidence of Visby? Clearly in 1361, a well-organised feudal army was a very capable one. Preliminary attacks by ranks of archers were probably preceded by mounted charges to the flanks or other areas of weakness established by the archers, followed by a concerted attack from men-at-arms armed with swords and maces. A poorly organised peasant militia was always going to be second best to Waldemar's professionals. Visby was not a particularly remarkable battle by medieval standards. The battle of Stamford bridge in 1066 at which many thousands of Norwegians perished, the catastrophic battle of Manzikert in 1071 at which the Byzantine army was utterly outdone by the Seljuk Turks, and the Battles of Crécy, Poitiers and Agincourt all rank as remarkable instances of aspects of weapon usage, strategy and tactics for their time. However, what we have at Visby is something which we crave for so many of the other battles that we read about: archaeological evidence. What would we know of warfare in tenth-century England if we could only locate the field of Brunanburh, the place in north of the country where in AD 937 the English king Athelstan defeated a huge host of Vikings, Welsh and Scots? How would we be able to assess the effects of the Dane Axe against the new foe, the mounted knight, trained to charge home in squadron formation, if we only had bodies from the field of Hastings?

There are many questions left unanswered, but as more evidence comes to light from the examination of battlefield skeletons, we will learn a great deal about warfare from its effects on the human body.

Conclusion

Throughout this book, we have demonstrated the relatedness of landscapes to the history and archaeology of warfare. It seems that, underlying any sociological, ethical or philosophical issues, there are fundamental human preoccupations with territory as a way of providing the means of survival and for the accumulation of wealth and power. We can speculate that the evidence we have seen for aggression even in the earliest human groups was related to control of hunting and gathering territories and access to water and shelter.

The beginnings of farming in the Neolithic period also began the process of formalisation of land ownership and boundaries; in turn, this began to reduce the options for using alternative survival strategies. The commitment to the investment of labour and time implicit in agriculture improves the certainty of being able to feed the family for the next season, but at the same time it traps the farmer into a confined area and way of life. He becomes vulnerable to crop failure, disease and attack but lacks the option of running away and foraging elsewhere. Because of this, Neolithic people began to group together in larger communities for protection, and then to build defences, or at least in defensible locations as at Mesa Verde or with defensible forms of architecture as at Çatal Hüyük and Jericho.

Agricultural food production has tended to lead to faster population growth and larger social groups; in turn, this has meant the development of social organisation – of polities. In most civilisations, this has resulted in the development of social stratification – the rise of elites and chiefs. Control of territory and the produce of agriculture and industries within it has very often been crucial to the creation and maintenance of the power of leaders. This perspective continues to be an important factor in many incidences of war to the present day.

> Warfare is without doubt the most complex form of activity evolved by man in the 2 million years of his evolutionary existence.[1]

The arts of attack and defence have become ever more sophisticated; we have seen how technological and strategic advances have occurred in phases and cycles, altering in response to developments in armament and mobility, and availability of manpower throughout antiquity to the point where professionalisation under Roman expansionism set the standard for military organisation.

The way in which troops and their generals have been prepared to deal with the landscapes in which they have found themselves and to utilise their advantages has been crucial for the success of campaigns. In this respect, irregular forces have often enjoyed major advantages. The Apaches' knowledge and ability to survive in the Sonoran mountains and deserts, or Arminius' understanding of the German bogs and forests, demonstrate this fact. But a good, or at least a fortunate, commander of regular forces can turn landscapes and weather to great advantage – as did the Yorkist bowmen at Towton when they used the snowstorm, or Wellington at Waterloo concealing his Guards in the corn, or the English at Agincourt denying the French the use of their cavalry.

It is in the design of defences and fortifications, perhaps more than anything else, that evidence survives to demonstrate the way the technology of war has developed in increasingly sophisticated stages, as measure and counter-measure were contrived. There has always been a defence race to complement the arms races of history.

From simple banks, ditches and palisades to complexes of ravelins and bastions, the military architect has been an important contributor to the history of war. As weapons increased their range and penetrating power, so new ways have been devised to protect against them – the artillery forts of Henry VIII were the ancestors of the massive installations of the Maginot Line and the Atlantic Wall. These fortifications were intended to act as defensive frontiers, perhaps the most difficult type of defence to operate successfully, because of the sheer distances involved. Structures such as Hadrian's Wall and the Great Wall of Ming China could never, as such, defy an invasion. They operated better as control points, dividing that which was considered to be 'civilised' from that which was 'barbarian', allowing taxation of imports, providing lateral communication around the borders of empire and creating a barrier to stop smaller-scale raiding incursions. They also defined the limit of expansion of the 'civilised' agricultural and centrally administered society – despite attempts to expand beyond their walls, cultures have in fact found themselves limited by them.

Attempts to defend such barriers against determined invaders seemed doomed to failure – pressure on a weakly defended section that achieves a breakthrough makes the rest of the line immediately redundant, as can be clearly seen in the events in the Ardennes in 1940. The concept of defence on a broad front appears to be a more efficient strategy, as Alfred's system of burhs, or Vauban's interlinked fortress plans, have shown. Alfred's defence of Wessex against the Vikings succeeded because it *connected* the country rather than attempting to give it bounds. Even so, the need for a supporting force that can move at speed to counter invasion threats has been essential. In Saxon England, Alfred's insistence on the provision of horses for military service and the creation of a naval force was a necessary adjunct to the burhs. Britain's first line of defence in many later conflicts has been with her navies; modern defences depend on satellite warning systems and air and sea-borne pre-emptive strike power.

New forms of armament have only ever lead to temporary military superiority; mankind's most inventive efforts have often been made during arms races. But they have changed the ways wars are fought, and the way that landscapes have affected or been affected by warfare. Developments in range, force, rate of fire and mobility of weaponry have meant that a series of trade-offs have often been necessary when coping with particular forms of terrain. Speed of advance may be sacrificed for the achieving of greater destruction of targets. At various periods, one or other advantage has come to dictate the forms of war. During the nineteenth and early twentieth century, there was an increasing tendency towards static warfare – during the American Civil War, the Boer War and on the Somme. Mechanised transport changed the nature of battles during the Second World War and succeeding conflicts, especially the increasing availability of air transport, enabling battles to be fought over much greater distances and in more inaccessible terrain. The horse and mule have not become totally redundant, as the recent conflict in Afghanistan has shown, but the whole nature of logistics and supply has changed with the provision of airlifted support. This can still go wrong, of course, as the over-extension of German supply lines at Stalingrad demonstrated.

The ability to deliver war over thousands of miles by air, by missile and via other strategies means that wars of the future may be much less concerned with the limiting effects of landscape. However, recent developments mean that the landscape itself has become more of a target than ever before, both the natural resources that it holds, and the human settlements and activities that it supports. Biological weapons have been in the news recently, with the use of anthrax spores delivered in the mail. Terrorist military strategies tend to favour such weapons because of their anonymity and their ease of delivery, and as a counter-measure, official forces have used such weapons in their struggles against terrorist armies. The defoliant Agent Orange was used to devastating effect during the Vietnam War. Such agents, capable of destroying crops and animal herds, exist in frightening quantities; the delivery by any one of a number of means of such chemicals could wipe out a country's agricultural economy and its ability to wage conventional war very quickly. Only the uncertainties of controlling the effects of such weapons so that they do not recoil upon the users has so far limited their application. Western authorities have been thinking very seriously of using such weapons to destroy opium and marijuana fields in Asia and Central America for some time.

The most awful weapon of our day remains the atomic bomb and its variants. The world saw what could be done to human settlements at Hiroshima and Nagasaki; for many years, the horror of those scenes has limited war between the major powers to a battle for technological stalemate – the so-called Cold War. But now less stable, more fanatic groups have the capability to use the bomb. There have been a number of very close calls over the years – with Cuba, with Iran and, as we finish this book, troops along the Pakistan-India border are squaring up to each other belligerently, and threats of nuclear attack have once more been made.

One more modern weapon should be considered: many observers in Nato and the Pentagon have expressed concern over the possibilities of cyberwar – attack upon a country's infrastructure via corruption of its information systems. Like biological weapons, such attacks need not be targeted on the military to be devastating. When a very large part of our food production, from milking parlours to canneries, from fishing fleets to delivery systems, are controlled by computers, an enemy perhaps does not need to stir from his own home in an enemy country to bring our states to their knees. Computerisation has brought an edge to conventional forces in the field, too. The accuracy of aerial bombardment in the modern age assisted by technology –

despite some notable mistakes being made in what is still the 'fog of war' – has given the aircraft a supremacy which it has been threatening since the Second World War.

In the hope that we do not destroy ourselves and our world in the near future, it is now time to turn to the issue of the role and future of an archaeology of warfare. Several writers have considered the contribution that archaeology could, or should, make to the study of war.

Studies of prehistoric war have concentrated on interpretation of the basic material forms of evidence (weapons and armour, defences, skeletal trauma, iconography) generally accepted as being indicative of conflicts; in addition, much use has been made of ethnographic and anthropological studies and of sociological perspectives on human group aggression. There has been some debate over whether archaeologists should restrict themselves to the description and interpretation of warfare in past societies, or whether our understanding of past societies could and should have a bearing on present and future social thought and action.

Do we simply study ancient conflict to enlighten ourselves about the behaviour of specific early societies and their developments, or can we draw comparisons between ancient causes and prosecution of aggression with our own modern world, so that we can avoid the mistakes of the past?

> We depend on anthropology and history for the models we build of what to look for as evidence of war. It could therefore be argued that the role of archaeology in the study of war is only to provide examples of practices that others have already attested in both theory and actuality . . . [but] clearly we all believe that archaeologists do have something to say about the study of war, and that archaeological data, archaeological method and archaeological approaches can add something to a more general understanding of war as a phenomenon.[2]

We have, as members of a discipline, to decide what that something is. Archaeology depends on *physical* evidence for the interpretation of the past. Perhaps our first task in the continuance of the archaeological study of war, however, should be to extend our search for that physical evidence into new fields.

The physical evidence for ancient war is very limited (as is, indeed, the physical evidence for virtually every other human action). We should perhaps begin to investigate a wider set of evidential sources, based on modern parallels, to see whether we can expand our understanding of prehistoric conflicts. Studies have been made, both actual and theoretical, of the effects of war on modern environments and human settlements; the authors suggest that utilisation of some of these approaches may prove fruitful for the past as well. We can begin to use new scientific techniques to look specifically for the kinds of changes that war brings to societies – changes of ethnicity, health, diet, land use and abandonment, architecture, community size and focus, formation of boundaries and territories, using advances in DNA and other pathological studies to investigate changes in not only human but plant and animal populations. We can use improved methods of studying soil horizons and midden deposits to note and explain change. We may be able to extend our abilities to date landscape change – contraction, expansion and utilisation of territories.

None of these techniques alone will, or could, prove that warfare has taken place, but alongside more traditional data, we could perhaps move some way further down the road towards probability. In this book, we have concentrated on the landscape of war because it has seemed to us that it is a central concept in the study of warfare, as cause, arena and prize of hostility between human groups. We accept the importance of psychological, sociological, political and historical factors; those are, however, for others to debate.

If archaeology can contribute towards the understanding of warfare in human society, then a study of the landscape – the environmental component of warfare – will be essential. So far, we have only just begun to realise the possibilities of such studies.

Notes

1 Origins of warfare

1. Clavell, J. (Foreword) 1981 *The Art of War by Sun Tzu*. London: Hodder and Stoughton. p.11.
2. Thorpe, I.J.N. 1999 'The origins of Violence – Mesolithic conflict in Europe' Paper presented at *European Association of Archaeologists* meeting 16 September 1999, Bournemouth – www.hum.au.dk/fark/warfare/thorpe_paper_1.htm. Site accessed 26/3/01.
3. Leakey, R. 1981 *The Making of Mankind*. London: Abacus. p.221. Leakey describes the theories in Dart's papers and suggests that the era in which he was writing, immediately after the Second World War, which he describes as 'tense and doom-laden', was a contributory factor to the interpretations in his papers.
4. Leakey, R. 1981 *The Making of Mankind*. London: Abacus. p.223-5.
5. Brothwell, D. 1999 'Biosocial and bio-archaeological aspects of conflict and warfare' in Carman & Harding *Ancient Warfare*. Stroud: Sutton.
6. Van der Dennen, J.M.G. 2000 'The Function of Human War Ritual in Ritualised "Primitive" Warfare and Rituals in War: Phenocopy, Homology, or . . . ?', http://rint.rechten.rug.nl/rth/dennen/ritual2.htm. Site accessed 09/11/00.
7. Brothwell, D. 1964 'Further comments on the right parietal from Swanscombe' in C.D. Ovey (ed.) *The Swanscombe Skull: Further research on a Pleistocene Site*. London: Royal Archaeological Institute. p.173-4.
8. Keeley, L.H. 1996 *War Before Civilisation*. New York and Oxford: Oxford University Press. p.37.
9. Brothwell, D. 1999 'Biosocial and bio-archaeological aspects of conflict and warfare' in J. Carman & A. Harding *Ancient Warfare*. Stroud: Sutton. p.31.
10. Keeley, 1996 *War Before Civilisation*, New York and Oxford: Oxford University Press. p.37. Keeley also cites evidence from Late Paleolithic Nubia of frequent occurrences of skeletons found with embedded projectile points, and the apparent execution of children.
11. Vencl, S. 1999 'Stone Age Warfare' in J. Carman & A. Harding (eds) *Ancient Warfare*. Stroud: Sutton. pp.57-72. p.70.
12. Ferrill, A. 'Neolithic Warfare' published in MHQ: *The Quarterly Journal of Military History*.
13. Dixon, P. 1989 'Crickley Hill' in C. Burgess *et al.* (eds) *Enclosures and Defences in the Neolithic of Western Europe*. Oxford; BAR Int. Series 403. pp.75-87. p.82.
14. Mercer, R.J. 1981 'Excavations at Carn Brea, Illogan, Cornwall, 1970-73: A Neolithic Fortified Complex of the Third Millennium bc', reprinted from *Cornish Archaeology* No. 20. p.67.
15. Mercer, R.J. 1981 'Excavations at Carn Brea, Illogan, Cornwall, 1970-73: A Neolithic Fortified Complex of the Third Millennium bc' reprinted from *Cornish Archaeology* No. 20. p.76.
16. Chapman, J. 1999 'The Origins of Warfare in the Prehistory of Central and Eastern Europe' in J. Carman & A. Harding *Ancient Warfare*. Stroud: Sutton. p.124.
17. Humble, R. 1980 *Warfare in the Ancient World*. London. p.7.

18. Whitehouse, R. 1977 *The First Cities*. Phaidon Press. p.167.
19. Whitehouse, R. 1977 *The First Cities*. Phaidon Press. p.168.
20. Watkins, T. 1989 'The Beginnings of Warfare' in Hackett (ed.) *Warfare in the Ancient World*. London. p.23.
21. *The Times*, Thursday 26 July 2001.
22. Osgood, R. & Monks S. with Toms J. 2000 *Bronze Age Warfare*. Stroud: Sutton. p.148.
23. Osgood, R. & Monks S. with Toms J. 2000 *Bronze Age Warfare*. Stroud: Sutton, p.29-30.
24. Harding, A. 1999 'Warfare: A defining characteristic of Bronze Age Europe?' in J. Carman & A. Harding (eds) *Ancient Warfare*. Stroud: Sutton.
25. Coles, J. 1990 *Images of the Past: a guide to the rock carvings and other ancient monuments of Northern Bohuslän*. Hällristningsmuseet.
26. Osgood, R. & Monks S. with Toms J. 2000 *Bronze Age Warfare*. Stroud: Sutton. p.69.
27. Parker Pearson, M. 1993 *English Heritage Book of Bronze Age Britain*. London: B.T. Batsford/English Heritage. p.107-8.
28. Hines, J. 1989 'The Military Context of the *Adventus Saxonum*: Some Continental Evidence' in Chadwick, S.C. (ed.) *Weapons and Warfare in Anglo-Saxon England*. Oxford University Committee for Archaeology Monograph No. 21. p.35.
29. The differing views of the theorists are summed-up and analysed on the web site http://devlab.dartmouth.edu/history/bronze_age/lessons/28.html#2. Site accessed 27/12/01.
30. Vermeule, E.T. 1960 'The Fall of the Mycenaean Empire' *Archaeology 13* p.66-75.
31. Iakovides, S. 1986 'Destruction Horizons at Late Bronze Age Mycenae' in *Philia Epe eis Georgion E. Mylonan A*. Athens. p.233-60.
32. Betancourt, P. 1976 'The End of the Greek Bronze Age' *Antiquity 50* p.40-7.
33. Carpenter, R. 1966 *Discontinuity in Greek*. Cambridge.
34. Andronikos, M. 1954 'E'dorike Eisvole kai ta archaiologika Euremata' *Hellenika 13* p.221-40.
35. Mylonas, G.E. 1966 *Mycenae and the Mycenaean Age*. Princeton.
36a. Desborough, V.R.d'A. 1964 *The Last Mycenaeans and their Successors*. Oxford.
36b. Desborough, V.R.d'A. 1972 *The Greek Dark Ages*. London.
37. Rutter, J. 1975 'Ceramic Evidence for Northern Intruders in Southern Greece at the Beginning of the Late Helladic IIIC Period' *AJA 79*. p.17-32.
38. Winter, F.A. 1977 'An Historically Derived Model for the Dorian Invasion' in E. Davis (ed.) *Symposium on the Dark Ages in Greece*. New York. p.60-76.
39. Deger-Jalkotzy, S. 1977 *Fremde Zuwanderer im Spätmykenischen Griechenland*. Vienna.
40. Drews, R. 1993 *The End of the Bronze Age: Changes in Warfare and the Catastrophe ca. 1200 BC*. Princeton.
41. Healy, M. 1991 *The Ancient Assyrians*. Osprey Books. p.56.
42. Hanson, V.D. 1999 'Hoplite obliteration: the case of the town of Thespiae' in J. Carman & A. Harding (eds) *Ancient Warfare*. Stroud: Sutton. p.203.
43. *ibid*.
44. *op. cit*. p.203-18.

2 The defensive response

1. Goodall, J. 1990 *Through a Window*. Harmondsworth: Penguin. Jane Goodall's studies of aggression in wild chimpanzees indicate that these primates are capable of extremely brutal acts against each other.
2. Fowler, P. 1983 *The Farming of Prehistoric Britain*. Cambridge: Cambridge University Press.

3. Drewett, P., Rudling, D. & Gardiner, M. 1978 *The South East to 1000 AD*. London: Longman.
4. Cunliffe, B. 1995 *Iron Age Britain*. London: Batsford/EH. p.53-4.
5. Le Patourel, H.E.J. & Roberts, B.K. 1978 'The significance of moated sites' in Aberg F.A. (ed.) *Medieval Moated Sites*. CBA Res. Rep. No. 17. p.46-55.
6. Raferty, J. 1942 *North Munster Archaeological Journal 3*. p.53-72.
7. Hencken, H. 1942 *Proc. Royal Irish Acad.* 47C. p.1-76.
8. Sweetman, D. 2000 'The Origin and Development of the Tower House in Ireland' *Barryscourt Lectures VIII*. Kinsale: Barryscourt Trust and Cork County Council.
9. Barry, T.B. 1987 *The Archaeology of Medieval Ireland* London: Routledge. p.186.
10. Pounds, N.J.G. 1990 (1994 reprint). *The Medieval Castle in England and Wales – A Social and Political History*. Cambridge: Cambridge University Press. p.291.
11. Williams, G. 1999 *Stronghold Britain – Four Thousand Years of British Fortifications*. Stroud: Sutton. p.184-5.
12. Dyer, J. 1990 *Ancient Britain* London: Batsford. p.114-15.
13. Osgood, R. & Monks S. with Toms J., 2000 *Bronze Age Warfare*. Stroud: Sutton. p.13.
14. *op. cit.* p.14-15.
15. Dyer, J. 1990 *Ancient Britain*. London: Batsford. p.143.
16. Ritchie, A. & G. 1979 'The Enigma of the Brochs' in *Popular Archaeology* Vol. 1 No. 6, Dec. 1979. p.9-12.
17. Collis, J. 1984 *The European Iron Age* London: Batsford. p.88.
18. Audouze, F. & Büchsenschütz, O. (tr. Cleere, H.) 1991 *Towns, Villages and Countryside of Celtic Europe: From the beginning of the second millennium to the end of the first century BC*. London: BCA.
19. *op. cit.* p.89-90.
20. Cunliffe, B. 1995 *Iron Age Britain*. London: Batsford/EH. p.93.
21. Julius Caesar *De Bello Gallico* (tr. S.A. Handford, 1951 *Caesar - The Conquest of Gaul*. Harmondsworth: Penguin) II,3.
22. *op. cit.* VI,2.
23. *op. cit.* II,4.
24. Hinton, D.A. 1982 'Hamwih' in Campbell, J., John, E., & Wormald, P. (eds) *The Anglo Saxons*. p.102-3.
25. Hill, D. 1967 'The Burghal Hideage – Southampton' *Proceedings of the Hampshire Field Club XXIV*, p.59-61. Although this has been disputed – see Burgess, L.A. 1964 *The Origins of Southampton*. Leicester. Department of English Local History; Occasional Papers: XVI.
26. Wacher, J.S. 1975 'The excavations 1956-68' in C. Platt & R. Coleman-Smith *Excavations in Medieval Southampton 1953-1969, I*. p.142-7, 149. Leicester.
27. Kenyon, J.R. 1990 *Medieval Fortifications*. Leicester: Leicester University Press.
28. Wacher, J. 1995 *The Towns of Roman Britain* (2nd revised edition). London: BCA. p.74.
29. Cüppers, H. *et al.*, 1983 *La Civilisation Romaine de la Moselle a la Sarre*. Exhibition Catalogue, Paris – Musée de Luxembourg, Mayence: Editions Philipp von Zabern.
30. Faulkner, N. 2000 *The Decline and Fall of Roman Britain*. Stroud: Tempus. p.106.
31. Hill, D. 1981. *An Atlas of Anglo-Saxon England*. p.85.
32. Griffiths, D.W. 1995 'The North-West Mercian Burhs. A Reappraisal' in *Anglo-Saxon Studies in Archaeology and History*, Volume 8. Oxford University Committee for Archaeology. p.75-84.
33. Williams, G. 1999 *Stronghold Britain – Four Thousand Years of British Fortifications*. Stroud: Sutton. p.235-6.
34. Wills, H. 1979 'The Pill-Boxes that went to War' in *Popular Archaeology* Vol.1 No.5, November, p.16-17.

35. Newark, T. 2000 *War in Britain*. London: Harper Collins. p.174.
36. Williams, G. 1999 *Stronghold Britain - Four Thousand Years of British Fortifications.* Stroud: Sutton. p.59.
37. *Hygini gromatici, liber de munitionibus castrorum* (ed. Domaszewski, Leipzig, 1887) in Jones, M.J. 1975 *Roman Fort Defences to AD 117, with special reference to Britain.* BAR 21.
38. *op. cit.* p.46.
39. Crummy, P. 1997 *City of Victory – the Story of Colchester, Britain's first Roman town.* Colchester: Colchester Archaeological Trust. p.45.
40. de la Bédoyère, G. 1991 *The Buildings of Roman Britain*. London: Batsford. p.53.
41. Brice, M. 1999 *Forts and Fortresses*. London: Chancellor Press. p.117.
42. *ibid.*
43. Brown, D. 1972 *The Fetterman Massacre*. London: Pan Books. p.223.
44. Keen, M. (ed.) 1999 *Medieval Warfare, a History*. Oxford: Oxford University Press. p.73.
45. Morillo, S. 1994 *Warfare Under the Anglo-Norman Kings*. Woodbridge: The Boydell Press. p.94.
46. Kenyon, J.R. 1990 *Medieval Fortifications*. Leicester: Leicester University Press. p.24.
47. Spurgeon, W.J. 1991 'Glamorgan's First Castles' *Fortress* 8, February 1991, (p.3-14). p.11.
48. Kenyon, J.R. 1990 *Medieval Fortifications.* Leicester: Leicester University Press. p.7.
49. Higham, R. & Barker, P. 1992 *Timber Castles*. London: Batsford. p.60-1.
50. Turner, D.J. 1987 'Archaeology of Surrey 1066 to 1540' in Bird J., & D.G. (eds) *The Archaeology of Surrey to 1540.* Guildford: Surrey Archaeological Society.
51. Pounds, N.J.G. 1990 *The Medieval Castle in England and Wales – A Social and Political History*. Cambridge: Cambridge University Press. p.69-70.
52. *op. cit.*
53. Platt, C. 1995 *The Castle in Medieval England and Wales*. London: Chancellor Press.

3 Frontiers

1. Corres., XII, No. 10419, p.492 – Luvaas p.100.
2. Ferrill, A. 1986. *The Fall of the Roman Empire. The Military Explanation*. London. p.26. Ferrill also outlines the terms 'Preclusive Security' and 'Defence-in-Depth' with relation to the military provision at the end of the Roman Empire in the West.
3. Haythornthwaite, P.J. 1989 *Wellington's Military Machine*. Staplehurst: Spellmount. p.100-1.
4. Ferrill, Arther 1986. *The Fall of the Roman Empire. The Military Explanation.* London. p.45.
5. McKee, A. 1964 *Caen, Anvil of Victory*. Pan Books: London. p.78.
6. Quoted in Pounds, N.J.G. 1990 *The Medieval Castle in England and Wales – A Social and Political History.* Cambridge: Cambridge University Press.
7. Clausewitz, Carl Von 1832 *On War*. Everyman's Library edition, 1993. London. p.472-9.
8. Frere, S. 1987 *Britannia – a History of Roman Britain*, 3rd ed. London: Pimlico. p.113.
9. *op. cit.* p.114
10. Johnson, S. 1989a *Hadrian's Wall*. London: Batsford/EH. p.66.
11. Gates, T. 1999 'Hadrian's Wall amid fields of corn' *British Archaeology No. 49.* p.6-7. Reports on aerial photographic studies of about $100km^2$. from the river Tyne to the Cumbrian border which have revealed over 200 previously unknown earthwork sites, including six dated to the Late Iron Age or Early Romano-

British periods, which are associated with field systems and some 70 patches of cord-rigg (hoe) cultivation close to the Wall.
12. Reported in Johnson, S. 1989b 'Recent work on Hadrian's Wall' *Fortress.* May 1989. Issue 1, p.3-13.
13. Frere, S. 1987 *Britannia – a History of Roman Britain*, 3rd ed. London: Pimlico. p.114.
14. Johnson, S. 1989a *Hadrian's Wall.* London: Batsford/EH. p.70.
15. Faulkner, N. 2000 *The Decline and Fall of Roman Britain.* Stroud: Tempus. p.47.
16. Hunter Blair, P. 1966 *Roman Britain and Early England 55 BC - AD 871.* New York & London: W.W. Norton. p.72-3.
17. *De Bello Gallico* V, 3.
18. Frere, S. 1987 *Britannia: A history of Roman Britain.* London: Pimlico. 3rd rev. ed. p.370.
19. Fowler, P. 2000 f/c 'Wansdyke in the Woods' Paper for *festschrift.* Ed. Ellis, P. 2001 f/c, Wiltshire Archaeological and Natural History Society, Devizes.
20. Reynolds, A. 1999 *Later Anglo-Saxon England – Life and Landscape.* Stroud: Tempus, p.85.
21. Blair, J. 1991 *Early Medieval Surrey: Landholding, Church and Settlement before 1300.* Stroud: Sutton and Surrey Archaeological Society. p.14.
22. Drewett, P., Rudling, D. & Gardiner, M. 1988 *The South East to AD 1000.* London: Longman, p.288.
23. Blair, J., 1991 *Early Medieval Surrey: Landholding, Church and Settlement before 1300.* Stroud: Sutton and Surrey Archaeological Society. p.7-8.
24. Hill, D., 1974 'Offa's and Wat's Dykes – some exploratory work on the frontier between Celt and Saxon' in Rowley, T. (ed.) *Anglo-Saxon Settlement and Landscape.* Oxford: BAR 6. p.102-7.
25. Williams, G. 1999 *Stronghold Britain: Four Thousand Years of British Fortification.* Stroud: Sutton. p.89.
26. Philp, B. 1981 'The Excavation of the Roman Forts of the Classis Britannica at Dover, 1970-1977' *3rd Research Report, Kent Monograph Series.* Dover: Kent Archaeological Unit.
27. Faulkner, N. 2000 *The Decline and Fall of Roman Britain.* Stroud: Tempus. p.101.
28. Philp, B. 1981 'The Excavation of the Roman Forts of the Classis Britannica at Dover, 1970-1977' *3rd Research Report, Kent Monograph Series.* Dover: Kent Archaeological Unit. p.118; Johnson, S. 1977 'Late Roman defences and the Limes' in Johnston, D.E. (ed.) *The Saxon Shore*, CBA Research Report No. 18. p.69.
29. *op. cit.* p.63-9.
30. Morley, B.M. 1976 *Henry VIII and the Development of Coastal Defence.* London: DoE/HMSO. p.7.
31. *op. cit.* p.32.
32. Saunders, A. 1997 *English Heritage Book of Channel Defences.* London: Batsford/EH. p.31.
33. Morley, B.M. 1976 *Henry VIII and the Development of Coastal Defence.* London: DoE/HMSO. p.15.
34. Williams, G. 1999 *Stronghold Britain.* Stroud: Sutton. p.177.
35. Saunders, A. 1997 *English Heritage Book of Channel Defences.* London: Batsford/EH. p.81.
36. Williams, G. 1999 *Stronghold Britain.* Stroud: Sutton. p.209.
37. Blizard, D. 1993 *The Normandy Landings. D-Day The Invasion of Europe 6 June 1944.* Reed International Books. p.22.
38. Macksey, K. 1979 *Rommel, Battles and Campaigns.* London: Arms and Armour Press. p.200.

4 Using the landscape

1. Liddell Hart, B.H. 1954 *Strategy, the Indirect Approach.* Quoted in Chandler, D.G. 1974 *The Art of Warfare on Land.* p.8-9.
2. Chandler, D.G. 1974. *The Art of Warfare on Land.* p.8-9.
3. *op. cit.*
4. Allmand, C. 1999 'War and the non-combatant in the Middle Ages' in Keen, M. (ed.) *Medieval Warfare – a History.* Oxford: Oxford University Press. p.261.
5. *op. cit.* p.260-1.
6. Schaumann A. 1924 *On the Road with Wellington – The Diary of a War Commissary.* London. Quoted in Parkinson, R. 1973 *The Peninsula War.* London: Hart-Davis MacGibbon. p.118.
7. Parkinson, R. 1973 *The Peninsula War* London: Hart-Davis MacGibbon. p.128.
8. *ibid.*
9. Ferguson, N. quoted in Regan, G. 2000 *Great Military Blunders.* London: Channel 4 Books/Macmillan. p.48.
10. Parkinson, R. 1973 *The Peninsula War.* London: Hart-Davis MacGibbon. p.152.
11. From the narration of James Kaywaykla, an Ojo Calientes Apache who was about 5 years old during the campaigns of Victorio and Kaywaykla's grandfather Nana in the late 1870s (Ball, E. 1973 *In the Days of Victoria: recollections of a Warm Spring Apache.* London: Corgi. p.91).
12. Hibbert, C. 1964 *Agincourt.* Tiptree: Purnell Book Services Ltd. p.32. Christopher Hibbert suggests this number of horses, though it has been suggested elsewhere that it was as low as 20,000.
13. A good idea of life in a tank in enclosed countryside. Quoted in McKee, A. 1964. *Caen.* London: Pan Books. p.345.
14. McKee, A. 1964 *Caen.* London: Pan Books. p.350.
15. Kraft *et al.* 1987 *Journal of Field Archaeology 14.* p.181-97.
16. Boardman, A. 2000 'The historical background to the battle and the documentary evidence' in Fiorato, V., Boylston, A. & Knüsel (eds) 2000 *Blood Red Roses: the Archaeology of a Mass Grave from the Battle of Towton AD 1461.* Oxford: Oxbow. pp.15-28. A comprehensive and fascinating account of a variety of historical and archaeological investigations into the battle.
17. Edward Hall, a Tudor chronicler, quoted in Ellis, H. (ed.) 1809 *Edward Hall's Chronicle.* London p.255-6 and Fiorato *et al.* 2000, p.20.
18. In Fiorato *et al.* 2000, p.133.
19. Miller, H. 2000 *Secrets of the Dead.* London: Channel 4 Books. p.27.
20. Hardy, R. 1992 *Longbow: a Social and Military History*, 3rd edn. Yeovil: Patrick Stephens, p.68.
21. Smurthwaite, D. 1984 *The Ordnance Survey Complete Guide to the Battlefields of Britain.* BCA, p.108.
22. In Fiorato *et al.* 2000, p.24.
23. http://www.geschichte.uni-osnabrueck.de/projekt. Site accessed 26/11/01.

5 Cycles of war

1. Quoted in full in Finberg, H.P.R. (ed.) 1975 *Scandinavian England.* Phillimore. Chichester. p.81-3.
2. Clausewitz, Carl Von 1832. *On War.* Everyman's Library edition, 1993. p.83.
3. Data extracted from Table 2.6 'Combat Unit Size and Social Unit Population' Keeley, L.H. 1996 *War Before Civilization.* New York and Oxford: Oxford University Press. p.189.

4. Keeley, L.H. 1996. *War Before Civilization.* New York and Oxford: Oxford University Press.
5. Fagan, B.M. 1991 *Kingdoms of Gold, Kingdoms of Jade: The Americas Before Columbus.* London: Thames & Hudson. p.206.
6. Miller, H. 2000 *Secrets of the Dead.* London: Channel 4 Books. p.77.
7. Wenger, G.R. 1991 *The Story of Mesa Verde* (revised edition) Mesa Verde National Park, Colorado: Mesa Verde Museum Association.
8. Haas, J. 1999 'The Origins of War and Ethnic Violence' in Carman, J. & Harding, A. (eds) *Ancient Warfare.* Stroud: Sutton. p.11-24.
9. Holden Reid, B. 1999. *The American Civil War and the Wars of the Industrial Revolution.* London: Cassell. p.23.
10. Duffy, 1985 *The Fortress in the Age of Vauban and Frederick the Great 1660-1789.* Routledge and Kegan Paul. p.292.
11. Guderian, Gen. H. 1952 *Panzer Leader* (1977 edition). London: Futura Books. p.25.
12. Written in foreword of Guderian, Gen. H. 1952 *Panzer Leader* (1977 edition). London: Futura Books. p.14.
13. Keegan, J. & Holmes, R. 1985 *Soldiers – a History of Men in Battle.* London. p.221.
14. *op. cit.* p.224.
15. Galtrey, Captain S. 1918 *The Horse and the War.* London: Country Life. p.78.
16. Haythornthwaite, P.J. 1995 *Wellington's Military Machine.* Staplehurst: Spellmount.
17. Nicolle, D. 1998 *Medieval Warfare Source Book Volume 2: Christian Europe and its Neighbours.* London: Brockhampton Press. p.256.
18. Warner, P. 1968 *Sieges of the Middle Ages.* New York: Barnes & Noble (1992 edn). p.32.
19. Winchester, C. 1998 *Ostfront – Hitler's War on Russia 1941-45.* Oxford: Osprey Publishing. p.72. A well illustrated and extremely readable account.
20. *ibid.* Of those who had been trapped, fewer than 6,000 returned to Germany.
21. Roberts, C. & Manchester, K. 1997 *The Archaeology of Disease* 2nd edn Stroud: Sutton. p.113.
22. Wenham, S.J. 1988 'Weapon Injuries' in Hawkes, S.C. *Weapons and Warfare in Anglo-Saxon England.* Oxford University Commitee for Archaeology Monograph No. 21. p.123-40. Oxford.
23. Fiorato, V., Boylston A. & Knüsel (eds) 2000 *Blood Red Roses: the Archaeology of a Mass Grave from the Battle of Towton AD 1461.* Oxford: Oxbow Books.
24. Keegan, J. 1976 *The Face of Battle.* London: Pimlico. p.113.
25. Bahn, P. (ed.) 1996 *Tombs, Graves and Mummies.* London: Weidenfeld and Nicolson. p.89.
26. Keegan, J. 1976 *The Face of Battle.* London: Pimlico. p.264.
27. Shepherd, E. (ed. by Rossor, B.) 1987 *A Sergeant-Major's War: From Hill 60 to the Somme.* Marlborough: Crowood Press. p.39-40.
28. Day Lewis, C. (ed.) 1963 *The Collected Poems of Wilfred Owen.* London: Chatto & Windus.

Conclusion

1. Chandler, D.G. 1974 *The Art of Warfare on Land.* London: Penguin. p.8.
2. Carman & Harding (eds) *Ancient Warfare.* Stroud: Sutton. p.249-50.

Index

Page numbers in **bold** refer to illustrations